ORATIONS OF THE FATIMID CALIPHS

The Institute of Ismaili Studies

Ismaili Texts and Translations Series, 10

Previously published titles:

1. Ibn al-Haytham. *The Advent of the Fatimids: A Contemporary Shiʿi Witness*. An edition and English translation of Ibn al-Haytham's *Kitāb al-Munāẓarāt*, by Wilferd Madelung and Paul E. Walker (2000).
2. Muḥammad b. ʿAbd al-Karīm al-Shahrastānī. *Struggling with the Philosopher: A Refutation of Avicenna's Metaphysics*. A new Arabic edition and English translation of al-Shahrastānī's *Kitāb al-Muṣāraʿa*, by Wilferd Madelung and Toby Mayer (2001).
3. Jaʿfar b. Manṣūr al-Yaman. *The Master and the Disciple: An Early Islamic Spiritual Dialogue*. Arabic edition and English translation of Jaʿfar b. Manṣūr al-Yaman's *Kitāb al-ʿĀlim waʾl-ghulām*, by James W. Morris (2001).
4. Idrīs ʿImād al-Dīn. *The Fatimids and their Successors in Yaman: The History of an Islamic Community*. Arabic edition and English summary of Idrīs ʿImād al-Dīn's *ʿUyūn al-akhbār*, vol. 7, by Ayman Fuʾād Sayyid, in collaboration with Paul E. Walker and Maurice A. Pomerantz (2002).
5. Naṣīr al-Dīn Ṭūsī. *Paradise of Submission: A Medieval Treatise on Ismaili Thought*. A new Persian edition and English translation of Naṣīr al-Dīn Ṭūsī's *Rawḍa-yi taslīm*, by S. J. Badakhchani with an introduction by Hermann Landolt and a philosophical commentary by Christian Jambet (2005).
6. al-Qāḍī al-Nuʿmān. *Founding the Fatimid State: The Rise of an Early Islamic Empire*. An annotated English translation of al-Qāḍī al-Nuʿmān's *Iftitāḥ al-daʿwa*, by Hamid Haji (2006).
7. Idrīs ʿImād al-Dīn. *ʿUyūn al-akhbār wa-funūn al-āthār*. Arabic critical edition in 7 volumes by Ahmad Chleilat, Mahmoud Fakhoury, Yousef S. Fattoum, Muhammad Kamal, Maʾmoun al-Sagherji and Ayman Fuʾad Sayyid (2000–2008).

9. Ḥamīd al-Dīn Aḥmad b. ʿAbd Allāh al-Kirmānī. *Master of the Age: An Islamic Treatise on the Necessity of the Imamate.* A critical edition of the Arabic text and English translation of Ḥamīd al-Dīn Aḥmad b. ʿAbd Allāh al-Kirmānī's *al-Maṣābīḥ fī ithbāt al-imāma,* by Paul E. Walker (2007).

Orations of the Fatimid Caliphs:

Festival Sermons of the Ismaili Imams

An edition of the Arabic texts and English translation of Fatimid *khuṭba*s

by

Paul E. Walker

I.B.Tauris *Publishers*
LONDON • NEW YORK
in association with
The Institute of Ismaili Studies
LONDON

Published in 2009 by I.B.Tauris & Co Ltd
6 Salem Rd, London W2 4BU
175 Fifth Avenue, New York NY 10010
www.ibtauris.com

in association with The Institute of Ismaili Studies
42–44 Grosvenor Gardens, London SW1W 0EB
www.iis.ac.uk

Distributed in the United States of America and in Canada Exclusively by
Palgrave Macmillan, 175 Fifth Avenue, New York NY 10010

ISBN 978 1 84511 991 1

A full CIP record for this book is available from the British Library
A full CIP record for this book is available from the Library of Congress

Library of Congress catalog card: available

Typeset in Minion Tra for The Institute of Ismaili Studies
Printed by the MPG Books Group in the UK

The Institute of Ismaili Studies

The Institute of Ismaili Studies was established in 1977 with the object of promoting scholarship and learning on Islam, in the historical as well as contemporary contexts, and a better understanding of its relationship with other societies and faiths.

The Institute's programmes encourage a perspective which is not confined to the theological and religious heritage of Islam, but seeks to explore the relationship of religious ideas to broader dimensions of society and culture. The programmes thus encourage an interdisciplinary approach to the materials of Islamic history and thought. Particular attention is also given to issues of modernity that arise as Muslims seek to relate their heritage to the contemporary situation.

Within the Islamic tradition, the Institute's programmes promote research on those areas which have, to date, received relatively little attention from scholars. These include the intellectual and literary expressions of Shiʿism in general, and Ismailism in particular.

In the context of Islamic societies, the Institute's programmes are informed by the full range and diversity of cultures in which Islam is practised today, from the Middle East, South and Central Asia, and Africa to the industrialized societies of the West, thus taking into consideration the variety of contexts which shape the ideals, beliefs and practices of the faith.

These objectives are realized through concrete programmes and activities organized and implemented by various departments of the Institute. The Institute also collaborates periodically, on a programme-specific basis, with other institutions of learning in the United Kingdom and abroad.

The Institute's academic publications fall into a number of inter-related categories:

1. Occasional papers or essays addressing broad themes of the relationship between religion and society, with special reference to Islam.
2. Monographs exploring specific aspects of Islamic faith and culture, or the contributions of individual Muslim thinkers or writers.
3. Editions or translations of significant primary or secondary texts.
4. Translations of poetic or literary texts which illustrate the rich heritage of spiritual, devotional and symbolic expressions in Muslim history.
5. Works on Ismaili history and thought, and the relationship of the Ismailis to other traditions, communities and schools of thought in Islam.
6. Proceedings of conferences and seminars sponsored by the Institute.
7. Bibliographical works and catalogues which document manuscripts, printed texts and other source materials.

This book falls into category three listed above.

In facilitating these and other publications, the Institute's sole aim is to encourage original research and analysis of relevant issues. While every effort is made to ensure that the publications are of a high academic standard, there is naturally bound to be a diversity of views, ideas and interpretations. As such, the opinions expressed in these publications must be understood as belonging to their authors alone.

Table of Contents

Preface and Acknowledgements

Several years ago I received a fellowship award from the National Endowment for the Humanities to conduct a study of the imperial rhetoric in Fatimid public pronouncements. Part of my plan involved collecting all known copies of decrees, orders, letters, and manifestos issued by the government, in addition to any other written record of official communiqués. We possess almost none in their original form but many, perhaps upwards of 300, exist in various secondary contexts having been transcribed by clerks of the chancery or by historians and others for their own purposes. One result of my effort was a preliminary catalogue of such materials. Another, however, was the realization of how important one subset of it could be. Those were the sermons delivered by the Fatimid imam-caliphs. The great majority of the other documents were the product of the royal chancery; they were composed by people employed in it and thus not by the caliphs, at least not directly. This situation does not diminish the value of such decrees as a true expression of Fatimid policy; all of them were certainly offered in accord with explicit orders and each said what the caliph wanted said. But, while voicing his sentiments and that of the tradition to which the Fatimids ascribed, few actually conveyed his own words. In short, except for a small handful, the caliph rarely wrote them himself. In general, however, the opposite was true of the sermons, which were not only delivered by the imams in person whenever possible, but also composed by them. Therefore we have the possibility, in this latter case, of listening to (or more precisely of reading) the very words of the imams.

The sermon—in Arabic, the *khuṭba*—was (and is) a standard feature of Friday congregational observance. It was offered each and every Friday. The Fatimid caliphs naturally did not deliver such sermons that often. However, the duty to do so on the twice-yearly occasion of the festivals—the two Muslim *ʿīd*s, the feasts of fast-breaking and of sacrifice—was taken seriously and seldom missed by the imams. In later Fatimid times some Friday sermons were added for Ramaḍān. Yet precious few examples, even of the sermons delivered by an imam, have survived. Still, those that have come down to us are more than enough to begin to appreciate the event and the words uttered on it.

Our principal purpose in this book is, therefore, to provide access to these sermons by presenting the Arabic originals and complete English translations of all those now available. To understand their context it is also necessary to learn as much as possible about the practice of the *khuṭba* and its history. For this reason, the first two chapters are devoted to a history of the Fatimid *khuṭba*—what was said, by whom and on what occasions, and to an analysis of the themes and rhetorical strategies given expression in the surviving examples.

Acknowledgements

It is most important to recognize at the outset the work of Muḥammad al-Yaʿlāwī. Had it not been for his *al-Adab fi-Ifrīqiya fi'l-ʿahd al-Fāṭimiyya* (French title, *La literature en Ifriqiya sous les Fatimides*, published in Beirut, 1986) I would, most likely, never have noticed the importance of these *khuṭba*s or, more significantly, how many of them exist. In his book al-Yaʿlāwī assembled all the known examples of early Fatimid literature—texts which were actually composed in North Africa during the period of the caliph's residence there—including the sermons, some letters, and poetry.

To better comprehend the Islamic tradition of sermons, I consulted many friends and colleagues. In one instance I organized a panel of experts on the topic for the Middle East Studies Association annual meeting (2006). To my fellow panelists, Jonathan P. Berkey, Philip Halldén, Linda Gale Jones, and Tahera Qutbuddin, I owe special thanks for having educated me in this subject, either on that occasion or through their writings.

As I delved ever more deeply into the rituals surrounding the delivery of these sermons, I came to rely increasingly on Paula

Sanders' study of Fatimid ceremonial, *Ritual, Politics, and the City in Fatimid Cairo* (Albany, NY, 1994). Ultimately it seemed only natural to consult her directly. I asked her to read an early version of Chapter 1 and she kindly responded positively, offering queries, corrections, and new information.

I must also thank Abbas Hamdani who offered me the chance to participate peripherally in his project to edit and publish Ḥātim b. Ibrāhīm al-Ḥāmidī's *Kitāb tuḥfat al-qulūb wa farjat al-makrūb*. One of the caliphal *khuṭba*s included here is found in it alone.

At a late stage I had the opportunity to show the Arabic of these sermons to Husain Qutbuddin, who, in addition to his own scholarship in the topic of Ismaili commentary on the Qur'an, is himself a *ḥāfiẓ*. Keenly aware of which phrases are verbatim quotations from the sacred book and which echo or borrow from it, he provided much needed guidance.

Several other colleagues, especially at the University of Chicago, generously allowed me to consult them concerning matters arising from this study, among them Ahmed Hashem, Khaled Keshk, Tahera Qutbuddin, Saifiyah Qutbuddin and Bruce Craig.

Writing to thank those who helped with a project such as this months before the final steps of editing and printing means having to leave out many names that ought to be mentioned but who appear too late to be included. Given that this book follows another of mine in the same series (*Master of the Age: An Islamic Treatise on the Necessity of the Imamate*), it will not be amiss to cite here the staff of The Institute of Ismaili Studies, most particularly of the editorial team at the Department of Academic Research and Publications, Kutub Kassam, Patricia Salazar and Fayaz Alibhai, as well as Shellina Karmali of the library, who provided invaluable help on that book. I can only hope that this volume will have benefit of as much help and attention as that one did.

Note on the Arabic texts of the *khuṭbas*

The first nine *khuṭbas* (nos. 1–9) in this collection come from the North African period of Fatimid rule. As noted above, the well respected Tunisian scholar Muḥammad al-Yaʿlāwī first brought special attention to them as a part of his work *al-Adab bi-Ifrīqiya fi'l-ʿahd al-Fāṭimiyya.*

For that volume he assembled the surviving examples of the caliphal *khuṭbas*, providing in the process a basic edition of the Arabic text for each one. For the Arabic text of these nine I have relied in the main on that edition. A year earlier, al-Yaʿlāwī also published a critical edition of the North African portion of the highly important history of the Ismaili imams by the 15th-century Ṭayyibī authority Idrīs ʿImād al-Dīn, the *ʿUyūn al-akhbār*. His edition of that work carries the title: *Taʾrīkh al-khulafāʾ al-Fāṭimiyyīn biʾl-maghrib: al-qism al-khāṣṣ min Kitāb ʿuyūn al-akhbār* (Beirut, 1985). As it is also the principal source for eight of these nine *khuṭbas* (all but no. 8), three of which appear in it alone (nos. 1, 3 and 9), al-Yaʿlāwī's text, either there or in his *al-Adab bi-Ifrīqiya*, may be accepted as the basic edition of them, as I have done in this work. He had also consulted the *Sīrat Jawdhar*, which includes among its many documents from the period three of these *khuṭbas* (nos. 2, 5 and 7). Ustādh Jawdhar was the eunuch servant of the early Fatimid caliphs. Eventually he rose as high in such service as possible, becoming a quasi-wazir, responsible for much of the government, as well as the personal affairs of his masters. Two of the *khuṭbas* (nos. 2 and 7) were given to him personally by the caliph al-Manṣūr for him to hold in safe-keeping and to copy for himself. Jawdhar's collection of letters and documents—the *khuṭbas* among them—were edited by one of his own servants, a disciple named Abū ʿAlī al-Manṣūr al-Jawdharī ('al-Jawdharī' to signify that he once belonged to Jawdhar), to form what is called his *Sīra*. That was published as *Sīrat Ustādh Jawdhar*, Arabic text edited by M. K. Husayn and M. ʿAbd al-Hādī Shaʿīra (Cairo, 1954), with a French translation by M. Canard, *Vie de l'ustadh Jaudhar* (Alger, 1958). Given that Jawdhar was himself a contemporary witness, his copies would have great claim to authenticity if, in fact, we could be certain of the transmission of his text, which was preserved and recopied exclusively by the same Ṭayyibī *daʿwa* to which Idrīs belonged. In his *ʿUyūn al-akhbār*, Idrīs obviously made use of it; his versions of these same *khuṭbas* are thus also a witness to those of Jawdhar.

In his *al-Adab bi-Ifrīqiya*, al-Yaʿlāwī added readings and additions from yet another source for three of the eight *khuṭbas* (nos. 4, 6 and 7) in the *ʿUyūn al-akhbār*: namely the 15th-century Mamluk era historian al-Maqrīzī's unfinished biographical dictionary, the *Muqaffā*. Although never completed, we possess substantial portions of this work, including its lengthy biography of al-Manṣūr. Among other pieces by the caliph, this section of the *Muqaffā* contains four of his *khuṭbas*. Three of them are versions of those known already from Idrīs, but one is unique (no. 8). It does not appear in any other source.

Five years after publishing his *al-Adab bi-Ifrīqiya*, al-Yaʿlāwī completed an edition of what survives of the *Muqaffā* (Beirut, 1991). Volume two includes the biography of al-Manṣūr (pp. 129–180). Although the editor is not quite clear about the changes he might have incorporated—the printed text of this material in the *Muqaffā* is later than his earlier editions of the same texts—it seems reasonable to assume that any adjustments he thought necessary for the later publication represent a better reading of the text. I have tried to adopt here the latest version.

For the first of these sermons, we possess, in addition to the al-Yaʿlāwī edition, a version offered by Samuel Stern and published in chapter six of his posthumous *Studies in Early Ismāʿīlism* (Jerusalem, 1983), pp. 116–121. Stern's source, as with al-Yaʿlāwī, was Idrīs's *ʿUyūn al-akhbār*. But he apparently based his work on a different manuscript. I have noted the main variants between the two and marked them as 'Stern' in the apparatus.

One *khuṭba* (but one only)—a sermon by al-Manṣūr (no. 7) on the ʿĪd al-fiṭr 336—appears in all three of these sources: in the *Sīrat Jawdhar*, in the *ʿUyūn al-akhbār*, and in the *Muqaffā*. A careful investigation of the differences indicates how close the three are for most of the text, and yet there are also serious discrepancies. That Idrīs follows Jawdhar fairly accurately is to be expected. But al-Maqrīzī, whose versions of these texts are generally less exact than those of Idrīs, includes a whole paragraph or more that is missing from the *ʿUyūn al-akhbār*. Obviously, then, al-Maqrīzī had access to a source that Idrīs most likely did not.

Two more of the *khuṭbas* (nos. 12 and 13) in this collection come from the *ʿUyūn al-akhbār*, not from the earlier North African period but from much later: the first decades of the 6th/12th century and the reign of the caliph al-Āmir. That section of the work was edited and published by Ayman Fu'ad Sayyid in *The Fatimids and Their Successors in Yaman: The History of an Islamic Community* (London,

2002). In the case of these latter two *khuṭba*s, I was able to consult a manuscript that Sayyid did not have. For it I have entered several new readings indicated in the notes with the letter ف, here meaning the Fyzee manuscript now in Haydarabad. (The letter أ represents Ayman Fu'ad Sayyid's reading).

The remaining two *khuṭba*s (nos. 10 and 11) derive respectively from the 6th/12th-century Ṭayyibī *dāʿī* Ḥātim b. Ibrāhīm al-Ḥāmidī's *Kitāb tuḥfat al-qulūb wa farjat al-makrūb*, as edited by Abbas Hamdani (forthcoming), and from Ibn al-Jawzī's *al-Muntaẓam fī ta'rīkh al-mulūk wa'l-umam* (Hayderabad, 1939). The same *khuṭba* of Qirwāsh is also found in Ibn Taghrī Birdī's *al-Nujūm al-zāhira fī mulūk Miṣr wa'l-Qāhira* (Cairo) with some variations. I have taken note of the differences between the two in the apparatus.

Qur'anic quotations in the Arabic and in the translations

These *khuṭba*s are full of Qur'anic references, either as verbatim quotations or borrowings that reflect less exactly the wording of a particular passage. The speaker in most cases fully intended his audience to recognize them. In this type of discourse, which is religious by its very nature and which, especially when delivered by the imam himself, carries the highest doctrinal authority, does not require that these quotations have formal markers. Thus the text does not indicate exactly which phrases derive from the sacred book. For the present purpose, however, it seems essential to identify them. Accordingly, I have noted in the main body of each *khuṭba* those that quote verbatim, enclosing them with quotation marks and adding in brackets the *sūra* and verse numbers. Others that recall or allude to a Qur'anic phrase, but not with the precise words, I have identified only in the notes. Certain standard, oft-repeated phrases that have a Qur'anic counterpart, but are here not clearly quoted from it, have not always been acknowledged in this manner.

Paul E. Walker
Chicago

List of Abbreviations

Daʿāʾim	Qāḍī al-Nuʿmān. *Daʿāʾim al-Islām*, ed. A. A. A. Fyzee. Cairo, 1951–1961; tr. Fyzee and Ismail K. Poonawala, *The Pillars of Islam*, 2 vols. New Delhi, 2002–2004.
EI2	*The Encyclopaedia of Islam*, New Edition.
Ittiʿāẓ	al-Maqrīzī. *Ittiʿāẓ al-ḥunafāʾ bi-akhbār al-aʾimma al-Fāṭimiyyīn al-khulafāʾ*, vol. 1, ed. Jamāl al-Dīn al-Shayyāl, and vols. 2–3, ed. Muḥammad Ḥilmī Muḥammad Aḥmad. Cairo, 1967–1973.
JSAI	*Jerusalem Studies in Arabic and Islam.*
Khiṭaṭ	al-Maqrīzī. *al-Khiṭaṭ* (*al-maʿrūf biʾl-mawāʿiẓ waʾl-iʿtibār biʾdhikr al-khiṭaṭ waʾl-āthār*), New edition by A. F. Sayyid, 5 vols. London, 2002–2004.
al-Muqaffā	al-Maqrīzī, *Kitāb al-Muqaffā al-kabīr*, ed. M. al-Yaʿlāwī, 8 vols. Beirut, 1991.
Q	The Qurʾan.
ʿUyūn (ed. Yaʿlāwī)	Idrīs ʿImād al-Dīn. *ʿUyūn al-akhbār*, ed. M. al-Yaʿlāwī as *Taʾrīkh al-khulafāʾ al-Fāṭimiyyīn biʾl-maghrib: al-qism al-khāṣṣ min Kitāb ʿuyūn al-akhbār*. Beirut, 1985.
ʿUyūn (ed. Ghālib)	Idrīs ʿImād al-Dīn. *ʿUyūn al-akhbār, al-sabʿ al-sādis* (vol. 6), ed. Muṣṭafā Ghālib. Beirut, 1984.
ʿUyūn (ed. Sayyid)	Idrīs ʿImād al-Dīn. *ʿUyūn al-akhbār, al-sabʿ al-sābiʿ* (vol. 7), ed. A. F. Sayyid in his *The Fatimids and Their Successors in Yaman: The History of an Islamic Community*. London, 2002.

PART ONE

Introductions

CHAPTER 1

A History of the Fatimid *Khuṭba*

A Fatimid *khuṭba* in Abbasid Iraq

In the year 401 (1010–1011), the ʿUqaylid ruler of north Mesopotamia, Qirwāsh b. al-Muqallad, abruptly announced that he would switch his allegiance from the Abbasid caliph in Baghdad to the Fatimid caliph al-Ḥākim bi-Amr Allāh in Cairo. He was in fact setting up a *daʿwa*, an appeal, in the latter's name. In typical fashion the formal public declaration of the change occurred in the next Friday *khuṭba* delivered in Mawṣil, the capital city of Qirwāsh's domain. The ʿUqaylid ruler simply handed the *khaṭīb* (the preacher) the text of his new sermon and the man dutifully read it to the assembled worshippers. That was the 4th of Muḥarram (18 August). Two months later, on the 2nd of Rabīʿ al-Awwal (13 October), the same or a similar announcement greeted the Muslim community in the congregational mosque of al-Anbār and one week after that in al-Madāʾin and Qaṣr ibn Hubayra.[1] A quick glance at a map of Iraq indicates that the cities that had unexpectedly gone over to the Fatimids form what amounted to a noose around Baghdad. The Abbasid caliph could not but be alarmed; his position had, seemingly overnight, become perilous.[2]

1. ʿIzz al-Dīn Ibn al-Athīr, *al-Kāmil fi'l-ta'rīkh*, ed. C. J. Tornberg (Leiden, 1867; reprinted Beirut, 1965–1967), 9, p. 223, adds to these cities al-Kūfa and claims there were others as well.

2. Abu'l-Faraj Ibn al-Jawzī, *al-Muntaẓam fī ta'rīkh al-mulūk wa'l-umam* (Hayderabad, 1939), 7, pp. 248–251; Jamāl al-Dīn Abu'l-Maḥāsin Ibn Taghrī Birdī, *al-Nujūm al-zāhira fī mulūk Miṣr wa'l-Qāhira* (Cairo, 1929–1949; Cairo, 1963–1971), 4: 224–227; Shihāb al-Dīn Aḥmad al-Nuwayrī, *Nihāyat al-arab fī funūn al-adab: al-Juz al-thāmin wa'l-ʿishrūn*, ed. Muḥammad Muḥammad Amīn and Muḥammad

Later Sunni historians, principally Ibn al-Jawzī and Ibn Taghrī Birdī, both of whom were decidedly anti-Fatimid, had a hard time making sense of this incident, even though they provide far more details about it than any other sources. Ibn al-Jawzī reports that agents for al-Ḥākim worked persistently to win over the ʿUqaylids and eventually succeeded. Both historians insist that the inhabitants of Mawṣil agreed to the change with the 'positive response of an enslaved flock, while concealing their true aversion and disgust', and both marvel at how easily the *khaṭīb*, who had previously pronounced the sermon in the name of the Abbasid caliph, al-Qādir bi-llāh, would acquiesce in the change, which amounted almost to converting from Sunni to Shiʿi Islam. They offer a list of rather sumptuous new accoutrements—by implication a bribe—bestowed on him for the occasion.[3]

For al-Qādir the matter was urgent and critical. Still, he himself possessed no real army. His throne depended on the good will of Buyid overlords. To make his case to them, he enlisted the help of the famous Mālikī jurist and Ashʿarite theologian, Abū Bakr al-Bāqillānī, whose anti-Ismaili sentiments were well known. Al-Bāqillānī went to Bahāʾ al-Dawla, the supreme Buyid amir, who, although himself inclined to Shiʿism, was nevertheless bothered by Qirwāsh's act, seeing it as a challenge to his own authority. The Buyid ruler then ordered 100,000 dīnārs to be spent either on a military force or a bribe to convince the ʿUqaylid to reverse course and return to the Abbasids. Our historians claim that al-Ḥākim had offered no more than 30,000. In any case, Qirwāsh quickly realized where his best interest lay; the *khuṭba* in his lands soon once again called for God's blessings on

---

Ḥilmī Muḥammad Aḥmad (Cairo, 1992), 28: 190; al-Maqrīzī, *Ittiʿāẓ*, 2: 88; Ibn Athīr, *al-Kāmil*, 9, p. 223; Heinz Halm, *Die Kalifen von Kairo: Die Fatimiden in Ägypten, 973–1074* (Munich, 2003), p. 275.

3. The list is clearest in Ibn Taghrī Birdī. One explanation for Qirwāsh's having bestowed what amounts to a *khilʿa*, a formal robe of honour, on his *khaṭīb* is that the Fatimid colours were white whereas those of the Abbasids were black. Accordingly, *the qabāʾ dabīqiyyā*, a tunic of *dabīqī* linen mentioned by him, would have been white to symbolize the change officially. In addition he was given a yellow turban, pants of red brocade, and red shoes. See Adam Metz, *The Renaissance of Islam*, trans. S. Kh. Bukhsh and D. S. Margoliouth (London, 1937), p. 325.

al-Qādir. Within a couple of months at most—some say a month only—the matter had been resolved in favour of the Abbasids.[4]

In all, this incident seems to represent but a brief interval, hardly worth more than a passing mention. The rivalry between the two caliphates was old by then. The Abbasid al-Qādir required little to provoke him at any time into the strongest reaction and take what counter-measures he could. The famous Baghdad Manifesto of 402, one year later, which refuted the validity of the Fatimid claim of descent from ʿAlī b. Abī Ṭālib, is an example. Even so, while not itself a lasting stage in this competition, an unexpected benefit of Qirwāsh's declaration of 401 is that a verbatim copy of the actual text of the *khuṭba* he issued for the occasion survived. And, most intriguing, it was carefully preserved by Ibn al-Jawzī, and from him by Ibn Taghrī Birdī. It is true that many odd bits of information show up in the former's *al-Muntaẓam*, but for a vehemently anti-Fatimid writer to include this *khuṭba*, which is clearly pro-Fatimid, in its entirety, is at the least curious. Still more puzzling is that it is the sole complete example of a standard Friday *khuṭba* on behalf of the Fatimids to reach us.

*Khuṭba*s and *khaṭīb*s

The Friday sermon is a required element in Islamic ritual; it is universally acknowledged by Muslims and performed in every weekly service as part of the community's congregational worship. Its origin

4. The explanations provided by Sunni historians for Qirwāsh's rather quick reversal is that of al-Nuwayrī (*Nihāya*, 28: 190): 'In the year 401, the *daʿwa* for al-Ḥākim was established in al-Madāʾin, which lies half a stage from Baghdad. The *khuṭba* was also said for him in the Iraqi cities of al-Anbār and Qaṣr ibn Hubayra because of Qirwāsh's having accepted allegiance to him and having revealed his own Shiʿism. That was in the days of the Abbasid caliph al-Qādir. Subsequently, Qirwāsh learned of the unstable rule of al-Ḥākim, that he had killed the leading notables of his government and had been overcome by melancholia. Thereupon he reverted to the Abbasid *khuṭba*.' But al-Nuwayrī reports, in addition, that the *daʿwa* to al-Ḥākim, with its attendant *khuṭba*, commenced about this time in Hilla under ʿAlī b. Mazyad, ruler of another portion of Abbasid Iraq. He neglects to mention that the ʿUqaylids announced their support of the Fatimid caliph on other occasions, among which is one many years later. Their latent Shiʿism and inclination to recognize the Ismaili imamate was therefore either always present, though prudently hidden, or recurring.

is extremely old, going back to the practice of the Prophet, perhaps even earlier. Many of the provisions for it are common to the several *madhhabs*, including the Shiʿa. The Fatimids were no exception.[5] Typically, the sermon, which precedes prayers, is delivered by a professional preacher, the *khaṭīb*. Under the Fatimids *khaṭībs* (the Arabic plural is *khuṭabāʾ*) were government officials employed by the judiciary. They thus fell within the domain of the chief qadi, the *qāḍī al-quḍāt*.[6] Therefore, significantly, although the Fatimids continued to maintain the *daʿwa*, as its teaching and proselytizing organization, which was likewise a bureau of the government, the *khuṭba* was not the responsibility of the chief *dāʿī* or of his missionaries. Nevertheless, a late source reports that the salary allocated for individual *khaṭībs* was ten to twenty dinars per month,[7] which is a not inconsiderable amount, and indicates how important they were.[8] A passage from a section of al-Qalqashandī's manual of chancery practice includes the text of a decree of appointment for a judge under the Fatimids. One paragraph in it is devoted to the role of the *khaṭībs* whose job he is to supervise:

> The *khaṭībs* are the knights of the *minbars*, the tongues of those assembled, the spokesmen of the sacred rituals, and the leaders of the congregations. They are the emissaries of the heart to its lofty station by means of the ears, its purifier that makes hearts overcome

---

5. For some indication of Fatimid doctrine in regard to the *khuṭba*, see al-Qāḍī al-Nuʿmān's *Daʿāʾim* 1: 182–187, trans. 1: 227–233.

6. The *khaṭāba*, the office responsible for the *khuṭba*, is specifically listed among the duties of the chief qadi in the few decrees of appointment that we have. See, for example, the appointment decree of Ibn Abi'l-ʿAwwām, who became chief judge at the end of al-Ḥākim's reign, in *Ittiʿāẓ*, 2: 108.

7. *Ittiʿāẓ*, 3: 340.

8. There is unfortunately little specific discussion of the appointment of individuals to the office of *khaṭīb*, the *khaṭāba*. But see Tāj al-Dīn Muḥammad Ibn Muyassar, *al-Muntaqā min Akhbār Miṣr*, ed. Ayman Fu'ād Sayyid (Cairo, 1981), p. 96 (Abu'l-Fakhr Ṣāliḥ was made *khaṭīb* of al-Azhār along with supervision of the royal library in 517); *Ittiʿāẓ*, 3: 290 (appointment to the office for the Old Mosque in Fusṭāṭ in 563); Ibn Muyassar, *Akhbār Miṣr*, p. 126 (a case of someone whose father had been *khaṭīb* in Fusṭāṭ prior to 531 when the son was executed). On the qualities of the ideal *khaṭīb* see Shihāb al-Dīn Aḥmad al-Qalqashandī, *Ṣubḥ al-aʿshā fī ṣināʿat al-inshāʾ* (Cairo, 1912–1938), who provides a sample appointment decree for the judiciary, 10: 432–433, as quoted below.

its illnesses. His warfare drives away the satans of the communities when they commit aggression against them. He gives expression to guidance and uses his eloquence to the utmost to lead them rightly. He perfects the articulation of the letters so that they serve to enable their fulfilment and manifestation. His exhortation unties from the hardened eyes the knots that bind them and he calls to the rusted hearts until his cry unleashes their tears. He wears proudly the robes of high dignity so that *minbar*s appear properly dressed because of him. His sermons nourish the souls when they come to him seeking assistance and appealing for help.[9]

There is no reason to assume that the sentiments articulated in this quite late document are in any way different from what might have been expressed a century or two earlier. Just as they would have been in other regions of the Islamic world, these 'knights of the *minbar*', whether Ismaili or not, were, under the Fatimids, men of distinction and religious probity.

Rules for the *khuṭba*, as stipulated in the writings of the various schools, stress that it be brief, among other conditions, for example, regarding dress of the *khaṭīb* and his ritual purity. Other provisions pertain to its content: recitation of Qur'anic passages, prayers (*duʿā'*) on behalf of the faithful, admonitions to piety, blessings on the Prophet, all normally regarded as obligatory. Generally these *khuṭba*s actually consist of two given consecutively. The *khaṭīb* mounts the *minbar*, pronounces the first, sits for a moment, and then rises for the second. Other occasions for the *khuṭba* include the two *ʿīd* festivals: ʿĪd al-fiṭr, breaking of the fast following the close of Ramaḍān, and ʿĪd al-aḍḥā (also called ʿĪd al-naḥr), the feast of sacrifice on the 10th of Dhu'l-Ḥijja. *Khuṭba*s may be a part of rituals for special purposes such as an eclipse, a drought, or an appeal for a *jihād*. A festival *khuṭba*, which, in contrast to that of Fridays, follows prayers, conforms to the occasion of it, featuring instructions to the congregation on the stipulations for either the *zakāt al-fiṭr* (alms due at the breaking of the fast) or for proper and acceptable sacrifice (i.e. what animals may be slaughtered and how).[10]

9. This document was written by Qāḍī al-Fāḍil on behalf of the caliph al-ʿĀḍid for the appointment of a judge who is not named (al-Qalqashandī, *Ṣubḥ al-aʿshā*, 10: 424–434); the paragraph about the *khaṭīb* is found on pp. 432–433.

10. On the role of the *khuṭba* in Islamic ritual, see '*Khuṭba*' by A. J. Wensinck

Though not necessary according to Islamic law, it was customary to mention in these *khuṭba*s the name of the ruling sovereign by imploring God to bestow His blessing on him. This custom gained enormous importance, so much so that the historical chronicles note any changes or alterations, such as is in the case of Qirwāsh, just cited. Whereas *khuṭba*s naming the ruler, the reigning caliph, or both were routine throughout a kingdom, any alteration or modification had immediate political consequences. A switch from the Abbasids to the Fatimids, or vice versa, had religious meaning as well. This aspect of the *khuṭba* and its variations is a vital tool for determining the history of dynasties. More than the coinage, which also names the ultimate authority under whom it was issued, the *khuṭba* established sovereignty in as short a span of time as one week. There are, moreover, instances where the *khuṭba* changed back and forth quickly.

The holy cities of the Hijaz, for example, possessed huge symbolic significance. The caliph could claim ultimate supremacy only if he controlled them. The Fatimids obtained recognition in Mecca and Medina with the advent of the caliph al-Muʿizz in Egypt. The *khuṭba* named them thereafter until the Seljuks grew powerful enough to contest it. As with other cities and regions, however, the *khuṭba* in Mecca and Medina could revert.[11] Aleppo in northern Syria witnessed

in the *EI2*, and for the Shiʿi (Fatimid) rules for it according to the imams, see the section on ritual prayer in the *Daʿāʾim*, particularly Arabic 1: 182–187, trans. 1: 227–232.

11. Various medieval chronicles preserve details of these changes back and forth. In 462/1070, for example, the *khuṭba* in Mecca reverted to the Abbasids, after, says our source al-Maqrīzī, 100 years (*Ittiʿāẓ*, 2: 303–304). The reason given is that the Fatimids had failed to send food and funds to the Hijaz during what was then a time of severe hardship throughout Egypt. Five years later, however, in 467/1075, with the advent of Badr al-Jamālī and the restoration of order, it came back to the Fatimids. That year a *minbar* embossed in gold with the name of the Abbasid caliph al-Muqtadī arrived in Mecca during Ramaḍān and was quickly smashed and burned because it represented the wrong caliphate (*Ittiʿāẓ* 2: 314 and 319). In Shaʿbān of 468, al-Mustanṣir wrote to the Yaman to boast of the restoration of his name in the Holy Cities and the eradication there of the shame of the Umayyads and the Abbasids. If Badr al-Jamālī, he says, 'were to accomplish nothing other than this glorious feat, done so recently, that would be sufficient.' See Ayman Fuʾād

frequent changes of allegiances throughout the 5th/11th century. The Zīrids in North Africa likewise both renounced their recognition of the Fatimids and returned to it on several occasions, beginning in the mid-5th/11th century and continuing onward to the time of al-Āmir in the early part of the next.

Nor were *khuṭbas* accorded this level of political importance solely within the lands of Islam. An interesting case is that of Constantinople and the Byzantine empire. Fatimid relations with the Byzantines began soon after the conquest of the Maghrib and continued, at times with animosity and in other periods with peace, for the next two centuries or more. In the year 378/988, a treaty concluded with Byzantium stipulated, among other provisions, that the *khuṭba* said in the mosque of Constantinople name the Fatimid caliph al-ʿAzīz as the Muslim supreme authority.[12] It is difficult to imagine that the congregation of Muslims in the Byzantine capital was large enough to be significant. However, renewals of this treaty maintained that provision. In 418/1027, a treaty with the Emperor made sure that *khuṭbas* in the lands of the Byzantines were to name only the Fatimid al-Ẓāhir. The mosque in Constantinople is to reopen, it says, and in exchange al-Ẓāhir will permit the reopening of the Church of the Holy Sepulchre in Jerusalem (both were evidently closed in the period prior to this).[13] Three decades later, in 447/1055, this stipulation remained in effect (or had been renewed in subsequent treaties), when an ambassador from the Seljuk sultan Tughril Beg arrived in Constantinople and asked if he could use its mosque. The Emperor granted him permission. The man went to the mosque on Friday to say his prayer and while there also gave a *khuṭba* in the name of the Abbasid caliph al-Qā'im. At the same time the qadi Abū ʿAbdallāh al-Quḍāʿī, who was the official representative of the

Sayyid, *al-Dawla al-Fāṭimiyya fī Miṣr: Tafsīr jadīd*, 2nd ed. (Cairo, 2000), p. 212; the source of the words of al-Mustanṣir is his *sijill* no. 58, also no. 57, in *Sijillāt al-Mustanṣiriyya*, ed. ʿAbd al-Munʿim Mājid (Cairo, 1954), pp. 192–193 and 187–188 respectively). But this restoration lasted only until 472/1079–1080 when the *khuṭba* once more was said for the Abbasids (*Ittiʿāẓ*, 2: 320; Ibn al-Jawzī, *al-Muntaẓam*, 8: 323).

12. Ibn Taghrī Birdī, *al-Nujūm*, 4: 152.

13. *Ittiʿāẓ*, 2: 176.

Fatimid caliph al-Mustanṣir, happened to be in Constantinople on behalf of his own master. He reported this breech of the treaty to Cairo, whereupon al-Mustanṣir revoked its provisions and ordered that all the goods and possessions in the Holy Sepulchre be seized by the government, leading predictably to a serious deterioration of relations with the Byzantines.[14] Yet it is unclear if the Byzantines fully appreciated how a small gesture on their part—allowing a visitor to use the mosque—could cause such an aggressive reaction elsewhere. Perhaps they failed to realize that al-Quḍāʿī was present and would report what had happened to Cairo.

Changing the *khuṭba* might come with other symbolic measures beyond the naming of the new ruler and altering the colour of the preacher's robes. In 450/1058, when the amir al-Basāsīrī captured Baghdad on behalf of the Fatimids, he had the *khuṭba* read in the name of al-Mustanṣir in its mosques and the *muṣallā* (festival grounds) one by one. Al-Maqrīzī reports that, on the ʿĪd al-naḥr, he smashed the *minbar* in the mosque in Baghdad and built a new one, stating 'this *minbar* is sinister; from it hatred of the family of Muḥammad has been proclaimed'.[15]

But the other side could be equally as vociferous. A case in point involves the Zīrids. This dynasty inherited the old Maghribi dominion of the early Fatimids. They were theoretically vassals of the caliph in Cairo. The Ṣanhāja Berbers from which tribe these rulers came were not, however, ever converted to Ismailism in contrast to the Kutāma. Most remained Mālikī Sunni even while supporting, at first loyally, the Fatimid cause. Shortly after the accession of the Zīrid al-Muʿizz b. Bādīs in 407/1016, anti-Ismaili riots, fomented by Mālikī clerics and possibly secretly abetted by the government, decimated what remained of any Shiʿi centres in the cities of North Africa. Nonetheless, al-Muʿizz preserved the trappings of continued allegiance, notably the *khuṭba*, until 440/1048–1049. In that year he cut his ties to Cairo for the first time. The Maghribi (Sunni) historian Ibn ʿIdhārī reports that he ceased the *khuṭba* in favour of the lord of Egypt and burned the banners of the Fatimids. He also quotes from

14. Ibn Muyassar, *Akhbār Miṣr*, p. 14.

15. *Ittiʿāẓ*, 2: 254.

the poet Ibn Sharaf al-Qayrawānī, who was extremely well connected at the Zīrid court and lived contemporary to the event.[16] He offers a detailed account of al-Muʿizz's switching the *khuṭba* to the Abbasids, thereby putting an end to the *daʿwa* of the Fatimids. The reason given is that, following the departure of the caliph from the Maghrib in the middle of the previous century, the appeal of the Fatimids—recitation of their names from the *minbars*—was resented so strongly that fewer and fewer attended the Friday service, leaving the mosques empty. After many years the Zīrid ruler finally, according to this view, came to agree with his subjects, broke off the *khuṭba* in their favour, and divorced himself from them. On top of that he ordered his *khaṭīb*, commencing with the *khuṭba* of the next ʿĪd al-aḍḥā, to insert into the *khuṭba* a cursing of the Fatimids. Ibn Sharaf preserved a copy of the portion that contained this curse and it is available in Ibn ʿIdhārī's *al-Bayān al-mughrib fī akhbār al-Andalus wa'l-Maghrib*.[17]

It is worth wondering, as the medieval authors often do, how the same *khaṭīb* could, after perhaps years of calling upon God to bless the Fatimid caliphs, suddenly recite a string of curses against them, asking that God do the same. But this problem occurred often enough. In the obituaries of famous preachers, their biographers might note, as in one example, that ʿAbd al-Karīm b. al-Ḥusayn Abu'l-Barakāt, a well-respected preacher, had said the *khuṭba* in Damascus for both the Abbasids *and* the Fatimids.[18] And, as with Qirwāsh's *khaṭīb* in 401 and the example here for the Zīrids, there are many more like him.[19]

In most of these examples what exactly was said in the new *khuṭba*, and how, was likely of great historical interest. Nonetheless,

16. On this man see 'Ibn Sharaf al-Ḳayrawānī' by Ch. Pellat in the *EI2*.

17. Abu'l-ʿAbbās Aḥmad b. Muḥammad al-Marrākushī Ibn ʿIdhārī, *al-Bayān al-mughrib fī akhbār al-Andalus wa'l-Maghrib*, vol. 1, ed. G. S. Colin and É. Lévi-Provençal (Beirut, 1948), pp. 277–278. The curse is fairly elaborate and full of invectives, given that al-Muʿizz and the Zīrids were later to revert to the Fatimids on more than one occasion.

18. Ibn Taghrī Birdī, *al-Nujūm*, 5: 138.

19. Not all *khaṭībs* so readily acquiesced. In 401 when the change of the *daʿwa* first reached al-Anbār and was presented to the resident *khaṭīb*, rather than accept, he fled from there to Kūfa to avoid it (Ibn al-Jawzī, *al-Muntaẓam*, 7: 251).

although the text carried obvious importance, there exist few records or information beyond the mere fact of the change. Most *khuṭba*s were never copied; and it is probable that on the vast majority of occasions the preacher spoke extemporaneously, perhaps embellishing a memorized sermon, or elements thereof. Famous *khaṭīb*s—those noted for their rhetorical skills and eloquence—did in certain instances assemble collections of their work in book form, providing in turn models for others in the profession. However, it is difficult now to determine which of them might have been originally read in a mosque rather than composed solely for the book. Thus, while such books of sample sermons may have value as literature, they tell us little about historical events. Under such conditions, the survival of a verbatim copy of Qirwāsh's *khuṭba* is extraordinary. Because it is the sole example of what were, in their time, thousands and thousands of *khuṭba*s on behalf of the Fatimids—one on each Friday in every city and town in their empire, or otherwise in support of them—it holds a unique position. Can it, because it is all we have, stand for the rest? Were the others like it?

Qirwāsh's *khuṭba* may have survived because it was not merely a written text but because copies of it circulated to the other cities of his domain. Possibly the same *khuṭba* was used in al-Anbār, Qaṣr, and al-Madā'in, and perhaps elsewhere in towns unnamed in our reports. It is more than likely that agents of the Abbasid caliph obtained an example of it, which thus made it available to later historians such as the Baghdad-based Ibn al-Jawzī. Significantly, we possess no complete example of an ordinary Friday *khuṭba* delivered inside the Fatimid empire. Given its importance, this situation is puzzling.

The Fatimids ruled a diverse population; Muslims within the empire belonged to a complete array of Islamic communities and schools. Even the chief justices, men who had ultimate responsibility for the *khuṭba* and the *khaṭīb*s employed under their supervision, were frequently not Ismaili. Many judges were Mālikī or Ḥanafī, in other words, Sunnis.[20] Yet a basic stipulation of holding such offices required acceptance of the *khuṭba* and that which was said in

20. A notable example is Ibn Abi'l-ʿAwwām, mentioned later, who was Ḥanafī, but there were many others.

the name of the Fatimid caliph. Muslims attending Friday services anywhere within the empire would hear the preacher ask God to bestow His blessings on these Ismaili imams. It is true that the average citizen need accept what he heard only passively. Even so, he could not escape at least a basic level of recognition of those who ruled over him without fleeing or hiding, and there is little evidence of that, not withstanding the resistance in the Maghrib cited above. Many other parts of the Fatimid empire accepted their rule without protest. They enjoyed considerable support and evident loyalty from all their subjects. Willingness to listen to that *khuṭba* would have constituted a minimal requirement for citizenship within their territory. Would then we could know more about exactly what was said in it.

Festival *khuṭba*s by the Fatimid caliphs

Fortunately, another category of *khuṭba*—those composed and delivered by the caliphs themselves—is much better represented in our sources. Where there are none for the ordinary Friday *khuṭba*, we have a dozen, more or less, for the imams. The Fatimid caliphs believed that it was their responsibility to deliver the *khuṭba* on the two *ʿīd* festivals,[21] a duty evidently well suited to most of them, particularly al-Qāʾim, al-Manṣūr, al-Muʿizz, al-ʿAzīz, al-Ḥākim, al-Ẓāhir, al-Mustanṣir, and al-Āmir. For the rest, evidence of their participation is lacking, which may mean that we simply have no record of their having given the *khuṭba* in person. In the case of the first Fatimid caliph al-Mahdī, however, one report indicates that he did not undertake so public a function, preferring instead to have his eldest son, the future al-Qāʾim, fill that role in his place.

Among those for whom we have examples of their *khuṭba*s, al-Manṣūr stands out. He was famous for his ability to compose and deliver the sermon, and was admired for it even by the Sunnis.[22] The North African historian Ibn Ḥammād commends him for his eloquence,[23] and the Mamluk era Egyptian authority, al-Maqrīzī,

21. In this regard the Fatimids were not alone; other caliphs and Muslim rulers, though not all, likewise delivered such *khuṭba*s in person.

22. By al-Nuwayrī, among others. See his *Nihāya*, 28: 118.

23. Abū ʿAbdallāh Muḥammad b. ʿAlī al-Ṣanhājī Ibn Ḥammād (also Ibn

who is one of our principal sources, included whole *khuṭba*s and other examples of al-Manṣūr's compositions in his biography of this caliph.[24] It is obvious that he also thought highly of them.

It is odd, nonetheless, that we do not have more examples. For Ismailis any statement by the imam has extraordinary value. Surely, if a text of what they said, in the *khuṭba* or on any another occasion, ever existed, it would have been preserved and recopied for posterity? The answer—perhaps the only explanation possible—is that, as with al-Manṣūr, who could deliver the *khuṭba* extemporaneously at will and without a text to read, the caliph rarely wrote down what he said. Those we have copies of are, therefore, all that may have existed; the rest were delivered by him but he left no written text of them. The same may be true of the other imams.

The very earliest *khuṭba* we now possess that was composed and delivered by an imam—actually a future imam—comes from al-Qā'im in his capacity as the heir-apparent. While leading a Fatimid army in the first attempt to conquer Egypt in 302/914–15, he spent time in Alexandria during the *ʿīd* festivals. Following what had evidently become his regular practice, he gave the *khuṭba* on these occasions. One example survives. It was delivered by al-Qā'im on the feast of breaking the fast upon the completion of Ramaḍān that year (19 April 915). What he said in it is, moreover, unusually interesting and historically valuable.[25] The text is quite remarkable for its anti-Abbasid (and anti-Umayyad) content and tone, in sum an admonition to the Egyptians to abandon their overlords in Baghdad.

The Andalusian historian from a slightly later period, ʿArīb b. Saʿd, reports that, while in Alexandria, al-Qā'im delivered many *khuṭba*s, and that they were preserved, evidently meaning that copies of them circulated. ʿArīb himself must have obtained his own copy of this collection because he remarks that if they had not been

---

Ḥamādu), *Histoire des Rois ʿObaïdides* (*Akhbār mulūk banī ʿUbayd wa sīratihum*), ed. and trans. M. Vonderheyden (Alger and Paris, 1927), p. 22.

24. *al-Muqaffā*, bio no. 780, 2: 129–180.

25. Heinz Halm, *Das Reich des Mahdi: Der Aufstieg der Fatimiden* (Munich, 1991), pp. 186–187, English trans. M. Bonner, *The Empire of the Mahdi: The Rise of the Fatimids* (Leiden, 1996), pp. 204–205.

so heretical, he would have borrowed them for his own use.[26] He himself worked under the patronage of the Umayyads in Spain who were vehemently anti-Shiʿa. Al-Qāʾim's castigation of what he calls 'the tyrants of the Banū Umayya' was quite likely pointed at both the Umayyads of a much earlier era as well as their descendants in the west. It is a pity that there is otherwise no trace of this collection of al-Qāʾim's *khuṭbas*.

Moreover, we have no more, either from the reign of his father or his own,[27] until the very end of his life, when, from the sickbed of the illness that killed him, he dictated another *khuṭba*,[28] which he was too weak to deliver in person. It was read to the faithful assembled in the mosque of al-Mahdiyya, which was then under siege by the Khārijite rebel Abū Yazīd, by the qadi al-Marwadhī. That al-Qāʾim actually dictated it himself is attested by his son, who would later deposit his copy of it with Ustādh Jawdhar along with the written text of one of his own *khuṭbas* (one from the year 336). Jawdhar was also given permission to make a copy of both for his own records.[29]

Even so we have good evidence of al-Qāʾim's delivery of the festival *khuṭbas* from the beginning of Fatimid rule. Ibn ʿIdhārī reports that, for the *ʿīd* festivals of the year 297/910, al-Qāʾim led prayers and gave the *khuṭba* at the *muṣallā* of Raqqāda—the earliest administrative capital of the newly formed Fatimid state—on the feast of fast-breaking and on the feast of sacrifice. This historian comments that, for the first occasion, he proceeded to the *muṣallā* 'accompanied by Abū ʿAbdallāh al-Shīʿī and a group of the leading commanders of the Kutāma'. It was, he continues, the first *ʿīd* in which he led the

26. ʿArīb b. Saʿd al-Qurṭubī, *Ṣilat taʾrīkh al-Ṭabarī*, ed. M. J. De Goeje (Leiden, 1897), p. 52.

27. Ibn ʿIdhārī says (*al-Bayān*, p. 208) that, once al-Qāʾim ascended to the caliphate, he went out of the palace (meaning in processions to, for example, the *muṣallā*) no more than twice.

28. That the Imam actually dictated the text himself is based on the testimony of his son al-Manṣūr who says so explicitly. See Abū ʿAlī al-Manṣūr al-Jawdharī, *Sīrat Ustādh Jawdhar*, ed. M. K. Husayn and M. ʿAbd al-Hādī Shaʿīra (Cairo, 1954), p. 53; French trans. M. Canard, *Vie de l'ustadh Jaudhar*, (Alger, 1958), p. 77, where the words of al-Manṣūr are recorded.

29. al-Jawdharī, *Sīrat Jawdhar*, pp. 53–55; French trans., pp. 76–80.

prayer in North Africa. In addition a statement of explanation by the father, al-Mahdī, was read out from the *minbar* of Qayrawān and in the districts surrounding it.[30]

So important was the responsibility for the festival *khuṭba*s that al-Qā'im was quite sensitive to the status they endowed, even though he was frequently also charged with the command of the armies sent great distances away and thus could not always be available in the capital for the *ʿīd*s. On one such expedition in the year 316/928–29, while away in the west, he learned of talk among the people that his father might switch the succession to a younger son, his half brother, Aḥmad Abū ʿAlī. These rumours evidently had started because this son had recently been delegated to lead the festival prayers. Alarmed, al-Qā'im immediately returned to al-Mahdiyya for reassurance and to put an end to any gossip of the kind.[31]

Fatimid *khuṭba*s in North Africa

There are two other important pieces of information about *khuṭba*s from the beginning of Fatimid rule. One is that Abū ʿAbdallāh al-Shīʿī (who spearheaded the initial conquest of the Maghrib), prior to the advent of al-Mahdī, gave a general order to include in all *khuṭba*s a blessing on Muḥammad and his family. 'He had the *khaṭīb*s of the mosques of Raqqāda and al-Qayrawān lead the way. He also wrote to other regions to the same effect. Abū ʿAbdallāh ordered that the *khuṭba* include blessings on Muḥammad, on his family, on the Commander of the Believers ʿAlī, on al-Ḥasan and al-Ḥusayn, and on Fāṭima the Radiant, may the blessings of God be on them all.'[32] Therefore the essential elements of a Shiʿi *khuṭba* were already present before the first

30. Ibn ʿIdhārī, *al-Bayān*, 1: 160 and 161; Halm, *Reich des Mahdi*, pp. 149–150, trans., pp. 160–161. Halm explains al-Mahdī's reluctance to take on this responsibility himself as part of a deliberate policy to deflect the unrealizable expectations of his most ardent followers away from him alone and onto his son to emphasize thereby the continuation of the dynasty.

31. Ibn ʿIdhārī, *al-Bayān*, p. 193; Halm, *Reich des Mahdi*, pp. 247–248, trans., p. 277.

32. Qāḍī al-Nuʿmān, *Iftitāḥ al-daʿwa wa ibtidā' al-dawla*, ed. Farhat Dachraoui (Tunis, 1975), pp. 249–250, and confirmed by Ibn ʿIdhārī, *al-Bayān*, p. 151.

for al-Mahdī as the new caliph, which occurred on the Friday immediately following his arrival in Raqqāda. 'When the morning dawned on Friday the day following his arrival, he sent out a note ordering that he be prayed for from the *minbar*s, and he dispatched it to the *khaṭīb*s of Raqqāda and al-Qayrawān telling them to invoke, after the blessing on Muḥammad, a blessing on ʿAlī, and Fāṭima and al-Ḥasan and al-Ḥusayn, and the imams among their progeny, as Abū ʿAbdallāh had ordered.'[33] That note, according to Qāḍī al-Nuʿmān, stipulated the following prayer as part of the Friday *khuṭba*:[34]

> O God, bless Your servant and Your deputy, the one responsible for the affairs of Your servants in Your land, the servant of God (*ʿabdallāh*), Abū Muḥammad, the Imam al-Mahdī bi-llāh, Commander of the Believers, just as You blessed his forefathers Your deputies, the rightly guided, the *mahdī*s,[35] who have discharged the duty of truth and in regard to it acted justly. O God, and just as You chose him for Your guardianship and for Your deputyship (*li-khalīfatika* [i.e. Your caliphate]) and You made him the defence of Your religion and its foundation, and for Your creation a refuge and sanctuary, so grant him victory over Your apostate enemies, and heal through him the breasts of the believers. Conquer through him the easts of the land and its wests as You promised him; support him against the iniquitous rebels, O God of creation, Lord of the worlds.[36]

In this passage, although we are missing what else might have been said in these earliest *khuṭba*s for the Fatimids, we have at least the key portion. The command the caliph gave evidently stipulated only that these phrases appear in the *khuṭba* without going further. Presumably, in all other matters concerning the *khuṭba*, the individual

---

33. As had already been cited in al-Nuʿmān, *Iftitāḥ al-daʿwa*, pp. 249–250.

34. al-Nuʿmān, *Iftitāḥ al-daʿwa*, pp. 293–294.

35. The words here are: *ʿalā khulafāʾika al-rāshidīn al-mahdīyīn*. The last term, the *mahdī*s, meaning 'those who were rightly guided', which is also the plural of *mahdī*, is particularly significant as becomes apparent when it reappears regularly in the texts of later *khuṭba*s, all the way to the end of the dynasty. For further discussion of its importance see the next chapter on the rhetoric of these *khuṭba*s.

36. Another translation of the same passage can be found in Halm, *Reich des Mahdi*, p. 138, trans., p. 147.

khaṭībs continued with their previous practice and traditions. Fatimid *khuṭbas*, even those given by the imams, in general followed Islamic traditions as to form and content.

Khuṭbas by al-Manṣūr and al-Muʿizz

The record of *khuṭbas* by al-Manṣūr is far richer than for any other Fatimid caliph. Even so it provides textual examples solely from the first couple of years of his reign. We have copies of one from the ʿĪd al-fiṭr in the year (334/946), given by him in place of his father who was gravely ill. Al-Qāʾim died less than two weeks later. Another, quite short—which may indicate that we lack the whole of the text—was delivered on Friday the 14th of Muḥarram (14 August 946) in Qayrawān, not by al-Manṣūr but by the chamberlain Jaʿfar al-Ḥājib. Rather than the standard *khuṭba*, it consists most importantly of an announcement of the remitting of taxes for the coming year, a measure intended to aid in the economic recovery after the revolt of the Khārijite Abū Yazīd and its attendant devastation. Two more examples come from the same year. Both were given while the imam was leading the army in the field in pursuit of the rebels. For the festival of the breaking of the fast, he preached at an ad hoc *muṣallā* laid out specifically for the occasion. By the feast of sacrifice (2 July) he was ready to assault the fortress of Kiyāna, the final refuge of Abū Yazīd. Again he delivered the *khuṭba* at an improvised *muṣallā*. With this ultimate victory he accepted at last the public proclamation of his imamate; only from then on did he use the regnal title al-Manṣūr. Beyond the four *khuṭbas* just mentioned, we have two more from the following year (336/948), both given in al-Mahdiyya, one for each of the *ʿīd* festivals. But that is all.

The lack of further examples does not indicate that al-Manṣūr ceased to deliver the *khuṭba* for the festivals but that he apparently no longer wrote down a copy of the text. Ustadh Jawdhar, the major domo of this period, almost a quasi-wazir to al-Manṣūr, reports that the caliph lent him copies of two *khuṭbas* to copy for himself.[37] They were two of those mentioned earlier. Significantly, moreover, we have no information to suggest that his *khuṭbas* from the last five

37. al-Jawdharī, *Sīrat Jawdhar*, pp. 53–54; French trans., pp. 76–78.

years of his reign were ever copied. Still there is a poignant account that describes him delivering his final *khuṭba* in the festival square of Qayrawān at a time when he was already quite ill.[38] That was the ʿĪd al-fiṭr of 341 (19 February 953); he was dead four weeks later.[39] His son and successor al-Muʿizz would later comment that, in this last *khuṭba*, his father had announced his own impending death.[40]

The first, and only complete, example of a *khuṭba* to come from al-Muʿizz was the one delivered by the new imam on the feast of sacrifice only weeks later. In it the caliph both announces the loss of his father and laments being separated from him. For the next two decades, he gave many more *khuṭbas*, but, aside from a relatively short passage from one that has no date or indication of where or on what occasion it was delivered, we have copies of no more. In fact there are none for the subsequent century and a half, not until the time of al-Āmir, when the next examples appear. Nevertheless, there are several reports of al-Muʿizz giving the *khuṭba*. Qāḍī al-Nuʿmān says in his *al-Majālis wa'l-musāyarāt*, that al-Muʿizz gave the *khuṭba* but he provides neither text nor details.[41] On another occasion al-Muʿizz preached to the troops who were about to leave for the *jihād* (in this case the conquest of Sijilmāsa); this *khuṭba* was, al-Nuʿmān reports, lengthy and he managed to preserve a part of it. What he saved is now available in this book.[42]

---

38. Abū Bakr al-Mālikī, *Kitāb riyāḍ al-nufūs fī ṭabaqāt ʿulamāʾ al-Qayrawān wa Ifrīqiya*, ed. Bashīr al-Bakkūsh (Beirut, 1981–1983), 2: 487; Ibn ʿIdhārī, *al-Bayān*, 1: 221; al-Nuwayrī, *Nihāya*, 28: 118; Halm, *Reich des Mahdi*, p. 299, trans., p. 336.

39. Al-Manṣūr died at the end of Shawwāl 341 (19 March 953).

40. See his comments about this *khuṭba* as recorded in Qāḍī al-Nuʿmān's *al-Majālis wa'l-musāyarāt*, ed. al-Ḥabīb al-Faqhī, Ibrāhīm Shabbūḥ, and Muḥammad al-Yaʿlāwī (Tunis, 1978), pp. 239–240.

41. p. 126.

42. al-Nuʿmān, *al-Majālis*, pp. 254–258. The portion preserved by al-Nuʿmān consists of an exhortation by al-Muʿizz to his most loyal troops, presumably the Kutāma Berbers whose past (and future) service to the dynasty he makes a special point of noting at length. The enemy against whom he is sending them has not only rebelled and disobeyed but has begun to refer to himself by the same titles as those of the caliph, thereby claiming the caliphate for himself. The enemy in this particular case must be the Berber ruler of Sijilmāsa, Muḥammad b. Abi'l-Fatḥ Wāsūl, who began to use caliphal titles in 342/955, one year after al-Muʿizz

The first Fatimid *khuṭba*s in Egypt

We have more information about the *khuṭba*s that were given in Egypt commencing with the Fatimid conquest. Ibn Taghrī Birdī says that, immediately after seizing control, Jawhar cut the *khuṭba* for the Abbasids and prohibited the wearing of black, replacing it with white. He commanded that the *khuṭba* have added to it: 'O God, bless Muḥammad, the chosen, 'Alī, the approved, and Fāṭima, the chaste, and al-Ḥasan and al-Ḥusayn, the two grandsons of the Messenger, from whom God has removed impurity and purged them of all sin. Bless the pure imams, the forefathers of the Commander of the Believers, al-Mu'izz li-Dīn Allāh.'[43] The equivalent text given by al-Maqrīzī has the word 'rightly guided' (*al-rāshidīn*) in place of 'pure' (*al-ṭāhirīn*) and adds after the name of the caliph: 'the rightly guided guides', (*al-hādīn al-mahdīyīn*). Another account relates a portion of the first *khuṭba* delivered in Fusṭāṭ with Jawhar and his troops present: 'When it was Friday with ten days left in Sha'bān, Jawhar went down with the army to the Old Mosque [in Fusṭāṭ] for Friday prayers. Hibat Allāh b. Aḥmad, the deputy of 'Abd al-Samī' b. 'Umar al-'Abbāsī [i.e. the *khaṭīb* of that mosque], gave the *khuṭba* wearing white.[44] When he reached the

succeeded to the throne (see Halm, *Reich des Mahdi,* p. 352, trans., pp. 397–398).

For an example of a *khuṭba* urging a *jihād* against the Fatimids, see accounts of the rebellion of the Khārijite Abū Yazīd. Following the capture of Qayrawān by the rebels, the townsmen of that city decided to support them. At a key moment, the imam of the city, Aḥmad b. Muḥammad b. Abi'l-Walīd, preached a *jihād* against the Shi'a. See al-Mālikī, *Riyāḍ al-nufūs*, 2: 341–345; Ibn 'Idhārī, *al-Bayān*, 1: 217–218; Halm, *Reich des Mahdi*, p. 271, trans., p. 304. The text of his *khuṭba*, at least a short version of it, appears in the *Riyāḍ al-nufūs*, pp. 343–344.

43. There is some, mostly minor, variation in the reported text according to different sources. The date for the first use of the new formula was Friday the 8th of Dhu'l-Qa'da 358/969 (according to Ibn Khallikān). Ibn Taghrī Birdī, *al-Nujūm*, 4: 36; *Itti'āẓ*, 1: 117.

44. The name al-'Abbāsī, 'the Abbasid', indicates that this man was a member of the Abbasid family and thus a relative of the Abbasid caliph. If his absence on this occasion was caused by his wishing to avoid preaching for the Fatimids, he soon changed his mind. Jawhar confirmed him as the *khaṭīb* of the mosque of 'Amr in Fusṭāṭ and he held that post at least until 365. Moreover, two of his sons, Abū 'Alī Aḥmad and Abū Ṭālib 'Alī, were later to serve as *khaṭīb*s, the former was particular

prayer portion [the second *khuṭba*], he read the following from a written note:'

> O God, bless Your servant and Your deputy, the fruit of prophecy, scion of the rightly guided guiding family, the servant of God, the Imam Ma'add Abū Tamīm al-Mu'izz li-Dīn Allāh, Commander of the Believers, just as You blessed his pure forefathers and his predecessors, the rightly guided imams.
>
> O God, raise high his rank and advance his word, make his proofs clear, bring the community together in obedience to him and their hearts loving friends of his, make guidance follow his sanction, have him inherit the eastern parts of the land and its west, have him be master of the beginning of things and their outcomes, for truly You speak and Your word is the truth. 'We had written in the Psalms after the remembrance that the servants of righteousness shall inherit the earth' [21: 105].
>
> Your religion has been subject to vexation. When that which is sacred to You was defiled, *jihād* on Your behalf extinguished, pilgrimage to Your house and visitation of the tomb of Your messenger … disrupted, he made his preparations for the *jihād*, got ready everything necessary and sent the armies to support You. He expended funds in adherence to You, taking pains to please You, to curb those who are foolish and restrain those who are arrogant, to cause the truth to appear and the false to come to nothing. So, O God, support the armies that he has sent and the detachments that he charge with fighting the polytheists, contending with the heretics, defending the Muslims, building up of the border territories and the holy places, eradicating injustice, suspicions and greed, and spreading justice throughout the nations.
>
> O God, make his banners stand high and prominent, his armies dominant and victorious; plant righteousness through him and by his hand; and grant us through him supreme protections.[45]

---

prominent during the reign of al-Ḥākim and the latter is specifically mentioned for an incident in 414 when confusion as to who held the job resulting in two *khaṭībs*, each separately but at the same moment, delivering the *khuṭba* from atop the same *minbar* (in the mosque of Rāshida). *Itti'āẓ*, 2: 50, 71, 72, 133, 134; *Khiṭaṭ*, 3: 41, 60, 4: 127; al-Mukhtār 'Izz al-Mulk Muḥammad, *al-Juz al-arba'īn min Akhbar Miṣr*. Pt. 1 (historical section), ed. Ayman Fu'ād Sayyid and Th. Bianquis (Cairo, 1975), pp. 4, 6, 9–10.

45. *Itti'āẓ*, 1: 114–115, with variations given by Idrīs, *'Uyūn* (ed. Ya'lāwī), pp. 684–685; al-Nuwayrī, *Nihāya*, 28: 131–132 (the editor has recorded there variations

The difference between this more complex benediction and the shorter one ordered by Jawhar about the same time probably reflects his direct involvement on the occasion. Accordingly, whereas there was to be included the briefer phrases in all *khuṭba*s everywhere in the newly conquered territories, the longer version applied to a specific event and depended on having a written text for the *khaṭīb* to read. The source suggests, in any case, that the preacher delivered his regular *khuṭba* for the first of the two and referred to the written text only for the second. What has come down to us is the latter portion only.

Al-Muʿizz himself did not arrive in Egypt until four years after the proclamations of these new *khuṭba*s in his favour. But, when he did, the record of his activities became ever more detailed, in part because the Egyptian historian Ibn Zūlāq, a contemporary, began to compile an account of what transpired between the caliph's arrival and his death, day by day. Al-Maqrīzī found and used a copy of that work written in its author's own hand.

On his way to Cairo al-Muʿizz first encountered a delegation of Egyptian notables in Alexandria where they had come to greet him. To them he gave a lengthy speech—a kind of *khuṭba*—in which he explained why he had come. From what he said on that occasion we have no more than a few notes.[46] As he approached the capital coming up the western side of the Nile, another group of greeters met him at Muḥallat Ḥafṣ. There, before al-Muʿizz, this same Ibn Zūlāq, who is our major source for the period, gave a short *khuṭba* of welcome, the text of which survives in al-Maqrīzī's biographical entry for Ibn Zūlāq in the biographical dictionary, *al-Muqaffā*.[47] It has obviously been taken from Ibn Zūlāq's own account of the event. In his speech, Ibn Zūlāq attested, most importantly, to his personal acceptance of the Fatimid descent of al-Muʿizz.[48]

Thanks to Ibn Zūlāq, from then onward we have a complete record of, at least, the occasions of al-Muʿizz's *khuṭba*s (though not

from the version in the *Ittiʿāẓ*).

46. *Ittiʿāẓ*, 1: 133; *ʿUyūn* (ed. Yaʿlāwī), p. 725; Aḥmad b. Muḥammad Ibn Khallikān, *Wafayāt al-aʿyān*, ed. Iḥsān ʿAbbās. 8 vols. (Beirut, 1968), 5: 227; Halm, *Reich des Mahdi*, p. 371, trans., p. 419.

47. *al-Muqaffā*, bio. no. 1145, 3: 284–286.

48. *al-Muqaffā*, 3: 285–286; Ibn al-Jawzī, *al-Muntaẓam*, 7: 57–58.

the text of any of them). He reports that the caliph led prayers and gave the *khuṭba* for each of the festivals for the years 362, 363 and 364. He died before the feast in 365. An account as complete as we have in this case indicates a practice that in all likelihood applies as well to the rest of his reign and that of his father, perhaps also his successors at least through al-Ḥākim. The *khuṭba* by the imam himself was a regular feature of the festival. The first of those in Egypt provides additional details about the event:

> On the day of fast-breaking [in 362], al-Muʿizz rode in procession to the *muṣallā* of Cairo that Jawhar had constructed for the *ʿīd* prayer. … al-Muʿizz approached in full attire[49] with his banners and coverings. He prayed with the people the prayer of the *ʿīd* at full length and completely, reciting for the first, after the Sūrat al-Fātiḥa, 'Has the story of the overwhelming event reached you' [88: 1].[50] Following the recitation, he pronounced the *takbīr*, bowed for a long time, and prostrated at length. Ibn Zūlāq said here: 'I uttered the *tasbīḥ* after him thirty times for each bow and each prostration. Qāḍī al-Nuʿmān relayed the *takbīr* from him. In the second he recited, after the Fātiḥa, the Sūrat al-Ḍuḥā [no. 93] and said the *takbīr* following the recitation. This was the prayer of his grandfather ʿAlī b. Abī Ṭālib. He held the bowed position and the prostration in the second also at length. … When he had completed the prayer he mounted the *minbar* greeting the people on the right and the left. Next he unfurled the two banners that were on the *minbar* and he delivered the *khuṭba* with them to the front of him. On the highest step of the *minbar*, there was a heavy brocaded cushion for him to sit on between the two *khuṭbas*. He began the sermon with 'In the name of God, the Merciful, the Compassionate.' With him on the *minbar* were Jawhar, ʿAmmār b. Jaʿfar, and Shafīʿ, the bearer of the royal parasol. Then he commenced with 'God is great, God is great',

49. The attire of the imam on these occasions was highly important if only for ritual purposes. Note the *ḥadīth* quoted from the imams by Qāḍī al-Nuʿmān in the *Daʿāʾim* (trans. 1: 228 and 230) to the effect that the imams on Friday and the two festivals should wear their finest. Requirements of royal prestige obviously added another dimension.

50. On the recitation of this passage as well as other details of the *ʿīd* prayer see the *ḥadīth* of Jaʿfar al-Ṣādiq related by al-Qāḍī al-Nuʿmān in his *Daʿāʾim*, 1: 186, trans., 1: 232.

opening with this. He preached so eloquently the people cried. His *khuṭba* was humble and submissive.

When he had completed the *khuṭba*, he departed with his troops, followed by his four sons wearing armour and helmets riding on horses in the finest attire. Two elephants preceded him. Upon reaching the palace he invited the people to enter and eat, urging them toward the food. He rebuked those who arrived late and issued a threat to those about whom he heard that they were fasting through the feast.[51]

Later that year he rode again with his troops to the *muṣallā* for the feast of sacrifice. The prayer and the circumstances of that occasion were more or less the same.[52] Those of the following two years (363 and 364) were likewise; by then the details of al-Mu'izz's practice on the *'īd* had become routine and customary as so noted in our sources.[53] But finally early in 365, we find the following report:

> 'Abd al-Samī' b. 'Umar al-'Abbāsī, the *khaṭīb* of the mosque of Fusṭāṭ, led the prayer from the *minbar* on Friday for al-Mu'izz. He said in his prayer the following: 'O God, bless Your servant and Your deputy, the fruit of prophecy, the source of excellence and the imamate, the servant of God, Ma'add Abū Tamīm, the Imam al-Mu'izz li-Dīn Allāh, just as You blessed his pure forefathers and his predecessors, those chosen before him. O God, assist him in that which You have appointed him to do, fulfil for him what You promised him, and make him master of the eastern parts of the earth and its west. Support him, O God, and assure his triumph through the amir Nizār Abi'l-Manṣūr, the heir apparent, the son of the Commander of the Believers, whom You have appointed to uphold his *da'wa* and speak his proof. O God, benefit through him the servants and put the land into good order before him, and fulfil for him

51. This account is from the *Itti'āẓ* (1: 137–138) but ultimately from Ibn Zūlāq. In al-Maqrīzī's notes from Ibn Muyassar's *History of Egypt* (*Akhbār Miṣr*, Ayman Fu'ād Sayyid edition, pp. 159–160) the same passage appears, indicating that this work was his source for it. See also al-Nuwayrī, *Nihāya*, 28: 144, and *Khiṭaṭ*, 2: 478–479.

52. *Itti'āẓ*, 1: 141.

53. *Itti'āẓ*, 1: 210 ('Īd al-fiṭr, 363), 215 ('Īd al-naḥr, 363), 222 ('Īd al-fiṭr, 364), and 223 ('Īd al-naḥr, 364).

through him Your promise to him for 'truly You never disappoint in promises made' [3: 193].[54]

This *khuṭba* prayer, uttered as the caliph lay on his deathbed, announced the coming succession of his son Nizār, who would take the regnal name al-ʿAzīz. Al-Muʿizz died later that very day.[55]

Khuṭbas by al-ʿAzīz, al-Ḥākim, and al-Ẓāhir

Fatimid practice in that era held that the death of the reigning caliph be kept secret until the transition of his successor was firm and secure. In keeping with this policy al-ʿAzīz did not announce publicly what had happened until, in what had also become customary, the next feast of sacrifice.[56] On that occasion he gave the *khuṭba* naming himself as imam-caliph in it and expressing his own sorrow over the loss of his father.[57] The 15th-century Ṭayyibī historian, Idrīs ʿImād al-Dīn, the author of a history of the Fatimid imams, provides a few details about what was said and, more importantly, quotes eleven lines from a long poem in praise of al-ʿAzīz composed by his eldest brother Tamīm in response to the moment of this announcement.[58]

More evidence about the *khuṭba* in this period comes also from Idrīs. In the year 368, shortly after the elevation of Yaʿqūb Ibn Killis to the rank of wazir, al-ʿAzīz, on the feast of fast-breaking, extolled him. Again Idrīs quotes lines of a poem for the occasion by Tamīm.[59] During that same year al-ʿAzīz also gave a *khuṭba* to the troops he was sending for the *jihād* against the Byzantines.[60] For the following ʿĪd al-fiṭr (369?)

54. Ibn Muyassar, *Akhbār Miṣr*, p. 168; *Ittiʿāẓ*, 1: 228–229. The *khaṭīb* on this occasion was the same ʿAbd al-Samīʿ b. ʿUmar al-ʿAbbāsī mentioned above.

55. *Ittiʿāẓ*, 1: 228–229.

56. Evidently we have no information about the ʿĪd al-fiṭr in that year, or an explanation of why al-ʿAzīz waited until the ʿĪd al-naḥr.

57. *Ittiʿāẓ*, 1: 231 and 1: 237, this latter report is there quoted from the historian Ibn Muhadhdhab, a contemporary of the event.

58. *ʿUyūn* (ed. Ghālib), 6: 206–207. The whole of this *qaṣīda* appears in Tamīm's *Dīwān*, ed. M. Ḥ. al-Aʿẓamī and others (Cairo, 1957), pp. 308–312.

59. *ʿUyūn* (ed. Ghālib), 6: 230–231; Tamīm, *Dīwān*, pp. 142–144.

60. *ʿUyūn* (ed. Ghālib), 6: 242. Idrīs calls the enemy *al-Ifranj* 'the Franks' but

he preached the sermon to the troops assembled, having just returned with booty and captives from a victorious campaign in Syria, a moment and image again made the subject of Tamīm's verse.[61]

Our next reports come from the year 380,[62] more than ten years later. The record from then until the end of the reign is, however, complete with respect to the caliph's participation in the festivals. The years 370 to 379 were likely the same. Al-ʿAzīz was famously fond of public events and the processions attendant on them in which he would ride out from the palace. Perhaps that love of pomp and ceremony provided the motivation for a new addition to the occasions for caliphal *khuṭbas*. According to later authorities, al-ʿAzīz was the first to deliver the sermon for the Friday service in Ramaḍān, a practice adopted by the Fatimids from then on.[63] Once this custom became settled, a caliph would typically ride to a different mosque each successive Friday and there deliver the *khuṭba* and lead prayers. But the rule limited riding for some reason on more than three Fridays, the fourth being reserved as a day of rest.[64] For the year 380, which may have been approximately when this innovation began, al-ʿAzīz gave the *khuṭba* on the second Friday of Ramaḍān and the next.[65] In the latter case he did so in the new mosque he had begun to erect just outside the Bāb al-Futūḥ, one of the two northern gates of Cairo.[66] That same mosque would later go by the name of al-Ḥākim,

---

that involves an anachronism that confuses the Byzantines with the much later Frankish crusaders.

61. *ʿUyūn* (ed. Ghālib), 6: 242–244; Tamīm, *Dīwān*, pp. 339–342.

62. He gave the *khuṭba* on the ʿĪd al-naḥr in that year; *Ittiʿāẓ*, 1: 269.

63. Jamāl al-Dīn ʿAlī Ibn Ẓāfir, *Akhbār al-duwal al-munqaṭiʿa*, ed. André Ferré (Cairo, 1972), p. 38. On this development see also Paula Sanders, *Ritual, Politics, and the City in Fatimid Cairo*, pp. 48ff.

64. As becomes apparent at a much later period, the main question was whether to rest on the first Friday or the last. If the caliph rode in procession on the first day of Ramaḍān, as was sometimes the case, then he rested on the first Friday, but thereafter rode and delivered the *khuṭba* on the next three Fridays, the last being among them. See Ibn Taghrī Birdī, *al-Nujūm*, 4: 102–104, citing information from Ibn ʿAbd al-Ẓāhir.

65. Al-Maqrīzī in his *Khiṭaṭ* (4.1: 123), cites al-Musabbiḥī as reporting that al-ʿAzīz in that year rode to the mosque of Cairo for the first Friday.

66. *Ittiʿāẓ*, 1: 267; *Khiṭaṭ*, 2: 280. If he did the same on the third Friday, the

who finished it. For the feast of fast-breaking, the service took place at the *muṣallā* outside the Bāb al-Naṣr, the other northern gate. *Maṣṭaba*s, raised benches, were built outside of homes and buildings along the route between it and the palace on which the *mu'adhdhin*s and scholars could sit and observe the procession of the imam to the *muṣallā*. When the *takbīr* sounded at the festival square, the students and the faithful whom the qadi had ordered to join the others on the *maṣṭaba*s, relayed it all the way back to the palace.[67]

For the following two years, we know al-ʿAzīz delivered the *khuṭba* in at least two mosques during Ramaḍān, the second in the Mosque of Cairo (later called al-Azhar). As had become his practice, al-ʿAzīz also gave the *khuṭba*s of the two festivals, as he did in 382, the year following.[68] This pattern continued in 383 and in 384 with the addition of the presence with him during Ramaḍān of his young son Manṣūr (the future al-Ḥākim).[69] By the end of Ramaḍān of 385, the court had moved out of Cairo to a staging area at Minā Jaʿfar devoted to the preparation of a grand army on its way to fight in Syria. On the *ʿīd*, in place of the caliph, the *khuṭba* was presented by his son, then less than ten years old. He observed his father's customary practice for the occasion and dressed as he would have.[70] Al-ʿAzīz, however, gave the *khuṭba* on the feast of sacrifice.[71] It was his last; he died in 386 at the very end of Ramaḍān still at the armies' encampment.

On the spot al-Ḥākim was proclaimed the new caliph. A great assembly of those at the camp immediately returned to Cairo for the funeral. On the morning of the feast, the chief qadi, Muḥammad b. al-Nuʿmān, led prayers and mounted the *minbar* to deliver the *khuṭba*, pausing in doing so to kiss the place were al-ʿAzīz would have sat. He wept and cried; a loud lamentation then arose from the people present. The qadi gave the *khuṭba* weeping in mourning for the deceased imam, but also in the same sermon announcing the new *daʿwa* for al-Ḥākim.[72]

---

information is missing.

67. *Ittiʿāẓ*, 1: 267; *Khiṭaṭ*, 2: 479–480.

68. *Ittiʿāẓ*, 1: 272–273, 276.

69. *Ittiʿāẓ*, 1: 279–280, 283–284.

70. *Ittiʿāẓ*, 1: 288.

71. *Ittiʿāẓ*, 1: 289.

72. *Ittiʿāẓ*, 1: 291–292.

But another account reports that, because of the noise of people crying, the audience could not hear most of what he said.[73]

A little more than two months later, in that same year, al-Ḥākim himself, who though quite young had already given the *khuṭba* at least once before, rode to the *muṣallā* for the feast of sacrifice. He mounted the *minbar* for the *khuṭba* on that occasion along with the chief qadi, Barjawān, his tutor, Ibn ʿAmmār, the regent, and others.[74]

In general, however, the record for the reign of al-Ḥākim is spotty and uncertain. One account from the year 395 says that in it:

> The Mosque of Rāshida was fitted out and the caliph rode to it on the feast of fast-breaking, wearing a plain yellow robe with an indeterminate turban on his head, which had been wrapped on his head with a hanging tail and with a jewel between his eyes.[75] In front of him in the procession were six horses bearing saddles studded with jewels, six elephants and five giraffes. He prayed with the people the *ʿīd* prayer and preached to them. In his *khuṭba* he cursed his enemy oppressor as was his due and those who would spread false rumours about him. The commander of the armies and the chief judge climbed the *minbar* with him.[76]

This report is important less for what it says about the giving of the *khuṭba* than for the details it provides concerning the procession. Obviously the ceremony on these occasions needed to be as elaborate as possible. The number and type of animals was one key element. From only a few years before, an account of the Zīrid ruler's procession to the *muṣallā* in 387 describes him as wearing the finest attire and being preceded by an elephant, two giraffes and 'a gleaming white camel the like of which had never been seen before'.[77] There are also descriptions of family members and other notables who walked behind the caliph and in what order.

73. ʿAlī b. Mūsā al-Maghribī Ibn Saʿīd, *al-Nujūm al-zāhira fī ḥulā ḥaḍrat al-Qāhira, al-qism al-khāṣṣ bi'l-Qāhira min Kitāb al-Mughrib fī ḥulā al-Maghrib*, ed. Ḥusayn Naṣṣār (Cairo, 1970), p. 55.

74. Ibn Muyassar, *Akhbār Miṣr*, p. 180; *Ittiʿāẓ*, 2: 7.

75. Sanders, *Ritual, Politics, and the City*, p. 25.

76. *Ittiʿāẓ*, 2: 58.

77. Ibn ʿIdhārī, *al-Bayān*, pp. 1; 238–239.

But the later record for al-Ḥākim is not consistent. For example, in the year 401, on the feast of sacrifice, the chief qadi led the prayer and gave the *khuṭba*. The caliph did not ride or offer the sacrifice.[78] In Ramaḍān of 403, however, he led prayers once in the Rāshida mosque, another time in the mosque beyond the Bāb al-Futūḥ and yet another in the Old Mosque in Fusṭāṭ. At the ʿĪd al-fiṭr he rode without the usual accoutrements. The ten horses led in front of him had saddles and bridles adorned with only small amounts of white silver. The parasol was white and without any gold. His robe was also white and without decoration and there was neither gold nor jewels in his turban. The *minbar* was not furnished.[79] On the feast of sacrifice he kept to the same relatively austere pattern.[80] His cousin ʿAbd al-Raḥīm b. Ilyās performed the sacrifice in his place. The report for this event, as for several other *ʿīd*s about his time, does not mention the *khuṭba* or who gave it.

The following year al-Ḥākim announced that this same ʿAbd al-Raḥīm, his cousin, had been made the heir-apparent and would therefore be his successor. He commanded that the invocation of the prayer should name ʿAbd al-Raḥīm after himself. 'Respond [O God] in regard to me in the matter of the son of my uncle and the holder of my covenant and the covenant of the Muslims and the caliph after me as You responded in regard to Moses concerning his brother Aaron.' On the feast this man mounted the *minbar* with al-Ḥākim and sat on his right.[81] That same year al-Ḥākim began to ride more and more often. In Ramaḍān he visited all four of the mosques: the one in Cairo, the one outside the north gate, the mosque of ʿAmr in Fusṭāṭ and the Rāshida. He himself pronounced the *khuṭba* from the *minbar* in favour of ʿAbd al-Raḥīm with the words quoted above.[82]About this time he issued an order to stop the practice of kissing the ground in front of him, praying in his name even in the *khuṭba* and that instead the salutation should name simply the 'Commander of the Believers' (*amīr al-muʾminīn*).[83]

78. *Ittiʿāẓ*, 2; 88.
79. *Ittiʿāẓ*, 2: 96–97; Sanders, *Ritual, Politics and the City*, p. 61.
80. *Ittiʿāẓ*, 2: 98.
81. Ibn Saʿīd, *al-Nujūm al-zāhira*, p. 64.
82. *Ittiʿāẓ*, 2: 103.
83. Ibn Saʿīd, *al-Nujūm al-zāhira*, p. 53.

In 405, during Ramaḍān, the heir-apparent ʿAbd al-Raḥīm rode for prayers on the first Friday in a procession fit for the caliph to al-Anwār, the new mosque outside of the northern gate, and then on subsequent Fridays first to the mosque of Cairo and then twice more to the new mosque.[84]

At the very end of the reign in 411/1021, just as the transition to al-Ḥākim's son and actual successor al-Ẓāhir was about to take place, an amir was charged with the responsibility of having the oath of allegiance said for the new caliph on the feast of sacrifice. At the *muṣallā*, however, the *khuṭba* was given by the chief qadi in the name of al-Ḥākim. Not three hours later on the same day, following the return of the qadi from the festival square, the oath was taken for al-Ẓāhir. Our source, Ibn al-Ṣayrafī, the head of the Fatimid chancery at a much later time, claims that nothing like this had ever occurred before.[85] He does not say why but evidently, since there had been no announcement of al-Ḥākim's death, the proclamation of al-Ẓāhir's succession so abruptly seemed quite unusual.

The testimony of al-Musabbiḥī

The amir al-Musabbiḥī, who held a high rank at the court, observed most of these events. Over much of the reign of al-Ḥākim and at least part of that of al-Ẓāhir, he compiled, apparently on an almost daily basis, a record—a history—of what he saw and what he heard during those years, including news arriving from abroad. His account grew to massive length, some 26,000 pages by one estimate. Of all that, however, we possess only one portion that covers part of the years 414 and 415. Other sections of the whole evidently were available to later medieval historians to judge by their quotations from it, but al-Musabbiḥī's account of these two years is unique in its completeness, and in the wealth of specific detail it provides of what took place. Accordingly, his description of al-Ẓāhir riding for prayers on the Fridays of Ramaḍān in 415 and for the two *ʿīd* festivals is invaluable.

84. *Ittiʿāẓ*, 2: 109.

85. Abu'l-Qāsim ʿAlī Ibn al-Ṣayrafī, *al-Ishāra ilā man nāla al-wizāra*, ed. Ayman Fu'ād Sayyid (Cairo, 1990), p. 65; *Ittiʿāẓ*, 2: 124.

Moreover, he proudly noted that, in these very processions, 'as was my custom, I walked in the company of all the notables in the presence of the imam both as he rode out and as he came back'.[86]

So important are these eye-witness passages that what follows is a full translation of them:

[The first Friday of Ramaḍān]

> On Friday two nights into the month of Ramaḍān, our master (*mawlānā*), may the blessings of God be upon him, rode for Friday prayer in the Anwār Mosque.[87] He was accompanied by all of his servants, as well as the elite notables of his government. He wore a fine linen shawl that was wrapped around him. On his head was a white turban embroidered with gold thread. On him was a white *dabīqī* linen robe and over him a *dabīqī* linen parasol, also embroidered with gold. That was for the procession going. When he came back, over his head, there was a white *dabīqī* linen parasol *mukhawwama* threaded with gold. The chief qadi Aḥmad b. Muḥammad b. Abi'l-ʿAwwām mounted the *minbar* with him as did Ibrāhīm, the companion and tutor, known as al-Jalīs (the boon-companion). These two lowered the curtains around the dome that was above the *minbar* and which was itself covered in plain white. Ambergris evaporated in front of him in jewelled silver and gold censers. He delivered the *khuṭba* for himself. It was a beautiful *khuṭba*, most complete and perfect. Then he offered a prayer for his forefathers, and for himself and all his servants and the prominent men of his government. The chief qadi and Ibrāhīm the tutor next raised the curtains of the dome that was above the *minbar* and the two descended before him. He, on whom be peace, then descended and prayed with the people a most complete and beautiful prayer. He departed for his palace safely, thanks to God. As was my custom, I walked along with the company of all the notables in the presence of the imam, both as he rode out and as he came back.[88]

86. al-Musabbiḥī, *Akhbār Miṣr*, pp. 62, 64, and 66. He also confesses when he could not attend an event in person, due, in one case, to an illness (p. 67).

87. This was later known as the Mosque of al-Ḥākim.

88. al-Musabbiḥī, *Akhbār Miṣr*, p. 62; paraphrased by al-Maqrīzī in *Ittiʿāẓ*, 2: 159.

[The second Friday]

On Friday the 16th of the month of Ramaḍān, our master, may the blessings of God be upon him, prayed in the Anwār Mosque outside of the Bāb al-Futūḥ. He, peace be upon him, rode wearing a white cloak hemmed with brocade and a white robe of *dabīqī* linen, an unadorned white gown and a white turban with gold thread. In his hand he carried the jewelled staff and over his head was the parasol circled with red. That was for his procession out, and for his return a parasol circled with gold thread. He mounted the *minbar* and gave the *khuṭba*, a beautiful *khuṭba*, most eloquent. He prayed a complete prayer, most completely and returned to his palace with all of the servants and prominent men of the government. I walked in his presence until he went in through the Gate of Gold safely, thanks to God. That was the second Friday in which he led prayers in this Ramaḍān.[89]

[The festival of breaking the fast]

Saturday was the ʿĪd al-fiṭr and our master, may the blessings of God be upon him, rode in procession with his troops and the prominent men of the government. In front of him there was the one elephant that remained of the elephants and the giraffes, golden banners brocaded with silver, drums, and other things. Various types of unmounted horses were paraded in front of him bearing saddles studded with jewels and heavy amber, along with all of the commanders of the Turks and the servants under commission in arms and others. He wore a wax-coloured silk robe and a wax-coloured turban embroidered with gold thread. In his hand was the staff and he was girded with a sword and he carried the lance as was usually done. Over his head there was the parasol heavily ornamented with gold carried by the Slav Muẓaffar as was customary. He proceeded in the finest of attire, a most perfect appearance and the most beautiful equipment. With him were his black eunuch servants wearing types of gilded, heavy adornments, fashions of great value. I walked in his presence to the *muṣallā* from the time before reaching its gate until he entered. He prayed a quite beautiful prayer, quite complete and perfect, and next delivered a most eloquent *khuṭba*. When he, peace be upon him, went up the *minbar*, he summoned the chief

89. al-Musabbiḥī, *Akhbār Miṣr*, p. 64; paraphrased by al-Maqrīzī in *Ittiʿāẓ*, 2: 160.

qadi, who also went up. This man was ill as result of a sting he had received. Next he summoned Ibrāhīm, the boon-companion and tutor, and he climbed the *minbar*. Then he summoned Shams al-Dīn Abu'l-Fatḥ Mas'ūd b. Ṭāhir al-Wazzān and he went up as well. He summoned Tāj al-Dawla Ibn Abī Ḥusayn, who was formerly the ruler of Sicily, but he was not present. He summoned 'Alī b. Mas'ūd b. Abi'l-Ḥusayn Zayn al-Mulk and he went up. Then he summoned 'Alī b. al-Faḍl and after him 'Abdallāh b. al-Ḥājib, so he went up as well. At that point he was covered with the two banners that were attached to the *minbar*. He, peace be upon him, gave the *khuṭba*, a most beautiful *khuṭba*, quite complete and eloquent. The banners were then opened and those on the *minbar* descended. Finally he descended. There was on him a trace of weariness. Then he rode and returned to his palace safely, thanks to God.[90]

[The festival of the sacrifice]

The 'Īd al-naḥr was Thursday the 10th of Dhu'l-Ḥijja. On it our master, may the blessings of God be upon him, rode in procession to the outskirts of the *muṣallā* by way of the Bāb al-Futūḥ with his servants, his troops, his eunuchs, and the prominent men of his government. In front of him were handsome unmounted horses, golden banners brocaded in silver, two flags, the giraffes, and the one elephant remaining of the elephants. With him were his Turkish servants in heavily adorned robes and fine arms, and his servants who had received commissions as officers in the finest of attire, most splendid and perfect. He reached the festival square after observing the other customs which had each lieutenant remain at his abode and district, and that the prayer of the troops take place with all of them gathered together with their commanders in their own district. They did that. Behind him were the Kutāma friends [i.e. Ismailis] and the notables of the government. He was girded with a golden sword and the lance was borne by Ibn Banūṭ whose duty was to carry it behind him. In his hand was the jewelled staff, until he arrived at the *muṣallā*. On his forehead was a jewel and over his head the red parasol heavily adorned with gold being carried by the Slav Muẓaffar Bahā' al-Dawla. The notables dismounted in front of him as was their custom. He prayed a beautiful prayer, quite completely

90. al-Musabbiḥī, *Akhbār Miṣr*, pp. 65–66; paraphrased by al-Maqrīzī in *Itti'āẓ*, 2: 161.

and perfectly. He climbed the *minbar* and gave an eloquent *khuṭba* that was most beautiful. He summoned up the *minbar* the chief *dāʿī* Qāsim b. ʿAbd al-ʿAzīz b. al-Nuʿmān and handed over to him the roster of the names of those who, according to protocol, climbed the *minbar*. He summoned the chief *dāʿī* Shams al-Mulk but he was not present. He summoned Muẓaffar the Slav, then ʿAlī b. Masʿūd and Ḥasan b. Rajāʾ b. Abiʾl-Ḥasan. Next ʿAlī b. Faḍl. Prior to the group just mentioned, he called for the boon-companion Ibrāhīm, the tutor and goldsmith. Then he summoned at the end, ʿAbdallāh b. al-Ḥājib and the son of his uncle. All of them mounted the *minbar* in accord with protocol. They covered our master, may the blessings of God be upon him, with the two banners until he had completed the *khuṭba*. Then he descended from the *minbar* to the place for the sacrifice at the *muṣallā*. He sacrificed a female camel and returned with his troops and regiments. In going out and returning he wore a white *sharb* linen turban, a cloak hemmed with gold thread, and a plain white robe until he arrived at his palace. The people walked with him as was their custom and he entered in complete security, thanks to God.[91]

Al-Musabbiḥī was not an Ismaili but rather Sunni.[92] Nevertheless his depiction of the caliph and his role in these ceremonies and in giving the *khuṭba* on each of these occasions is deferential, revealing this amir's respect for both the imam and the institution he represented. We should assume that the others who participated did likewise. The chief qadi, who is mentioned by name in the first report, was Ḥanafī and thus also Sunni, and yet he performed a key function: climbing the *minbar*, lowering the curtains around the caliph as he delivered the *khuṭba*, and then raising them after he finished. Although we possess additional descriptions of processions for the *khuṭba*, none from this period are quite as detailed. Here, moreover, are accounts covering four events in succession from one and the same year. It is unclear whether the caliph offered the *khuṭba* on yet another of the Fridays (a third Friday) of this particular Ramaḍān, as had apparently become the custom in the reign of his two predecessors and perhaps

91. al-Musabbiḥī, *Akhbār Miṣr*, pp. 80–81; paraphrased by al-Maqrīzī in *Ittiʿāẓ*, 2: 167.

92. On this man in general see ʻal-Musabbiḥīʼ by Th. Bianquis in the *EI2*.

in his as well. Otherwise it is quite valid to consider the pattern we observe in this case as applying more or less to the practice of his forefathers and possibly to his immediate successors with some exceptions to the end of the dynasty. Small changes may have occurred over time, especially in the later period, but general custom prevailed. Al-Musabbiḥī's account is thus a capital source for the ceremonies surrounding the *khuṭba*s of the imams, even though it offers us no text of what they said in it.[93]

The *khuṭba* from al-Mustanṣir to al-Āmir

The lack of sources becomes even more important in trying to assess the subsequent period. For the next hundred years, from 415 until almost 515, when al-Afḍal b. Badr al-Jamālī, the wazir under al-Āmir, was assassinated, there is little information, and none of it from the chronicles. Even so, evidence of the caliph's riding to perform the prayer on both *ʿīd* festivals exists in a collection of decrees and letters (*sijillāt*) issued by al-Mustanṣir and sent to the Yaman.[94] In them the caliph in his own name describes his riding to the *muṣallā* for the festivals. The late Mamluk specialist in chancery practice, al-Qalqashandī, quotes here from a 5th/11th century Fatimid manual of chancery

93. It should be noted that Fatimid ceremonial has been the subject of various modern studies, most recently by Paula Sanders in her *Ritual, Politics, and the City in Fatimid Cairo*. That work should be consulted for the circumstances, content, and meaning of most of the ceremonies mentioned here.

94. *al-Sijillāt al-mustanṣiriyya*: nos 1, 13, 18, 19, 31, all written on the feast of fast-breaking for the years 445 (decree no. 13), 451 (no. 1), 476 (no. 31), 478 (no. 19), 480 (no. 18), and on feast of sacrifice in the years 474 (no. 30), 476 (no. 64), and 478 (no. 27). These letter-decrees belong to a type that was composed specifically to convey the good news of the occasion to distant regions. See, from a much later period, the seven examples: one for the first to third Fridays of Ramaḍān and two each for the *ʿīd* festivals—with and without a wazir—included by al-Qalqashandī in volume eight of his *Ṣubḥ al-aʿshā* (pp. 316–328) and two more examples of a similar kind that are to be found in al-Maqrīzī's *Khiṭaṭ*, new edition 2: 492–494 (ʿĪd al-fiṭr, 536) and 437–438 (ʿĪd al-naḥr, 536). The edition calls them *mukhallaqāt* but there is obviously some uncertainty about this term; see also pp. 335 and 366 of the same volume. Even so al-Qalqashandī does use this same word (*Ṣubḥ al-aʿshā*, 3: 505) for exactly this type of document and that appears to confirm its authenticity.

practice, the *Mawādd al-bayān*, a reason why such letters were necessary. Public observance of the festivals of Islam were both essential and yet also fraught with danger. In a state that governed a wide variety of religious groups and factions, the opportunity for rebellion and discord was always present. Those who wanted to cause trouble might see the festival as an opportunity for it. Thus news conveyed by these letters both announced the successful completion of a given ceremony and also the safe arrival of the imam back inside his palace.[95]

With this information we have thus no reason to conclude that the subsequent caliphs ceased giving the *khuṭba* at least on the two *ʿīd*s. Still, it would be nice to have more direct evidence in the cases of al-Mustanṣir (r. 427/1036 to 487/1094) and al-Mustaʿlī (r. 487/1094 to 495/1101), and a clearer picture of the practice of al-Āmir in the period prior to the death of al-Afḍal. The flow of information from these years in our medieval histories steadily dries up, leading to the era of the wazir Badr al-Jamālī (466/1074 to 487/1094) when it all but disappears. The documentation for the wazirate of his son is hardly better. Nor is there much if any relevant information about the crisis caused by the split between the supporters of al-Mustaʿlī and Nizār and how that might have affected the delivery of the *khuṭba* either at the time of the schism or later. Nothing comparable to the writings of al-Musabbiḥī exists until the beginning of the wazirate of al-Maʾmūn who succeeded al-Afḍal in that position upon the latter's death.

Quite abruptly the historical record for the next years becomes nearly as complete as it was once a century before. For the years of al-Maʾmūn's wazirate, from 515 to 518 (he was arrested in Ramaḍān of 519/1125 and confined in prison until his execution in 522/1128), we again have a considerably detailed account of the ceremonies that accompany the occasions of the caliphal *khuṭba*s. These reports for the most part come from a history composed by this same wazir's son, Ibn al-Maʾmūn al-Baṭāʾiḥī, which, though it itself is no longer extant, was a major source for several other chroniclers, among them al-Maqrīzī and Ibn Taghrī Birdī who quote it for these years. The son may thus offer an eyewitness account, his own perhaps, or, at the least, he had direct access to persons who were there.

95. al-Qalqashandī, *Ṣubḥ al-aʿshā*, 8: 313.

Information from this source, however, says little about the *khuṭba* before al-Ma'mūn took over, except in suggesting a change in practice precisely to alter a policy instituted under al-Afḍal. Al-Ma'mūn evidently also convinced al-Āmir to let someone besides himself deliver the *khuṭba*s on the Fridays in Ramaḍān, although he continued to do those of the two *'īd* festivals. The much later Ṭayyibī *dā'ī* and historian Idrīs 'Imād al-Dīn found, among the possessions of the Ṣulayḥid queen al-Ḥurra, copies of two *khuṭba*s given by al-Āmir. Both had been transcribed on silk and sent to her from Cairo. One of the two is from a Ramaḍān Friday service; the other from the 'Īd al-fiṭr. In the first the caliph invokes God's blessing on 'the Illustrious Excellency al-Afḍal, the son of the Lord Commander of the Armies', i.e. al-Afḍal Ibn Amīr al-Juyūsh, the wazir at the time of this *khuṭba*. That text thus provides evidence of the *khuṭba* before 415, though how much before is impossible to say. The other *khuṭba* has no indication of a date but it would be reasonable to assume that the two come from the same period.

Al-Afḍal fell to assassins at the very end of Ramaḍān in the midst of preparing for the feast. Al-Āmir had thus to observe both the ceremonies of mourning for the deceased wazir and the *'īd* at the same time. For the latter he broke his fast in the palace in the midst of sadness. We have an account of the details of breaking the fast and the mourning at the palace.[96] In regard to the *'īd* prayer and the *khuṭba*, the same source reports that at one point the commander al-Ma'mūn took 'the hand of the *dā'ī* and brought him close to the caliph. Al-Āmir then handed him the text of the *khuṭba*, which had been on his left wrapped in a kerchief of white *sharb* linen with gold thread. The *dā'ī* kissed it, put it to his forehead and then clutched it to his breast. The commander went over to the chamberlain Ḥusām al-Mulk and asked him to gather all of the amirs and proceed with them to the *muṣallā* of Cairo to perform the prayer. They wended their way there wearing the attire for mourning; the *mu'adhdhin*s were in front of them. The *dā'ī* led prayers and then mounted the *minbar*, stopping on the third step. There he gave the *khuṭba*. That *khuṭba* expounded a prayer for al-Afḍal and a request for the mercy

96. Sanders, *Ritual, Politics, and the City*, pp. 68–70.

of God to be upon him.[97] But the caliph, who remained back in the palace, did not attend.

During these years the head of the Fatimid chancery was Ibn al-Ṣayrafī. In this man's history of the wazirate, we have some evidence about the *khuṭba* after that event. He reports that in the year 515,[98] on the 2nd of the month of Dhu'l-Ḥijja, the caliph al-Āmir bestowed special honours on his new wazir and then issued a copy of the exact words to be used in offering a prayer for him (i.e. as in the *khuṭba*):

> O God, support the one the Commander of the Believers has chosen for his government, has approved of him and selected him to manage the affairs of his kingdom and picked him and entrusted matters to him. He has administered them with the finest of governance, always watchful, with diligence and firm energy. He has rendered satisfactory matters of importance and met all requirements in that regard with keen discernment, independence, and resolve, freeing himself for that which is beneficial with an acuity that matches in sharpness his keenness. The auspicious star rises higher because of him and its resplendence is more sublime. Radiating him is the illustrious and reliable, Crown of the caliphate, Strength of Islam, Pride of mankind, the Good order of religion and loyalty to the Commander of the Believers,[99] Abū ʿAbdallāh Muḥammad al-Āmirī, may God assist him in providing good service to the Muslims, and keep him upright in service to the Commander of the Believers and prolong for him greatness, abundance, and strength. O God, make him the star of his good fortune, eternal, supreme, and of great height. Conquer for the dynasty by his hand the west and the east. May his opinions and resolutions be connected to success. In slaughtering the enemies of religion, have the points of his lances and sharp edges of his swords accomplish their purpose.[100]

Early in his wazirate, according to one report, al-Ma'mūn, who had noted some carelessness in al-Āmir's climbing the *minbar* and giving the *khuṭba*, was nevertheless embarrassed to speak about it to

97. *Ittiʿāẓ*, 3: 64.

98. The Arabic has 510 but that must be a mistake for 515.

99. These are the titles of al-Ma'mūn.

100. Ibn al-Ṣayrafī, *al-Ishāra*, p. 105.

the caliph in person. He hoped to make the caliph realize it without having to confront him. So he said to him: 'O our master, some days have passed from the month and it is time to ride for the first Friday.' Here our source, Ibn Taghrī Birdī, interjects: 'The arrangement for the Fatimid caliph to ride in procession for the Friday prayer and to pray with the people on three Fridays was discussed previously in the biography of al-Muʿizz li-Dīn Allāh [in this book].[101] For the final Friday of every month the *khaṭīb* prayed with the people. They referred to that Friday as the Friday of rest (*al-rāḥa*), meaning that the caliph rested in it.'[102] In the corresponding passage of Ibn 'Abd al-Ẓāhir, it is clear here that the wazir refers to the first Friday, not the last. That is the day he proposes for the caliph to observe the *khaṭīb*. Ibn Taghrī Birdī then resumes his account:

> ...the wazir suggested to the caliph that, without attendants, he go to the mosque on the last Friday and sit in the dome over the *miḥrab* opposite the *khaṭīb* in order to observe how the man who was deputized to take his place gave the *khuṭba*. That man was a *sharīf* and was quite skilled with the Arabic language, having memorized the Qur'an. Al-Āmir agreed to the plan. Once he was in the mosque, he took up a seat in the domed area with the skylight opened. The *khaṭīb* stood up and gave the *khuṭba*. In the midst of the prayer for the Prophet in the second *khuṭba*, a whiff of air opened the drapes and the *khaṭīb* raised his head and found himself face to face with the caliph. He recognized him and began to tremble in alarm. He did not know what to say until inspired to speak: 'O assembled Muslims, may God benefit you and me by what you hear and keep you from error. God says in His precious book: "We had previously accepted the covenant

101. What he claims about it going back to al-Muʿizz is not supported by other sources which insist that it began with al-'Azīz.

102. Other information suggests a different practice, one in which, if the caliph rode in procession on the first day of Ramaḍān, evidently a variation used in some years, then he 'rested' on the first Friday. In those years, he rode, gave the *khuṭba*, and led prayers therefore on the last three Fridays (*Khiṭaṭ*, 4.1: 123) rather than the first three. See further A. F. Sayyid's editor's notes to Ibn al-Ma'mūn, *Nuṣūṣ min Akhbār Miṣr* (ed. Ayman Fu'ād Sayyid, Cairo, 1983), p. 82, n. 1 [information from Qalqashandī 3: 505–508 and the *Khiṭaṭ*] and Abū Muḥammad 'Abd al-Salām Ibn al-Ṭuwayr, *Nuzhat al-muqlatayn fī akhbār al-dawlatayn*, ed. Ayman Fu'ād Sayyid (Beirut, 1992), p. 172, n. 2.

> of Adam but he forgot and We found that he had no consistence" [20: 115]. "God commands justice and the doing of good…" [16: 90] (to the rest of this verse). He descended and prayed with the people. When he had left that session, al-Āmir spoke with his wazir about what had happened to the *khaṭīb*. That opened the subject for the wazir and he mentioned what had concerned him. Thereafter al-Āmir refrained from giving the *khuṭba* and delegated it instead to this wazir. The wazir then went thereafter to give the *khuṭba* in the mosques of Cairo, Ibn Ṭūlūn, and Fusṭāṭ.[103]

Here Ibn Taghrī Birdī switches to another source, a history by Ibn Abi'l-Manṣūr(?), who implies that al-Ma'mūn began giving these Friday *khuṭba*s thereafter despite al-Āmir's express desire to ride for such purposes even more so than his forefathers. The caliph continued to deliver the *ʿīd khuṭba*s, leaving only those of the Fridays in Ramaḍān to his wazir.[104]

> When he rode to the *muṣallā* for the festival sermon, he was preceded there by his men with furnishings and implements. The *miḥrab* was swathed in golden *sharb* linen and three mats were laid out overlapping one another, on top of which was a fine mat, which was by them highly prized. It was a piece of a mat that they claimed had once belonged to Jaʿfar al-Ṣādiq. During the time of al-Ḥākim it had been taken along with other items from his house in Medina when it was opened by this caliph's order. The ground beneath the dome was furnished entirely with mats. The three doors beneath the dome in front of the *miḥrab* were shut. Curtains were hung from the *miḥrāb* and on both sides of the *minbar*. The latter's steps were covered as well. At the

---

103. Ibn Taghrī Birdī, *al-Nujūm*, 5: 175–176; see also the same work 4: 102–104, in the latter place quoting from Ibn ʿAbd al-Ẓāhir. See also the version now found in what remains of Ibn ʿAbd al-Ẓāhir's text (*al-Rawḍa al-bahiyya al-zāhira fī khiṭaṭ al-muʿizziyya al-qāhira*, ed. Ayman Fu'ād Sayyid, Cairo, 1996), pp. 38–40.

104. This comment is also found in Ibn ʿAbd al-Ẓāhir, *al-Rawḍa al-bahiyya*, p. 40, which may be the ultimate source for it. Curiously, the same report says that al-Ma'mūn thereafter (in the year 516) rode to and gave the *khuṭba* in, successively, the mosques of Fusṭāṭ, Ibn Ṭūlūn, and Cairo. Not only does the order here seem peculiar, we have otherwise no references that suggests the use of the Mosque of Ibn Ṭūlūn in this fashion. Even so, al-Afḍal as wazir did endow a new *miḥrāb* for that mosque. Perhaps it functioned as a congregational meeting place on some occasions in this one period.

top they placed a cushion for the caliph to sit on. Two banners were unfurled and attached. The supervisor of those preparations stood with the qadi at the bottom of the *minbar*. Incense was released. The wazir was responsible not to let anyone open any door except the door through which the caliph would come at which he stood. The *dāʿī* sat in the entryway with the *mu'adhdhin*s reciting beside him. The princes, the *ashrāf* nobility, the witnesses, and notables entered but no one else unless given a pass by the *dāʿī*. If the prayer fell due, the caliph approached in the attire we described..., the sceptre of power in his hand. Immediately behind him were all of his brothers and uncles. The *mu'adhdhin*s met him and those who had been around him of his uncles and brothers withdrew. He went out from the Gate of Power [of the palace] arriving at the *ʿīd* Gate. The parasol was then extended over him and a procession formed calmly, no one advancing or falling out of his proper place. Behind the procession were the camel-borne litters, the giraffes, the elephants, and the lions on which were fetters adorned with steel claws. No one entered the gate of the *muṣallā* riding except the wazir. Then he went through the second gate and dismounted. He took control of the bit of the caliph's horse while the caliph dismounted and walked to the *miḥrab* with the qadi and the *dāʿī* to the right and left of him relaying the *takbīr* to the group of *mu'adhdhins*. The Kātib al-Dast and a group of clerks were offering blessings beneath the supports of the *minbar*; no one but they were allowed to be with them. The *takbīr* was said seven times in the first and in the second five in accord with the practice of the nation. Next the wazir went up and handed over to the qadi the list of invitees. He summoned those who customarily mounted the *minbar*. No one overstepped his place. Then, following the *khuṭba*, the caliph descended and returned [to the palace] in the finest of form and attire. His going out and his return were by the gate opposite the festival courtyard and for that reason that place was called the courtyard of the *ʿīd* Gate.[105]

The description of this *ʿīd* festival (and the Friday services) appears to come from the year 516 and from an account of it composed

105. Ibn Taghrī Birdī, *al-Nujūm*, 5: 177–178; Ibn ʿAbd al-Ẓāhir, *al-Rawḍa al-bahiyya*, 40–41; Ibn al-Ma'mūn, *Akhbār Miṣr*, pp. 86–89; *Khiṭaṭ*, 2: 484–489 (the latter version, which is also reprinted in Ibn al-Ma'mūn [it is the passage on pp. 86–89] is more complete with greater detail than that of Ibn ʿAbd al-Ẓāhir and Ibn Taghrī Birdī).

by Ibn al-Ma'mūn, the wazir's son. Because it contains extensive detail of the event, it later served as a prime example of Fatimid practice in regard to the caliph's riding to the *muṣallā* and back. What took place that year, however, may have represented a change from earlier practice. The year 516 was the first fully under the control of al-Ma'mūn. He is known to have agreed to allow the caliph much greater participation in public ceremonies, particularly of these two festivals. Al-Maqrīzī remarks that the caliph prayed with the people at the *muṣallā* beyond the Bāb al-Naṣr and gave the *khuṭba* in 516. 'That' he adds, 'had been discontinued in the days of Badr and al-Afḍal.'[106] Still it seems unlikely that al-Afḍal had eliminated the ceremony altogether. But the matter remains unclear. It could be that the role of the caliph was severely reduced by the old wazir and then enhanced by al-Ma'mūn.[107]

We have, in addition, a description of the festival of sacrifice from later that same year, again from Ibn al-Ma'mūn,[108] and, for the first time, a report covering in some detail the observance of the *ʿīd* of Ghadīr Khumm, a commemoration of the moment when the Prophet publicly acknowledged ʿAlī's special relationship as the one who would succeed himself as leader of the Muslim community.[109] On these festivals, sacrifices were performed like those of the feast of sacrifice and, according to Ibn al-Ma'mūn, on that day in 516, after the qadi Abu'l-Ḥajjāj Yūsuf b. Ayyūb led prayers, 'the *sharīf* Ibn Anas

106. *Ittiʿāẓ*, 3: 83. It is possible, however, that the principal changes allowed by al-Ma'mūn applied to other events in the calendar of ceremonies, perhaps the observances of the births (*mawlids*) of the Prophet, ʿAlī, Fāṭima, and the current imam, which were cancelled by al-Afḍal. See Ibn al-Ma'mūn, *Akhbār Miṣr,* p. 62.

107. For an interpretation of al-Afḍal's purpose in this regard, see Sanders, *Ritual, Politics, and the City*, p. 68.

108. As found in the *Khiṭaṭ* (2: 432–434); Ibn al-Ma'mūn, *Akhbār Miṣr,* pp. 25–26, 40–42.

109. After writing these words, my University of Chicago colleague Tahera Qutbuddin reported that she had found at least one example of a Ghadīr *khuṭba* in volume three of al-Mu'ayyad fi'l-Dīn al-Shīrāzī's *Majālis*. She, moreover, believes there may be additional *khuṭba*s among these *majālis,* and thus when the rest are finally edited and fully published, we may discover more examples of various forms of the Fatimid sermon.

al-Dawla rose and delivered the *khuṭba* of the *ʿīd* festival'.[110] Evidently the caliph did not take an active role in these proceedings.[111] At a later period, following the caliphate of al-Ḥāfiẓ, the festival of Ghadīr Khumm assumed special importance. It was then used to affirm the possible accession of a cousin, as had been the case both with ʿAlī b. Abī Ṭālib and with al-Ḥāfiẓ.[112] Even in its expanded format, however, the ceremonies of this feast were quite private among loyal Ismailis and confined to the palace grounds. Moreover, although it featured a *khuṭba*, that *khuṭba* was delivered by the *khaṭīb*, not the imam, even though he sat close by in the *subbāk*, the royal grilled loge, which separated him from the audience.[113]

For 517 we have a report that the caliph rode to the *muṣallā* and gave the *khuṭba* on the ʿĪd al-fiṭr as usual.[114] But, from the rest of his reign, there is little evidence. What policy he might have adopted once he rid himself of his wazir could be of special interest, but we know nothing about it.

---

110. 'The *khuṭba* of the *ʿīd* festival' means here a *khuṭba* like that of the other *ʿīds*. Ibn al-Maʾmūn, *Akhbār Miṣr,* pp. 42–43; *Khiṭaṭ*, 2: 431–432. In general the observance of Ghadīr Khumm, which is important for the Shiʿa and which was a part of the ritual calendar of the Fatimids, is less well documented. Ibn al-Maʾmūn's description is therefore especially important. He indicates that it was observed much like the ʿĪd al-naḥr, but it is not clear if earlier practice was like that of late Fatimid times.

111. But see, from a later period, the report by Ibn al-Ṭuwayr, *Nuzhat al-muqlatayn,* pp. 186–189 (= *Khiṭaṭ*, 2: 300–305); Sanders, *Ritual, Politics, and the City,* chapter six, pp. 121–134.

112. For more on this development, see Paula Sanders, 'Claiming the Past: Ghadīr Khumm and the Rise of Ḥāfiẓī Historiography in Late Fāṭimid Egypt,' *Studia Islamica* 75 (1992), pp. 81–104.

113. This development is fully described by Sanders, *Ritual, Politics, and the City*, chapter six (pp. 121–134). For some idea of the content of *khuṭbas* given on Ghadīr Khumm, see the examples cited by al-Amīnī, *ʿĪd al-Ghadīr fī ʿahd al-Fāṭimiyyīn* (Najaf, 1962; also Tehran, 1997), pp. 136–142.

114. *Ittiʿāẓ*, 3: 105. On p. 102 there seems to be an indication that he might have ridden as well to the mosques for the Friday services in Ramaḍān. If so it may call into question what was said above.

Khuṭbas from the reign of al-Ḥāfiẓ onward

The assassination of al-Āmir in 524 brought to power his cousin ʿAbd al-Majīd as regent and then in swift succession a coup by the son of al-Afḍal, Abū ʿAlī Aḥmad, who was known by the name Kutayfāt. Although this man's control of the government lasted only until a counter-coup in the following year restored the former regent, who thereafter adopted the full trappings and titles of caliph with the regnal name al-Ḥāfiẓ, the brief interregnum of Kutayfāt was important in a number of ways. One later historian reported of it: 'Aḥmad the son of al-Afḍal conducted his affairs nicely, especially in relationship to the days of al-Āmir. He returned to the people much of what had been extorted from them. He openly espoused the doctrine of the Twelver Imamis. He removed from the call to prayer the phrase "Come to the best of works". He ordered that the prayer be made from the *minbar* [i.e. in the *khuṭba*] in his name using a formula of prayer that he devised himself. It ran as follows:

> The Illustrious Excellency, King of the supporters of the state, Defender of the domain of religion, Spreader of the wing of justice over the Muslims, both those near and those far away, Supporter of the imam of truth both in his absence and when he is present, Brandisher of the sharpness of his sword in backing him, the pertinence of his opinions and his good management, Trustee of God to His servants, Guider of judges in following the road to truth and basing themselves on it, Director of the *dāʿīs* of the believers through the clearness of his explanations and instructions, Master of favours, Remover of tyranny from the nations, Possessor of the two virtues of the sword and the pen, Abū ʿAlī Aḥmad, son of the Illustrious Lord al-Afḍal Shāhanshāh, Commander of the Armies (*amīr al-juyūsh*).'[115]

The *khuṭba* for the regent was stopped. In its place Kutayfāt appears to have opted for a generic Shiʿi appeal to the imam in occultation and this change presumably implied the end of the Fatimid dynasty. But the period of his rule was so short it is hard to determine

115. This version comes from al-Nuwayrī, *Nihāya*, 28: 297. Al-Maqrīzī (*Ittiʿāẓ*, 3: 143–144), reports the same with a couple of minor variants. Both ultimately depend on Ibn Muyassar (*Akhbār Miṣr*, p. 116). See also Ibn Ẓāfir, *Akhbār al-duwal al-munqaṭiʿa*, p. 94 (with again a couple of variants).

exactly what he intended. Removing the phrase 'Come to the best of works' from the call to pray goes against all the Shiʿa, not merely the Ismailis.

Soon enough the *khuṭba* returned to its Fatimid form, with, now, the specific citation in it of al-Ḥāfiẓ as imam-caliph. After the death of Kutayfāt and his own enthronement, al-Ḥāfiẓ ordered that the prayer be said in his name from the *minbar*s according to the following formula:

> O God, bless he through whom You reconstruct religion after enemies conspired to make it disappear. You empowered Islam by making him ascend over the nation and reappear. You made him a signpost for whoever brings about the truths by inner discernment, our master and our lord, the imam of our age and its time, ʿAbd al-Majīd Abu'l-Maymūn, [bless] his pure forefathers, his noble sons, with a blessing that persists until the Day of Judgment.[116]

With the advent of al-Ḥāfiẓ, now no longer merely a regent, but—as these formulas in his *khuṭba* indicate—claiming the imamate in full and in his own name, the Fatimid dynasty began a new lease on life. Yet the cost to its base of support in many regions of the Islamic world had strained the institution severely. Nizari Ismailis had withdrawn three decades earlier when al-Afḍal refused to accept the succession of Nizār. A major section of the Ismaili *daʿwa* in Yaman, and with it India, likewise declined to accept al-Ḥāfiẓ, maintaining instead that the imamate of al-Ṭayyib, the infant son of al-Āmir, had continued with him as an imam in hiding. A Ḥāfiẓī *daʿwa*, however, would remain in charge of Egypt until the close of the dynasty. Accordingly, the *khuṭba* over the final period of Fatimid rule reveals both interesting changes and innovations and yet important evidence of how practices of an older culture persisted.

The innovations would include the following *khuṭba* that al-Ḥāfiẓ, under intense pressure from forces he could not control, permitted, as one part of his recognition of his son Ḥasan as heir apparent:

116. *Ittiʿāẓ*, 3: 146; Ibn Taghrī Birdī, *al-Nujūm*, 5: 238–239; al-Nuwayrī, *Nihāya*, 28: 298; Ibn Ẓāfir, *Akhbār al-duwal al-munqaṭiʿa*, p. 95 (with some variants in the four).

O God, construct by the continued existence of the holder of the covenant of the Muslims the foundations of his caliphate. Gird him with the swords of might in support of him and his capacity, make him a benefit for the betterment of his land and his people, make him a gathering for them and for the whole of the lords his brothers whom You have raised in the heavens of his kingdom like moons without which it would wane and be moonless. You tame with their fortitude every renegade among the partisans of dissent and hypocrisy. You strengthen through them the vigour of the imamate and retain the caliphate in their offspring until the Day of Judgment, through Your mercy, O most merciful of the merciful.[117]

Al-Ḥāfiẓ did not actually favour this son but, in permitting him to claim the title of heir-apparent, he was bowing to brute force used against him by this same Ḥasan. Later the caliph would also contrive the death of this offending son. Even so the *khuṭba* said in his favour is the one preserved example of how such a sermon might read.

At a later time this same caliph appointed as his wazir the Christian Bahrām. How a Christian could perform the tasks expected of the wazir was the subject of much debate. How could he climb the *minbar* with the imam on the *ʿīd* festivals in order to cover him with the curtains that were to conceal him from the people while he delivered the *khuṭba*? It was a serious question and treated as such by members of the court. There were other problems as well. Al-Ḥāfiẓ decreed, however, that the wazir's role on the days of the festival would be performed by the chief qadi instead of the wazir.[118] Nevertheless, soon enough the presence of a Christian wazir and the coincident influx into Egypt of great numbers of Christian Armenian soldiers—Bahrām was himself Armenian—produced a backlash among Muslims. The governor of the Gharbiyya province, Riḍwān b. Walakhshī, himself a Sunni, took up the cause of the Muslims in opposition. He mounted the *minbar* and delivered a stirring *khuṭba* urging those who heard him to begin a *jihād* against Bahrām and any who supported him.[119] That was the year 531; Bahrām fell from power soon thereafter.

117. Ibn Ẓāfir, *Akhbār al-duwal al-munqaṭiʿa*, p. 96; *Ittiʿāẓ*, 3: 150.

118. al-Nuwayrī, *Nihāya*, 28: 301.

119. *Ittiʿāẓ*, 3: 159; al-Nuwayrī, *Nihāya*, 28: 302.

From the final thirty-six years of the Fatimids there is not much information about the *khuṭba*.[120] The exceptions are, first, two documents from the year 536, both copied by al-Maqrīzī into his *Khiṭaṭ*.[121] They are decrees or letters written in the name of the caliph for dispersal abroad. Each announces that in that year the caliph had ridden to the *muṣallā*, led prayers, and delivered the *khuṭba*, after which he returned safely and securely to the palace. One is for the ʿĪd al-fiṭr and the other for the ʿĪd al-naḥr. Both were composed by the head of the chancery, Ibn al-Ṣayrafī. It is odd that, from this period, we have these two, and both from the same year. Yet it is quite likely that that is merely an accident of survival. The practice of sending out such announcements was obviously common. An additional eight examples exist, also perhaps by an accident of preservation, from the years of al-Mustanṣir.[122] There are seven more in al-Qalqashandī's manual of chancery practice, the *Ṣubḥ al-aʿshā*, but only one of these has a date (ʿĪd al-fiṭr, 531). Typically al-Qalqashandī was less interested in exact dates, which he often removed in his presentation of the text of a document, than in the person who composed it. Five of his examples are by Ibn al-Ṣayrafī, most likely the sixth as well (the one dated 531), and one by Ibn Qādūs, who was head of the Fatimid chancery at a period after the former. Ibn al-Ṣayrafī died in 542/1147; Ibn Qādūs in 553.

120. One report from those years says that the child caliph al-Fā'iz (r. 549/1154–555/1160) rode in procession on the *ʿīd*s unaware of its importance and that the chief qadi gave the *khuṭba* on his behalf, even though the boy was next to him on the *minbar* (*Ittiʿāẓ*, 3: 239).

121. Ayman Fu'ād Sayyid edition, 2: 492–494 and 2: 436–438. The term *al-mukhallaqāt*, which this editor believes applies to such documents and is the proper reading of the manuscripts, is, as mentioned earlier, open to question but I have come up with nothing better. Compare what he says on pp. 335 and 366 of the same volume. Note as well al-Qalqashandī's use of the same term for this type of document, which, he adds, no longer exists in his time.

122. See above.

The eyewitness testimony of Ibn al-Ṭuwayr

The other item is a detailed account of a caliph delivering the *khuṭba* on the Fridays of Ramaḍān and the two *ʿīd* festivals. One of the most complete of its kind, it comes from Ibn al-Ṭuwayr, an eyewitness to the late Fatimid period. In fact this man reports that he personally saw the caliph give the *khuṭba* in one of the cases he describes. Unfortunately he does not indicate which caliph it was. Since he himself lived from 525/1130 to 617/1220, he could have seen only the last four: al-Ḥāfiẓ, al-Ẓāfir, al-Fāʾiz and al-ʿĀḍid.[123] It is unlikely that he refers to al-Fāʾiz, and perhaps not to al-Ḥāfiẓ. The former was probably too young ever to give the *khuṭba*[124] and the latter was caliph in Ibn al-Ṭuwayr's own youth (although he would have been nineteen by the end of this reign).

> Ibn al-Ṭuwayr reports:[125] If he rode on the first of the month of Ramaḍān, the caliph rests on the first Friday. On the second Friday, he rides to the great Anwār Mosque wearing the outfit of the festival seasons and those items of accoutrement mentioned previously. He is clothed in a robe of white silk, reverently gilded out of respect for the prayer, and a kerchief and rounded shawl of hair. He enters by the *khaṭīb*'s door, with the wazir accompanying him, after having been preceded at the start of the day by the treasurer, who was mentioned earlier as one of the eunuchs, who brings with him the furnishings special to the caliph if he appears on that day. These items are carried in the hands of servants selected for this duty and are wrapped in wide *dabīqī* linen. Three carpets have been laid out in the *miḥrāb*, either of the finest *sāmān* or of *dabīqī* linen of either kind, each embroidered in red. These carpets were stacked one on the other.

---

123. It cannot have been al-Āmir who died before Ibn al-Ṭuwayr was born.

124. Al-Fāʾiz was put on the throne at the age of five and he died age eleven. Hibatallāh b. ʿAbdallāh b. Kāmil, the chief qadi from 549 to 559 (or 558), was deputized to deliver the *khuṭba* for him on the *ʿīds*. See Ibn Muyassar, *Akhbār Miṣr*, 153, n. 524; Ibn Ḥajar al-ʿAsqalānī, *Rafʿ al-iṣr ʿan quḍāt Miṣr*, ed. ʿAlī Muḥammad ʿUmar (Cairo, 1998), p. 304.

125. This and the following passages from his work were collected and published by A. F. Sayyid in *Nuzhat al-muqlatayn fī akhbār al-dawlatayn*, pp. 172–185, although they come from the *Khiṭaṭ*, vol. 4.1, pp. 123–126; vol. 2, 489–492; and vol. 2, pp. 432–435.

Two curtains, one left and one right, have been attached to the top. The one on the right has written on it in red silk with clear markings the Basmala, the Fātiḥa, and the Sūrat al-Jumuʿa. The curtain on the left is similar, with, along with the Fātiḥa, 'When the hypocrites come to you…' [63: 1].[126] They have been lowered and spread in being attached to the sides of the *miḥrāb* affixed to its structure. Then the chief qadi goes up the *minbar* holding in his hand a fine bamboo censer that has been given to him by the treasurer containing embers on which has been placed three types of incense the like of which were never smelled except in this place. He perfumes the top, which has on it a covering like that of the dome for the caliph to sit in the midst of the *khuṭba*. The qadi makes three passes over it. Then the caliph arrives with respectful appearance of drum and bugle. In his train, just beyond the grooms, come the reciters. The reciters were present on each side chanting the recitations one after another, having begun that when he first departed from where he sat, along the route leading to the chamber of the *khuṭba* in the mosque. The enclosure is guarded from the outside by the chamberlain and the commander of the troops, and from inside from start to end by the Elite Youth Guard (*ṣibyān al-khāṣṣ*) and others who were so charged, from his entering it through the doorway until he exits going to the *minbar*, one by one, with the wazir at the end.

When the call to Friday prayer sounds, the chief qadi goes in to him and says: 'Greetings to the Commander of the Believers, the most noble judge, may God have mercy on him and bless him. The prayer, may God have mercy on you!' Then the caliph precedes out walking, around him are the eunuchs and *muḥannak*s, the wazir behind him, and those of the elite following them, those belonging to the Youth Guard with weapons in their hands—they are officers bearing this name. He mounts the *minbar* to the top, beneath the perfumed dome. Once he is seated, with the wazir at the door to the *minbar* facing him, he signals the latter to climb up. The qadi goes up until he reaches him and then kisses his hands and feet in full view of the people. Next he covers the caliph inside the dome, which then resembled a *hawdaj*. He descends facing him and stops holding the door of the *minbar*. If there is no wazir who is also military, the lowering of the curtains would have been done by

126. On the reciting of these verses in the Friday prayer, see the *Daʿāʾim*, 1: 228.

the chief qadi in like fashion and he would have stood holding the door of the *minbar*. The caliph then delivers a short *khuṭba* from a prepared text presented to him from the chancery. He recites in it a *sūra* of the Sacred Qur'an. I myself listened once to his *khuṭba* in the Azhar Mosque. He recited in his *khuṭba*: 'O my Lord, have me be thankful for Your favour which You have bestowed on me and on my parents' (to the end of this verse) [27: 19 or 46: 15]. Next he prayed for his father and grandfather, meaning by them here Muḥammad and ʿAlī b. Abī Ṭālib,[127] and he preached to the people an eloquent sermon of a few words. The *khuṭba* itself consisted of abundant phrases. He mentioned those who had come before of his forefathers until coming down to himself and said—and I was listening to him: 'O God, I am Your servant, and son of Your servant; I do not expect of You either harm or benefit'. He asks for grand good wishes appropriate to that and he requests blessings for the wazir, if there is one, and, for the armies, support and good order and, for the troops, victory, and, on the unbelievers and opponents, destruction and domination. Then he closes by saying: 'Remember God remembers you.' The person who had covered him then goes up and opens those curtains and descends again backward. The reason for covering them was their reading from a prepared text in contrast to the usual custom of the *khaṭīb*s. The caliph descends and stands on those three carpets in the *miḥrāb*, alone in front, the wazir and qadi in a line behind and behind them the eunuchs, the *muḥannak*s, the collared officers, various lords of rank among the military and clerical staff, with the *mu'adhdhin*s, standing and visible up against the *maqṣūra* to guard him. As the wazir hears the caliph, he relays [what he says] to the qadi, who relays it to the *mu'adhdhin*s, and they relay it to the people. So it was and the mosque was full of a host ready for prayer behind him. The caliph reads what is written on the right-hand curtain during the first *rakʿa* and in the second what is written on the left, doing that as a way of remembering, out of fear of any hesitation. When finished, the people depart and ride away one by one. The caliph returns in the direction of the palace, with the wazir behind him. Bugles and drums sound on the return.

---

127. The inverted reference to father and grandfather as Muḥammad and ʿAlī (rather than vice versa) reflects the Arabic original.

The ceremony of the second Friday was much the same. On the third, the caliph rode to Fusṭāṭ for the *khuṭba* in its mosque. The route and decoration of this procession were thus different but the other details remained. For the festival of fast-breaking:

> [T]he caliph rides in procession at the onset of Shawwāl at the close of Ramaḍān which they calculate always as thirty days. Once preparations have been completed for the caliph, the wazir, the commanders, and the elite of various ranks, as described previously, and the wazir with his retinue is stationed at the door of the palace, the caliph proceeds wearing the attire of the caliph, the parasol, the solitaire gem [in his turban], and other accoutrements previously mentioned. His clothing on this day, which is the ʿĪd al-fiṭr, consists of a white-banded robe *mujawwama*, which is the most glorious of their outfits, and the parasol is similar (it always matches his robe so that however it is, the parasol is also). He exits from the *ʿīd* Gate to the *muṣallā*. The extras that appear on this day are in the numbers of soldiers and troops, both on horse and foot, who line the route from the gate of the palace to the *muṣallā* in two rows. The master of the treasury had, as was the custom, furnished the *muṣallā* as was done on the Fridays.' [Here Ibn al-Ṭuwayr repeats in summary the furnishing and the two curtains with Qur'anic verses (on the right 87: 1 and the left 88: 1, plus Basmala and Fātiḥa on both).] Two banners have been firmly planted on the two sides of the *muṣallā* like those, on two lances adorned with joints of silver, both unfurled and loose. The caliph enters from the eastside of the *muṣallā* to a spot in which he rests a moment. Then he proceeds, guarded as he had been in the mosque of Cairo, meaning that he walks out with the *muḥannak* eunuchs around him and the wazir behind him.... He goes forward to the *miḥrāb* and gives the *ʿīd* prayer with *takbīr*s as prescribed, the wazir behind him and the qadi. In each *rakʿa* he reads what is inscribed on the curtains, which are there as reminders.
>
> Once finished, he extends greetings and mounts the *minbar* for the *ʿīd khuṭba* of the festival of fast-breaking. When he has taken his seat at the top where there is a cushion of *sāmān* or *dabīqī* linen of appropriate size, the rest of him is covered in white in his measure according to the division of its stairs exactly without having been altered. The people of that gathering see him sitting at the top. Standing at the base of the *minbar* are the wazir, the chief qadi, the chamberlain, the commander of the army, the head of the chancery,

the controller of the palace, the master of the bureau of state, the parasol bearer, the leaders of the *ashrāf* relatives, the treasurer, the lance bearer, the head of the ʿAlid nobility. The wazir faces him. The caliph signals to the wazir to climb up and so he does, approaching and stopping, his face opposite his feet. He kisses them in view of all those present. Then he rises and stands to the right of the caliph.

Once standing he signals to the chief qadi to come up. He goes up to the seventh step. Then the boon-companion .... He takes out of his sleeve a register that has been presented to him the day before from the chancery after having been passed by the caliph and the wazir. As he reads it he disclosed what it contains. He says: 'In the name of God, the Merciful, the Compassionate. This confirms who is to be honoured by mounting this sacred *minbar* on such and such day, which is the ʿĪd al-fiṭr, of such and such a year, of the servants of the Commander of the Believers, may God's blessings be on him and on his pure forefathers, and the noble prophets, following the mounting of the Illustrious Lord and his approved title and his pious benediction.' If the caliph wants to bestow honours on any of the sons of the wazir and his brothers, the qadi would call them up by the title mentioned therein. Next follows the name of the aforementioned qadi, who is himself the reader [of the document]. It is not his place to expand on his own titles nor his invocation but to say merely 'the slave so and so (*fulān b. fulān*)'. Once the qadi Ibn Abī ʿAqīl was reading when he came to his own name and he said: 'The humble servant who confesses to the wondrous art in the glorious position, Aḥmad b. ʿAbd al-Raḥmān b. Abī ʿAqīl.' [128] That was considered good on his part and subsequently al-Aʿazz b. Salāma, who was qadi at the end [of the dynasty], followed his example.[129] He said: 'The slave in the place of sacred honour, who holds the appointment to the most truthful symbol, Ḥasan b. ʿAlī b. Salāma.' Next he summons those we mentioned who were standing at the door of the *minbar* by their titles, citing their service, and inviting them according to rank.

In going up each of them knows his place on the *minbar*, left or right. Once there is no one left who should mount, the wazir signals those in whose hand is a part of the banner that hangs to the side of the caliph. He is then covered over and concealed. The wazir calls to

128. This man was chief qadi from 531 until his death in 533.

129. He was qadi from 559.

> the people to listen. The caliph delivers the *khuṭba* from the written text as usual. It is an eloquent *khuṭba* appropriate for that day. When he finishes, each of those whose hand was on a part of the banner outside of the *minbar* uncover it as they had previously covered it. They descend one by one, the nearer first, backward. Once the *minbar* is cleared of all except the caliph, he stands and goes down to the spot he will exit from, stopping only a brief moment and then rides... [back to the palace].

Here Ibn al-Ṭuwayr continues with details of the ceremony of returning to the palace, entering it, and the feast to follow.

His account of the ʿĪd al-naḥr is shorter, in general noting that the riding of the caliph on that day was much like that of the feast of fast-breaking, except that he would be dressed in red. His riding occurred on three days consecutively, only the first of which was to the *muṣallā* for a *khuṭba* as with the ʿĪd al-fiṭr. The other two went instead directly to the special grounds for the sacrifices, the *manḥar*.

As with the information gleaned from Ibn al-Maʾmūn, this report by Ibn al-Ṭuwayr entered most subsequent accounts of the caliphal *khuṭba* and its attendant ceremonies. Both appear, for example, in al-Maqrīzī's *Khiṭaṭ* in the section of that work devoted to the appropriate topic. Like Ibn al-Maʾmūn, and al-Musabbiḥī from a previous century, Ibn al-Ṭuwayr offers eyewitness observations of the events he describes. Significantly, a comparison of the three suggests that there had been little, perhaps no, change in the protocol surrounding either the Friday *khuṭba* of Ramaḍān or of the two *ʿīd* festivals. Once set, the customary practice of the Fatimid dynasty in regard to the giving of these *khuṭba*s remained in place to the very end.

The last *khuṭba*

At the very end of Fatimid rule, the wazir was Saladin (Ṣalāḥ al-Dīn), who would become famous as the founder of the Ayyubid dynasty that followed. Before that he had entered Egypt only as a commander of Syrian troops on behalf of his Zangid overlord and sponsor in Damascus from whom he had obtained his commission. Later, having risen to the position of wazir, he came to owe a second allegiance to al-ʿĀḍid, the last of the Fatimids. And, although under pressure from both Damascus, and also Baghdad, to abolish the Shiʿi caliphate in Cairo, he resisted as long as he dared. Finally, with al-ʿĀḍid sick and dying, and not expected to recover, Saladin at last gave the order to change the *khuṭba*. The *khaṭīb*, however, was poorly prepared. It was Muḥarram of the year 567 when the command came down, but, faced with what exactly to say in the new *khuṭba*, he hesitated. He knew not to mention al-ʿĀḍid and did not. In place of the Fatimid caliph, however, he named in the prayer simply 'the rightly guided imams' (*al-a'imma al-mahdiyyīn*), along with al-Mālik al-Nāṣir (the title of the wazir, i.e. Saladin). The formulation 'rightly guided imams' was as old as the Fatimids; it had appeared in the earliest of the *khuṭba*s said in their favour. It hardly sufficed to signal the end of their dynasty. But, on the following Friday, the *khaṭīb* came much better prepared and this time pronounced without confusion or hesitation the full names and titles of the Abbasid caliph. Egypt no longer recognized the Fatimid imam; it was once again Sunni and the Shiʿi Ismaili caliphate had finally come to an end.[130]

130. *Ittiʿāẓ*, 3: 325–327.

CHAPTER 2

Rhetoric and Themes in the Surviving *Khuṭbas*

Rhetoric is the art of expression, particularly in oratory. It is thus the skilful use of language in speech. Whoever delivers the Friday *khuṭba*, or that of the two *ʿīd* festivals, must assume the responsibility of employing terms and phrases aimed at a broad audience, the rhetoric, in other words, of public address. To understand fully what might have been involved, we ought to have a much larger sample of these sermons. It is unfortunate that those which survive, either whole or in part, represent a very small fraction of the total. Over the entire 270 years of Fatimid rule, the number of *ʿīd khuṭbas* alone would have easily exceeded 500. Of these, today we can study as few as ten, with some uncertainty about one or two of them. Of Friday sermons by the imams, only one, possibly two, remain. Of the literally thousands and thousands of ordinary Friday *khuṭbas* said in their names, we possess only one in complete form and parts from a handful of others. Even so the situation is by no means hopeless. Although the evidence is not as plentiful as we might want, what we do have is all the more precious for its rarity. If we cannot expect definitive answers, we nonetheless have important material to investigate in the sermons that survive.

What follows in this chapter constitutes a preliminary accounting of the themes and rhetorical strategies displayed in the texts of the *khuṭbas* that are available. This material begins to tell us what the imams actually said to their subjects and it thus reveals, secondarily, a little about what, in the context of a public forum, they felt the need to relate to those who, in that era long ago, followed them.

The audience

The Fatimid caliphs obviously always guarded carefully what they said, but perhaps no more so than on the occasions of the *khuṭba*s just described when they spoke before an audience that may well have included a vast array of their subjects, representing many different religious inclinations—Sunnis and Shiʿis of various kinds—and also a variety of ranks: men of the elites from both the military and the bureaucracy, merchants, religious scholars and the common folk among them. They knew well that the audience for these *khuṭba*s likely consisted not only of their most loyal subjects but also, at the same time, others less attached, and possibly some who harboured grave doubts about them, even hostility. One of the surviving *khuṭba*s, by al-Qāʾim in Alexandria in 302, acknowledges such conditions forthrightly. The future imam even anticipated the resistance and possible enmity of the Egyptians to himself and his dynasty. Likewise the *khuṭba* of Qirwāsh, as perhaps many Fatimid *khuṭba*s in similar situations outside the empire, must have seemed quite foreign to those who were used to hearing the Friday sermon said in the name of another caliphate.

Within the *daʿwa* of the Ismaili movement, loyal members would have attended a private session—a lesson—normally given by a *dāʿī*, on behalf of the imam. At the conclusion of these meetings, called the *majālis al-ḥikma*, which were held generally once a week, each person paid what was called 'a fee for private discourse' (in Arabic, the *najwa*). This practice was clearly based on Qur'anic legislation as noted, for example, in *sūra* 58: 12: 'O you who believe, if you confer with the Prophet in private, give alms before your consultation.' These occasions were not for the public and this is thus confirmed additionally in this way. By contrast, the ceremonial *khuṭba* was open at least theoretically to all Muslims, not simply to Ismaili believers, and the person speaking had to take that fact into account in choosing his words.

It is obvious then that the first step in analysing the rhetoric of these *khuṭba*s depends on determining the audience for each one. The sermon for the festival, moreover, was delivered at the *muṣallā*, which was always a large open space designed to accommodate the maximum number of worshippers at one time. The Friday *khuṭba* given inside a mosque naturally limited the size of the audience. Not so that of the *ʿīd*.

With crowds so large it is fair to ask how many could actually hear what was said. Even in a mosque that may have been a problem. The congregation was under a strict rule to maintain absolute silence. A *ḥadīth* on the authority of Jaʿfar al-Ṣādiq states clearly: 'When the imam stands up to deliver his sermon, it is obligatory for the congregation to observe complete silence.'[131] Even so, in the open air of the *muṣallā*,[132] surely only those close to the *minbar* heard the words of the imam directly? Perhaps the same was true in the largest congregational mosques. But this difficulty was in part overcome by having a series of voices relay the message out beyond the reach of the speaker's own immediate circle.

Still, it is likely that those allowed to be close to the imam had a special claim to this privilege, either through rank or proven loyalty. From the descriptions provided by eyewitnesses from the last phase of Fatimid rule, it is clear that the protection of the caliph was taken seriously whenever he appeared in public. The occasion of the *khuṭba* required careful control of exactly who came into close proximity to him. One note indicates that no one outside of the governing elite was admitted to the ceremony without being vouchsafed by the chief *dāʿī*. That stipulation would appear to confine the scope of the public audience—that is, those from outside the government—to Ismailis. Only Ismailis would have had access to the *dāʿī*. This condition, however, may have applied more to the Friday *khuṭba* that the caliph gave in Ramaḍān in a mosque than to the festivals. In any case there is no comparable evidence about such a restriction from the earlier periods.

One important detail in two of the *khuṭba*s from North Africa, however, features a direct appeal by name to the Kutāma, who must, therefore, have made up a major portion of the audience at the time. The first instance is particularly striking. It occurs in the *khuṭba*

131. *Daʿāʾim*, 1: 182, 186, trans. 1: 227–228, 231.

132. The Imam Jaʿfar had stated that 'The prayers on the two festivals should be offered neither under a roof nor in a house. For the Messenger of God used to go out of [Medina] until the horizon would come into view [far away from habitation] and place his forehead on the bare earth'. *Daʿāʾim*, 1: 185, trans., 1: 230.

read to the army during Abū Yazīd's siege of al-Mahdiyya in Rajab 333 (March 945). In the name of al-Qā'im, the judge al-Marwadhī praises the Kutāma, whose forefathers had performed so gloriously both in keeping the rights of the Fatimid line safe when it had been forced into hiding and in fighting for its return to triumphal victory. 'You were the cache where God placed this Muhammadan, Fatimid, *mahdī*-ist right [to the imamate] until He caused it to triumph.' 'You are,' it goes on to say, 'like the apostles of Jesus and the Anṣār of Muḥammad.' The appeal here is so specific we must conclude that the audience on that occasion was predominantly, if not exclusively, Kutāma Berber. The second instance is the festival sermon for the 'Īd al-fiṭr of 336, again at al-Mahdiyya. In it al-Manṣūr addresses part of his remarks to the Kutāma, noting effusively God's favours to them and thus their special status in the imam's eyes, and how pleased he is with them and their devotion to the Fatimid dynasty.

Aside from these quite specific cases and the general impression conveyed by al-Qā'im's tone in his *khuṭba* to the people of Alexandria, we need to assume that the audience tended to include a variety of the Muslim inhabitants of the empire and was not limited to Ismailis, except as might have occurred by virtue of place and time. Al-Mahdiyya, when the caliph resided there, was largely Ismaili; Qayrawān, the home of the old, mostly Mālikī elite, was not. Cairo in its earliest phase is likely to have been heavily Ismaili since it began as a Fatimid governmental enclave; nearby Fusṭāṭ was much older and already contained a substantial Sunni population. Later some of these distinctions faded or disappeared entirely.

Double meanings for different audiences

An element in the rhetorical strategy of these *khuṭbas* may have involved the use of phrases that a Sunni audience would understand differently from the Shi'a among them. For example, the commonly employed words *'Alī walīy Allāh* ("Alī is the *walīy* of God'), which eventually appeared on all Fatimid coins and is quite standard in Shi'a discourse of every type, is readily taken by Sunnis to mean "Alī is the friend of God'. Ordinarily, because this sense of the word *walīy*, which is perfectly valid for it, is not objectionable, it causes no resistance or hostility on their part. For the Shiʿa, however, it means more than 'friend'. ʿAlī was, in their view the 'guardian' (*walīy*, in a different sense) of God's community on earth. He was thus the agent of God with exclusive authority to act as regent for the Muslims; he is their guardian.

One good example, albeit by mistake, of how Sunnis might misread the words of a Fatimid *khuṭba* occurs with the line in Qirwāsh's Friday sermon about God, '…who, by His light, caused the rising of the sun of truth from the west….' Islamic messianic speculation, even among Sunnis, regarded the signal for the end of time as the rising of the sun from its place of setting, in other words of time being made to reverse course or to cease altogether. With the Shiʿa, in expectation of the return of this or that imam who had temporarily gone into occultation, such speculations are more pronounced. The doctrine of several early Shiʿi sects included a rising of the imam from the west, from where he will restore true Islam and reclaim his rightful position as head of the Muslim community. The Fatimids, who had first attained power in the Maghrib, i.e. in the west, naturally made the most of this concept. They were, beginning with al-Mahdī, but subsequently collectively, the embodiment of such messianic aspirations. With their rising to the imamate in the westernmost region of the Islamic realm, these speculations had become a reality.

But, in at least one major source that reports these opening words of Qirwāsh's *khuṭba*, Ibn al-Athīr's early 7th/13th century universal history, *al-Kāmil fi'l-ta'rīkh*, some copies have changed the word 'west' to 'Arabs', which in Arabic script is quite easy: instead of *al-gharb* (the west), read *al-ʿarab* (the Arabs), the difference is a dot above the Arabic letter غ or ع.[133] Thus the key phrase would have the 'sun of truth rising from the Arabs', which would sound quite reasonable to a Sunni audience.

The address to God: the *khuṭba* as a prayer

A major portion of the *khuṭba*, in any case, consisted of an address to God, a request to Him for blessings or favours, as in the standard

133. Ibn al-Athīr, *al-Kāmil*, 9: 223. This edition, in fact, prefers the reading *al-ʿarab*, listing *al-gharb* in the notes as an alternate given by one of the manuscripts.

benediction for Muḥammad and for his family, hardly a matter of controversy. Typically it commences with the vocative phrase *Allāhumma*, 'O God!'. A passage of this type is then a prayer, a *duʿāʾ*, a form of supplication made either in the name of the person giving the *khuṭba* or by him on behalf of someone else. More rarely, however, but not unknown, it asks God to curse an enemy. We have an example of the latter in al-Qāʾim's early sermon to the Egyptians where he castigates the Umayyads, and in his last *khuṭba* in which he invokes God's curse on the Khārijite rebel Abū Yazīd, there naming him simply the 'Nukkārī'. In these respects Fatimid *khuṭba*s are like those we know from elsewhere. Obviously the caliphs intended to observe common Islamic traditions and therefore followed established practices in the form and the content of their sermons. That is clear from the use of the double *khuṭba* in which the speaker sits briefly between the two, in having the Friday sermon precede, and on the festivals follow, prayers and in other technical matters such as the number of *takbīr*s, greetings to those present, and the recitation of Qur'anic passages.

Qāḍī al-Nuʿmān quotes the Imam Jaʿfar al-Ṣādiq for a rule concerning the content of the *khuṭba* prayer:

> *Allāhu akhbar* should be uttered only once, and with it the recitation of the Qur'an should begin; thus this is the *takbīrat al-iḥrām*. Thereafter the Fātiḥa should be recited, followed *by wa'l-shamsi wa ḍuḥā* [sūrat al-Shams, no. 91]. Then the *takbīr* [of the *ʿīd*] should be recited five times. The ordinary *takbīr* should also be said at the time of bowing and prostrating oneself. Then the worshipper should stand up [for the second *rakʿa*] and recite the Fātiḥa, followed by *hal atāka ḥadīth al-ghāshiya* [sūrat al-Ghāshiya, no. 88], and the *takbīr* [of the *ʿīd*] should be recited four times, and the ordinary *takbīr* should be uttered while bowing and rising from it and prostrating oneself. Then the *tashahhud* should be said, and finally the salutation.[134]

He likewise noted that Jaʿfar's father had included the following words in his own prayer for the occasion:

> O God! He who prepares and arrays himself this day to present himself to a creature hoping for his gift and reward [may do so;

134. *Daʿāʾim*, 1: 186, trans., 1: 232.

> but] I come to You, my Lord, preparing and making ready and arraying myself solely for Your gift, reward, and presents. I have not come to You with the assurance of good works already performed, nor have I sought the intervention of any of Your creatures [for the fulfilment of my hopes]. But I have come to You conscious of my misdeeds and the evil that I have wrought upon myself. O Mighty, Mighty, Mighty One! Forgive my weighty sin; for verily none save You, O Mighty One, can absolve me from a weighty sin. There exists no god but You.[135]

In general what Qāḍī al-Nuʿmān reports about the circumstances of the Friday prayer and that of the two *ʿīd* festivals indicates the standard expected of these events. There we find strictures concerning the silence to be observed while the *khuṭba*s are being delivered and that the congregation must face the speaker and pay close attention. 'The sermon is prescribed in lieu of the two *rakʿa*s that have been omitted from the *ẓuhr* prayer; and thus it is similar to offering a prayer itself. Hence nothing is permitted during the delivery of the sermon that is not permitted while praying.'[136]

> The Friday prayer should commence with the delivery of the two sermons. When the imam first ascends the pulpit he should sit down and the *muʾadhdhin*s should give the call to prayer. When they have completed the call, the imam should stand up and deliver his sermon and exhortation. Then he should sit down for a short while and then stand up again and offer a second sermon along with his prayer invocation [*duʿāʾ*]. Thereafter the *muʾadhdhin*s should say the *iqāma*, and the imam should come down from the *minbar* and pray the two *rakʿa*s in which the Qurʾan should be recited loudly.[137]

Unfortunately, aside from the relatively brief section in al-Nuʿmān's handbook of Ismaili law that speaks about the Friday and festival sermons, there is little else to indicate what rules might have applied to Fatimid *khuṭba*s. And those of the imams, who were

135. *Daʿāʾim*, 1: 185, trans., 1: 230.

136. This admonition is quoted from the Imam Jaʿfar, *Daʿāʾim*, 1: 183, trans., 1: 228.

137. This rule comes from the Imam Jaʿfar, *Daʿāʾim*, 1: 183, trans., 1: 228.

acknowledged authorities for doctrine and practice in their own right, did not necessarily follow earlier dictates in any case. But what al-Nuʿmān does report is likely what was expected.

Qur'anic imagery and language

Given its nature as a prayer to God, the *khuṭba* obviously tends to borrow heavily from Qur'anic imagery and depends on its language either by outright quotation or only slightly veiled allusion. In fact the texts of the surviving *khuṭba*s are replete with references to the Qur'an, though some less obvious than others. The predominant stylistic device involves the use of rhymed prose, *sajʿ*, which is itself an important element of Qur'anic eloquence, as it was even in the pre-Islamic period for most oral prose.[138]

Praising God

All *khuṭba*s that are designed for ceremonial use have a section, usually at the beginning, dedicated to praising God. In our Fatimid examples that portion could be brief or long depending, perhaps, on the needs of the particular moment. Several are quite elaborate, however, and especially eloquent. Do they also reveal any peculiarities of Ismaili doctrine, such as the denial of attributes for God? From the writings of Ismaili theologians—that is, those who wrote about such matters as God and the possibility of His having attributes—we know that they carefully observed a rigorous doctrine of restricting all qualification of God, thereby denying that He possesses the attributes commonly given to Him by Sunni authorities. He is outside and beyond the perceptions of human beings, even intellectually, and thus He cannot be known or indicated directly by human intellect.[139]

138. On *sajʿ*, see 'Sadjʿ' (parts 1–3) in the *EI2* by W. P. Heinrichs and Afif Ben Abdesselem.

139. For the position on this issue of several major figures in the Ismaili *daʿwa* of the Fatimid period, see the following studies by Paul E. Walker: *Abu Yaʿqub al-Sijistani: Intellectual Missionary* (London, 1996), chapter four, pp. 84–103; *Early Philosophical Shiism* (Cambridge, 1993), chapter five, pp. 72–80; and *Ḥamīd al-Dīn al-Kirmānī: Ismaili Thought in the Age of al-Ḥākim* (London, 1999), chapter five, pp. 80–103.

In parts of the following passages taken from the surviving *khuṭba*s there appears to be an echo of this doctrinal position:

> Praise be to God who unites through divine lordship, who is unique in oneness, who is almighty in ability and endurance, all-powerful in majesty and grandeur, the first without limit, the last without end, transcending the comparisons of the ignorant and the definitions of the describers, the conditions of the attributers, and the comprehension in visions of those who speculate.[140]
>
> Hallowed is God, He whose signs bear witness to His power. His essence refuses the association with it of attributes, the vision of Him by sight, the definition of Him by intellects, being most grand and almighty, glorious and powerful, splendid and magnificent.[141]
>
> His causing things to come into being from nothing all at once and altogether is evidence that nothing came before Him and their end at a term indicates that there is no limit to Him. That they are apprehended by definitions establishes that He has no definition. The weakness, impotence, poverty, and want of which created beings are not free is the most eloquent admission and most truthful evidence for the Creator, who is alone, glorious is His praise, in divinity and singularity, in power and lordship, in completeness and perfection, in eternity and perpetuity.[142]
>
> Distinct in His essence, alone in His attributes, manifest in His signs, solitary in His indications, time passes by Him not so that the seasons preceded Him, forms do not resemble Him so that places contain Him. Eyes do not see Him so that tongues can describe Him. His existence is prior to all existences; His goodness surpasses all goodness. His oneness is fixed in every intellect; His presence exists in every vision.[143]

If, however, there is here some deliberate reference to Ismaili doctrine, these statements of it are, even so, much too vague for a firm conclusion. The rhetoric of the *khuṭba* often suggests rather than insists. Those in the audience heard in the first instance phrases and

140. *Khuṭba* of al-Manṣūr, ʿĪd al-aḍḥā in the year 335 (no. 6).

141. From the *khuṭba* by al-Manṣūr, ʿĪd al-fiṭr in the year 336 (no. 7).

142. From the *khuṭba* by al-Muʿizz, ʿĪd al-naḥr in the year 341 (no. 9).

143. From the Qirwāsh's *khuṭba* of 401 (no. 11).

meanings that agreed with what they thought. The speaker was not in most cases intent on expounded doctrines that might provoke dissent. The praising of God in Islam always required a firm declaration of His absolute unqualified oneness—as is frequently stated in the Qur'an itself—and that is exactly what these and the other passages in our *khuṭba*s indicate. To say in a *khuṭba*, for example, that God cannot be seen, which is Ismaili doctrine as well as the doctrine of many other groups, does not necessarily imply that He will never be seen, even in the next life, which is also the Ismaili position at least as expressed by its *daʿwa* in that era. For that conclusion, we would need more information than we are provided in these *khuṭba*s alone.

Muḥammad as grandfather

To bear witness or testify that Muḥammad was the prophet and messenger of God is a standard feature of the *khuṭba* in general. Most of the attributes ascribed to Muḥammad in Fatimid *khuṭba*s, moreover, agreed well with such statements in those not by them. What is different and uniquely Fatimid is the reference to him as the 'grandfather', e.g. of the current caliph, or, as it most often appears, as 'our grandfather', as in the invocation of God's blessings on 'our grandfather' (*jiddinā*). The meaning, of course, is ancestor or forefather, but it carries a special connotation in conjunction with references to ʿAlī b. Abī Ṭālib, who is always called 'our father' (*abūnā*, *abīnā*). See, for example, the *khuṭba*s of al-Āmir where this type of reference appears prominently in both parts of the sermon. Additional examples occur in those of al-Manṣūr from 335 and 336.

ʿAlī as father

References and characterizations of ʿAlī are particularly important as a sign of the ancestral lineage of the Fatimids and of the Shiʿi assertion of legitimacy for its imamate. ʿAlī bears the title Commander of the Believers, which, for the Shiʿa, applies to him alone among the Companions of the Prophet since they do not recognize any of the others as valid successors to the imamate. In his position as heir to the Prophet, both physically and spiritually, he carries also the title of Legatee (in Arabic *waṣī*). In Qirwāsh's *khuṭba* he is called the Lord of the Legatees (*sayyid al-waṣīyīn*). Another appellation denotes his close family relationship to Muḥammad, which for the Shiʿa means, in reference to ʿAlī, brother. For them the Prophet had adopted him as his own brother. He was, moreover, in the same position as had been Aaron with respect to his brother Moses. The Prophet had stated, according to a *ḥadīth* of special importance to the Shiʿa, that, "ʿAlī is to me as Aaron was to Moses.'

Here follow some examples from the *khuṭba*s:

> ʿAlī, the Commander of the Believers and master of the legatees and best of Muslims.[144]

> ...and bless the first to respond to him [i.e. the Prophet], ʿAlī, the Commander of the Believers and lord of the legatees, the establisher of excellence and mercy, the pillar of knowledge and wisdom, the root of the noble and righteous tree generated from the sacred and pure trunk. And [blessings be] on his successors, the lofty branches of that same tree, and on what comes from it: the fruit that grows there.[145]

> O God, bless your radiant guardian and your greatest friend, ʿAlī b. Abī Ṭālib, the father of the rightly guided imams.

> God bless our grandfather, Muḥammad, the guide to the shining path, and our father, the Commander of the Believers, ʿAlī b. Abī Ṭālib, his brother and son of his paternal uncle, whom he sanctioned for the position of executor, and the chaste imams among the descendants of both, the clear evident proofs of God to His creatures.[146]

> And bless, O God, our father, the Commander of the Believers, ʿAlī b. Abī Ṭālib, who held the place with respect to him that had Aaron with Moses, the one who spoke to God.[147]

> ...and He aided him through our father, the Commander of the Believers, ʿAlī b. Abī Ṭālib, his brother and his legatee and the spokesman of his law, who explained its peculiar intricacies.[148]

---

144. *Khuṭba* of al-Manṣūr, ʿĪd al-aḍḥā in the year 335 (no. 6).
145. Qirwāsh's *khuṭba* (no. 11).
146. Qirwāsh's *khuṭba* (no. 11).
147. *Khuṭba* of al-Āmir (no. 12).
148. *Khuṭba* of al-Āmir (no. 13).

The Companions of the Cloak (*aṣḥāb al-kisāʾ*)

From a brief mention of a ritual of mutual cursing which is apparently what is taking place in Qur'an 3: 61 ('If any one disputes this with you after the knowledge has come to you, say, "Come, let us gather our sons and your sons, our women and your women, ourselves and yourselves; then let us pray and invoke the curse of God on those who lie"'), an entire tradition developed around the implied story of Muḥammad having brought his immediate family members under his cloak on that occasion. They were the *aṣḥāb al-kisāʾ* (the Companions of the Cloak). The question then became who exactly belonged to this set. For the Shiʿa this has never been much of an issue since they included only the Prophet, ʿAlī, Fāṭima, al-Ḥasan, and al-Ḥusayn. The non-Shiʿa dispute the matter and they have alternate interpretations of the tradition.[149] However, in the Fatimid *khuṭba*s, as one would expect, the Shiʿi point of view prevails, as in the following passages:

> O God, bless Your servant and Your messenger with a perpetually perfect blessing, increase him with an honour to his honour and a nobility to his nobility. Bless also all of the Companions of the Cloak (*aṣḥāb al-kisāʾ*), the pure ones, the immaculates: ʿAlī, the Commander of the Believers, Fāṭima the Radiant, mistress of the women of the two worlds, and al-Ḥasan and al-Ḥusayn, the two most noble and most righteous, and [bless] the rightly guided imams among the progeny of al-Ḥusayn, the luminaries of guidance, the full moons of the darkness, the masters of mankind, friends of the Most Merciful, the proofs of times, and pillars of the faith.[150]

> I testify that Muḥammad is His chosen servant, and His approved messenger, His confidant for what He reveals, the deliverer from error and destruction, may God bless him and his revered family, the rightly guided ones, the imams of righteous guidance: ʿAlī, the Commander of the Believers and master of the legatees and best of Muslims; Fāṭima, the radiant, mistress of the women of the two worlds; and al-Ḥasan and al-Ḥusayn, the two lords of the youth

149. For additional information see the articles in the *EI2* on 'Mubāhala' by W. Schmucker, 'Ahl al-kisāʾ' by A. S. Tritton, and 'Ahl al-bayt' by I. Goldziher, C. van Arendonk, and A. S. Tritton.

150. From the *khuṭba* by al-Manṣūr, ʿĪd al-fiṭr in the year 335 (no. 5).

among the people of paradise; and the imams from the progeny of al-Ḥusayn, the chaste ones, the remainder of the messenger of God and his fruit, his two heirs, his proof to the servants, the mountains of religion, lords of the believers, and saints of the worlds.[151]

...the rightly guided (*mahdī*-ist) imams among his noble and chaste progeny who have been chosen for the caliphate and approved for the imamate, confirming their proof in the testament of the messenger, making obedience to them necessary in the revelation, after His conferring excellence on them over the world through the parentage of Muḥammad, the lord of the messengers, and ʿAlī, the most excellent of the legatees, those whose mother was the mistress of women, the fifth of the Companions of the Cloak.[152]

Fāṭima as mother

Al-Manṣūr speaks of her as 'the Radiant, mistress of the women of the two worlds' in two successive sermons, and in yet another *khuṭba*, in reference to his own father and grandfather, the imams al-Qā'im and al-Mahdī, he calls her 'Fāṭima, the radiant virgin,[153] your mother'. In a sermon by al-Muʿizz the rightly guiding imams are 'those whose mother was the mistress of women, the fifth of the Companions of the Cloak'. Similar characterizations appear in the *khuṭbas* of al-Āmir.[154]

al-Ḥasan and al-Ḥusayn

In Fatimid era *khuṭbas* both Ḥasan and Ḥusayn are cited as imams and members of the five Companions of the Cloak, although they make quite clear that the imamate continued after them solely among the descendants of Ḥusayn.

---

151. *Khuṭba* of al-Manṣūr, 'Īd al-aḍḥā in the year 335 (no. 6).

152. From the *khuṭba* by al-Muʿizz, 'Īd al-naḥr in the year 341 (no. 9).

153. 'Virgin' here means 'immaculate' (*al-Baṭūl*), untainted by menstrual impurity.

154. 'And [bless] our mother Fāṭima, the radiant and chaste'; '[Bless] our mother Fāṭima, the radiant, nurturer of the prophecy singled out for revelation and nobility of character and honour.'

> …al-Ḥasan and al-Ḥusayn, the two most noble and most righteous, and [bless] the rightly guided imams among the progeny of al-Ḥusayn, the luminaries of guidance, the full moons of the darkness, the masters of mankind, friends of the Most Merciful, the proofs of times, and pillars of the faith.[155]

> …al-Ḥasan and al-Ḥusayn, the two lords of the youth among the people of paradise; and the imams from the progeny of al-Ḥusayn, the chaste ones, the remainder of the messenger of God and his fruit, his two heirs, his proof to the servants, the mountains of religion, lords of the believers, and saints of the worlds.[156]

> O God, bless the two pure grandsons al-Ḥasan and al-Ḥusayn.[157]

> …her [Fāṭima's] two sons, the imams Abū Muḥammad al-Ḥasan and Abū ʿAbd Allāh al-Ḥusayn, the best of creatures.[158]

> [Bless] al-Ḥasan and al-Ḥusayn two imams of the community and shinning lights of the sphere of religion and its perfection in assemblies and festivals.[159]

The imams from al-Ḥusayn to al-Mahdī

Clearly the imams after al-Ḥusayn are his offspring, not those of al-Ḥasan. However they are seldom mentioned by name in the surviving *khuṭba*s, even those prior to the period of concealment which commenced with Ismāʿīl, the son of Jaʿfar al-Ṣādiq, or with his son Muḥammad b. Ismāʿīl, who was actually the first never to have appeared in public. In Qirwāsh's sermon they are all simply 'the righteous imams, the best and most excellent, those of them that stood forth and appeared and those of them that were concealed and hidden'. In the first *khuṭba* by al-Manṣūr he calls his grandfather al-Mahdī, the 'son of the Rightly Guided Ones (*al-Mahdiyyīn*), the noble son of the most noble' without going further into the matter. That seems to have been, to judge from these *khuṭba*s, the preferred

155. From the *khuṭba* by al-Manṣūr on the ʿĪd al-fiṭr in the year 335 (no. 5).
156. *Khuṭba* of al-Manṣūr, ʿĪd al-aḍḥā in the year 335 (no. 6).
157. Qirwāsh's *khuṭba* (no. 11).
158. *Khuṭba* of al-Āmir (no. 12).
159. *Khuṭba* of al-Āmir (no. 13).

policy for public pronouncements. Only in a *khuṭba* of al-Āmir are any of them cited by name. There he refers to the imams prior to al-Mahdī as "'Alī b. al-Ḥusayn Zayn al-'Ābidīn, and Muḥammad b. 'Alī Bākir 'Ulūm al-Dīn, and Ja'far b. Muḥammad al-Ṣādiq al-Amīn, and the true imam Ismā'īl, and Muḥammad his son, possessor of the nobility of the authentic caliphate, and those who had all excellences and superiority, and [bless] the imams who were concealed from the enemy, who in his actions opposed all of them in like manner,' whom he contrasts with 'the piercing stars of truth, the suns rising from the places of setting'. The latter he names one by one starting with al-Mahdī.

The imams from al-Mahdī onward

It was evidently customary practice to cite each of the preceding imams by name from the current caliph back to al-Mahdī. Ibn al-Ṭuwayrī near the end of the dynasty suggests as much. In one of the two *khuṭbas* of al-Āmir, this caliph lists all of those who came before him from al-Mahdī through al-Musta'lī, his own father. All those to the reign of al-Ḥākim are named likewise in the *khuṭba* of Qirwāsh. Since the full name of each caliph contained the word Allāh, as in al-Manṣūr bi-Naṣr Allāh or al-Ḥākim bi-Amr Allāh, in the sermon where the name appears as part of a request addressed directly to God for Him to bless each of the imams so named, the proper form requires a personal pronoun, thus al-Manṣūr bi-Naṣrika ('The One who is victorious through Your support', rather than 'The One who is victorious through the support of God') or al-Ḥākim bi-Amrika ('The Ruler by Your Command' rather than 'The Ruler by the Command of God').

The name of the dynasty

From the medieval period until now it has been customary to call the dynasty of Ismaili imams who ruled North Africa beginning in 297/909, and then a larger empire that included Egypt, and at times much of Syria, the Hijaz, and Yaman, the Fatimids. But the history of this term is not yet clear. Did, for example, the earliest caliphs of this line refer to themselves by that name? In 1996 the Spanish scholar Mirabel Fierro published an important study of this problem, and of the use in general of the terms *al-fāṭimī* (Fatimid) and *al-fāṭimiyyūn* (the Fatimids).[160] Although she carefully surveyed many of the major sources, she found little evidence of these terms in works written by adherents of the dynasty. Further investigation by others has since turned up more information. These terms do, in fact, appear but more so, and more often, in the later phases of this rule. By the end of the dynasty it was fairly common to call it *al-dawla al-fāṭimiyya* ('the Fatimid state' or 'the Fatimid dynasty'), and thus later authors grew quite accustomed to this term.

Nevertheless, it is strikingly rare in the earliest documents produced by those who held positions of authority in the government, including most particularly the imams in their public pronouncements and declarations. The *khuṭba* would have been a natural occasion for its use. Yet only one of those we now have contains the word in a form that suggests an appropriate meaning. In the *khuṭba* that al-Qā'im dictated for his chief judge to read to the army in 333, while al-Mahdiyya remained under the siege of the Khārijite forces of Abū Yazīd, his words addressed to the Kutāma appeal to them as the depository where God put the rights of the Fatimid line until it could be revealed once again. 'You were the cache,' it states, 'where God placed this Muḥammadan, Fāṭimid, *mahdī*-ist right [to the imamate] until He caused it to triumph and raised it high again.' The Arabic reads for the key terms: *al-ḥaqq al-muḥammadī al-fāṭimī al-mahdī*. Therefore it is certainly technically correct to say that the Fatimids called themselves 'Fatimid' from a quite early date. It would not have been used in this fashion otherwise. The terms *al-imām al-fāṭimī* and *al-fāṭimiyyīn* also appear in early pro-Fatimid poetry.[161]

Significantly, however, it appears in this one instance joined by two other adjectives, 'Muḥammadan' and '*mahdī*-ist' (*al-muḥammadī* and *al-mahdī*), either or both of which have the same claim to apply to the dynasty. The latter term *al-mahdī* or its plural *al-mahdiyyūn*/

160. 'On al-Fāṭimī and al-Fāṭimiyyūn,' *JSAI*, 20 (1996), pp. 130–161.

161. See Muḥammad al-Ya'lāwī (Yalaoui), *al-Adab bi-Ifrīqiya fi'l-'ahd al-Fāṭimīyya* (Beirut, 1986), pp. 37 and 139. These two references were brought to my attention by Tahera Qutbuddin.

al-mahdiyyīn, moreover, was, to judge from the *khuṭba*s and other surviving documents, the standard way these early Fatimids referred to themselves. The phrase *khulafā' al-rāshidīn al-mahdiyyīn*, 'the rightly guided *mahdī*-ist caliphs', was a part of the very first Fatimid *khuṭba*. Al-Qā'im in 302 asked for God's blessings on *al-khulafā' al-rāshidīn al-mahdiyyīn*. In al-Manṣūr's first *khuṭba* he uses the words *ibn al-mahdiyyīn* 'son of the *mahdī*s' for his grandfather. Later in the same sermon he cites *al-hudāt al-mahdiyyīn*, 'the rightly guided guides'. In a subsequent *khuṭba* he speaks of al-Mahdī as *wārith faḍl al-a'imma al-mahdiyyīn min ābā'ihi al-khulafā' al-rāshidīn*, 'the inheritor of the excellence of the *mahdī*-ist imams from his forefathers, the rightly guided caliphs'. In the same sermon he calls al-Mahdī 'the distinguished offspring of the rightly guided imams' (*najīb al-a'imma al-mahdiyyīn*). The phrase *al-a'imma al-mahdiyyīn* becomes standard in subsequent *khuṭba*s. And it appears regularly in many contexts—documents and *khuṭba*s—throughout the Fatimid period.

Strictly from this context then the terms 'Mahdī' (in the singular), 'Mahdīs' (plural), or 'Mahdīd' (adjective) might be more appropriate than 'Fatimid'. However, in its meaning simply as the 'rightly guided one(s)', it is fairly common and thus not uniquely Fatimid. Likewise, in its heightened sense wherein the *mahdī* is the person who will restore Islam and return it to its original form after a period—perhaps lengthy—of decay and degradation, it was applied reasonably often by several competing groups and dynasties. There were Umayyad *mahdī*s and Abbasid *mahdī*s, not to speak of those belonging to the Shi'a even before the rise of the Fatimids. It can also mean the messiah who appears at the end of time. Any of these meanings—and possibly all of them together—may have played a part in the Fatimid choice of the term, but in the *khuṭba*s it seems to represent the equivalent of *rāshidīn*, those persons who have the benefit of God's guidance in contrast to most others who do not. The implication is that humans should follow those, and only those, whom God provides with guidance. As a name of the dynasty, therefore, it hardly distinguishes the Fatimids from their opponents if both make the same claim about God's favouring them. Evidently, then, the term Fatimid—which certainly applies as is attested by its use in this one early *khuṭba*, added, in other *khuṭba*s, to the more frequent mentions of Fāṭima as the mother ancestor of the imams—eventually became the name for the dynasty, in part because it readily set them apart from the competing caliphates of the Umayyads and the Abbasids.[162]

Enemies

Many of the *khuṭbas* feature condemnations of various enemies of the Fatimids. The very earliest text requests God to 'grant him [the imam] victory over Your apostate enemies (*aʿdāʾika al-māriqīn*), and heal through him the breasts of the believers, conquer through him the easts of the land and its wests as You promised him, support him against the iniquitous rebels'. Those who oppose the Fatimid cause are in fact enemies of God. That much is made clear again and again. In the earliest sermon by al-Manṣūr he says: 'Bring down upon his [meaning his father, al-Qāʾim's] enemies, in the east and the west, on land and on the sea, the most severe assaults and retributions that You have done or caused to occur with any of those who were enemies of Yours, with destructive misfortune, dishonouring exemplary punishments; destroy them by annihilation and burn them in the fire of hell.'

The first *khuṭba* by al-Qāʾim, which is, relative to the rest, quite early and thus attests to the attitude of the Fatimids at the beginning of their rule, is, in part, a case in point but with the extension of this idea to specific dynastic opponents, here the Abbasids and the Umayyads. Responding to the situation in which he was at the time, having invaded Abbasid Egypt, al-Qāʾim castigates both the rulers in Baghdad and their predecessors, the Umayyads. Although he does not say so in this *khuṭba*, descendants of the Umayyads he denounces were still governing Spain and portions of far western North Africa. They thus remained to be overcome and defeated just like the Abbasids:

> The lying apostate community, reneging on its intentions, deviating from the command of their Lord, suppose that it has been correct in

---

162. One other term that might have been considered is 'Ismaili' (*Ismāʿīlī*). However, it appears nowhere in the *khuṭbas* and is exceedingly rare in Fatimid era literature as a whole.

what it claims about its caliphs whom they insist are the caliphs of the Lord of the worlds, such as a youth not yet mature, like the boy lacking knowledge, or like the child who, according to their claim, governs Islam. And yet among them women bring them wine from every valley and region on the backs of horses and in the bottoms of ships. As God the Exalted said: 'They take their priests and monks as lords besides God' [9: 31]. They spend the funds of orphans and the poor, wrongly on their part and unjustly, for singing lute players, skilled *ṭunbūr*ists, and *miʿzafān*ists,[163] and talented drummers. You have seen their governors of cities, how one of them mounts the wooden pulpit of the Prophet's *minbar* to preach to the people but he does not preach to himself. Rather he descends from that position and inquires of those in that land for male and female singers, *ṭunbūr*ists, *ʿūd* players, thieves, short change artists, and shavers of weights so that those can be brought to serve him. God curses the unjust and prepares for them a blazing fire. That man is someone who neither commands the good nor prohibits the bad.

So much for the Abbasids. For the Umayyads he names specific names:

O God, curse Your enemies, the people who disobey You among the ancients and the later comers: the nation of Noah in the two worlds—truly they were an impious group—and ʿĀd and Thamūd, and the Associates of al-Rass,[164] and the tyrants of the tribe of Umayya and tribe of Marwān, and Muʿāwiya b. Abī Sufyān, who took from Your servants the rightful share of dinars and dirhams, and waged war with them against the Emigrants and Helpers. Curse ʿAmr b. al-ʿĀṣ, … [Here he lists fourteen more], and those who were faithless and deviant, the apostates, transgressors, and heretics, and those who put off [acknowledging ʿAlī's succession] and those who refrained from going to war under the Commander of the Believers.

It should be noted that this list, by including the names of certain Umayyads or Umayyad supporters and not others, suggests that the enemies named are worse than those not mentioned. Al-Qā'im is

163. Players of the short-necked lute.

164. For the meaning, identity, and significance of those named here and in the following passage, see the notes to this *khuṭba* in Part Two below.

likely to have known what he was doing. He did not, for example, explicitly condemn Abū Bakr or ʿUmar, the two earliest caliphs whom the Shiʿa generally castigate vehemently, or the third caliph ʿUthmān, who was himself an Umayyad and usually considered an enemy. To invoke the curse of God on any of these three in Egypt at the time of this *khuṭba* would have provoked a strongly negative reaction. In contrast the men named, who al-Qāʾim likens to a set of enemies cited in the Qurʾan (the nation of Noah, ʿĀd, Thamūd, and the Associates of al-Rass), were not even remotely as well regarded.

The other major enemy of the Fatimids in these early *khuṭba*s was the Khārijite rebel Abū Yazīd. The revolt of Abū Yazīd Makhlad b. Kaydād al-Nukkārī looms excessively large in the history of the Fatimids during the Maghribi period. It dominated the reigns of al-Qāʾim and al-Manṣūr. No wonder then that the *khuṭba*s of that era focus on it. Abū Yazīd was for the Fatimids the Dajjāl, the arch-deceiver of the end of time apocalypse. Having brought to his side a force of anti-Fatimid Berbers, Abū Yazīd, himself an Ibāḍī Khārijī preacher and teacher, burst rather suddenly upon the scene in 332/943. Known as the 'Man on the Donkey' (*ṣāḥib al-ḥimār*), he quickly defeated armies sent against him and ultimately laid siege to al-Mahdiyya in 333 and early 334 before retreating. Al-Qāʾim died during this siege. Without announcing either the death or his ow succession, al-Manṣūr led the pursuit of the fleeing rebel whom he final captured only in Muḥarram 336 (August 947).[165]

Abū Yazīd was already the main subject of the final *khuṭba* of al-Qāʾim:

> O people! Truly this accursed Nukkārī[166] has exacerbated his wickedness and his disease has infested the land. Deceptive hopes sustain him, and the soul that urges to evil prompts him to esteem lightly the favour of God the exalted to him; and the devil, who is his associate, intimates to him that he has no conqueror. But it is merely that the

165. For additional details and information about the revolt, see 'Abū Yazīd al-Nukkārī' by S. M. Stern in the *EI2*, and Halm, *Reich des Mahdi*, 265–287, trans., 298–322.

166. The rebel Abū Yazīd Makhlad b. Kaydād, Ṣāḥib al-Ḥimar, belonged to the Nukkārī (also Nakkārī) sect of the Ibāḍiyya Khārijites. On the term and its history see T. Lewicki, 'al-Nukkār' in the *EI2*.

> Commander of the Believers loosens for him his reins in order to cause him to stumble in the abundance of his halter. So may God curse him with a calamitous curse and humiliate him with lengthy ignominy and make of him a blazing fire: 'None shall burn in it but the most wretched' [92: 15].
>
> The accursed arch-deceiver has settled in front of you with a misled, erring party that does not draw on the light of true guidance. They are like startled [and heedless] cattle, figures that merely imitate the real, planks of wood propped up, frightened donkeys. If they stand in place, they are destroyed, and if they are called back, they are overtaken. Do not recoil after advancing! You are the party of God; they are the party of Satan. Your dead are in paradise; their dead are in hellfire.[167]

Most of the *khuṭba*s by al-Manṣūr also have something to say about Abū Yazīd. They include his sermon for the festival of fast-breaking in 336, well after the rebellion had been crushed and the offender killed:

> Praise be to God; You made Your servant victorious, against the hatred of the unbelievers, the minions of the cunning, depraved, profligates, the partisans of the lying arch deceiver [*aḥzāb al-Dajjāl*], the misguiding object of anger, the filthy and unclean, the contemptible and wretched, the damned and infamous, those accursed throughout the earth and heaven.[168]
>
> God, the mighty and glorious, ... illuminated the hearts of the believers following upon the darkness, and the cessation of hope due to the length of the period of tribulation with the great sedition and its horrors, and its chaos and its convulsions, black darknesses, deaf blindnesses, ignorant barbarism, due to the hypocritical arch deceiver and his apostate partisans, the enemies of religion, and supporters of the accursed Iblīs. … There was, thanks to God and His favour against our enemies, a trial that blinded them, made them deaf, led them astray, caused their apostasy, ruined them, made them degenerate, debased, dishonoured, while we and our friends had an ordeal that secured for us recompense and treasure, and brought about might and glory. Its means were vile but its results noble. Since God, the Mighty and Glorious, wanted the

167. *Khuṭba* by al-Qā'im from 333 (no. 2).

168. *Khuṭba* by al-Manṣūr, 'Īd al-fiṭr 336 (no. 7).

> renewal of our dynasty and our might and to show His favour to us, His being burdened with our victory, and the testing of our friends, and the destruction of our enemies, so that when the end of it arrived and it had reached the furthermost degree, the satan came out hopeless, uttering rants, his fire blazing, his persistence continuing. Having been aroused to anger over his transgressors, God allowed retribution among them by giving control to His servant and appointing him to the task. Thus did God clear up its darkness and cast light on its blackness, open its denseness, and avert the distress of it, through me and by my hand, as a mark of esteem by which God singled me out, an excellence whose nobility He bestowed on me, a favour for me to store up. …
>
> Prior to that, swords were unsheathed, so He broke them; soldiers advanced toward me, so He defeated them; the armies of unbelief made common cause against me, so He left them in the lurch; eyes aspired after me, so He effaced them; heads were raised, so He made them bow down; noses were turned up in disdain, so He abased them; cheeks became contemptuous, so He made them humble.[169]

Death and loss: fathers and imams

Two of our surviving *khuṭba*s announce formally the death of the previous imam. It was Fatimid policy to delay such revelations until the situation on the ground was calm and stable. In the first instance al-Manṣūr in fact waited for his sermon on the festival of fast-breaking in 336, almost two full years after the loss of his father, although by then surely everyone knew. It may therefore be significant that he speaks of having lost both his father and his grandfather:

> May the peace of God and His blessings, benedictions, salutations, and charity (*zakiyyāt*) be on you both, O Commanders of the Believers, O you two caliphs of the Lord of the universe, O you two sons of the *mahdī*-ists' guidance, O father, O grandfather, O sons of Muḥammad, the Messenger of God! … He imposed on me in losing you both, patience . … the misfortune and flow of tears over me, O father, O Muḥammad, O Abu'l-Qāsim, O mountain, O what longing, O what agony!

169. *Khuṭba* by al-Manṣūr, ʿĪd al-fiṭr 336 (no. 7).

...I am not in doubt as to the choice of God for you and His transporting you to the abode of His favour and residence of His mercy, which provides accommodations for Muḥammad, His Messenger, your grandfather, as well as the Commander of the Believers, ʿAlī b. Abī Ṭālib, your father, and Fāṭima, the radiant virgin, your mother, and your pure righteous *mahdī*-ist forefathers. But the grief of the grief-stricken is a spur to sorrows, causing tears in the eyes.

In the second case al-Muʿizz reveals his father's death in the first and only full *khuṭba* we have from him:

O God, single out the excellent imam, ... Abu'l-Ṭāhir al-Manṣūr bika, ... he whom You have made us miserable by his loss and left us alone after him. You have separated us from him and made us grieve. ...

Truly, the distress and severe agony due to you O my father, O master, O Ismāʿīl, O Abu'l-Ṭāhir, O sea of the knowledge of the chaste imams, of *mahdī*-ist guidance, O remnant of the sons of the Messenger and sons of the Legatee and the immaculate lady, O imam of the community and key of the door to mercy, O lamp of right guidance, sun of mankind, he who casts light in the deep darkness, O he whom God made special by swift favours, painful for us by God who are afflicted by you. The misfortune is great; because of losing you consolation does not exist, and tongues fail in enumerating your excellences or counting your virtues. So, by Him who singled you out with His mark of honour and presented you with the abundance of His gifts, ennobled you with the parentage of His messenger, were it not for what You inspire in me because of him and confirm for me as to upholding the truth of God and defending the community of your forefather, the messenger of God, rescuing them from the flood of ignorance, the sea of error, abysses of disorder, and the wreckage of misfortunes, ... if it were not for that I would strike my face as a traveller in the land, loathing a place of rest, being content with a bag full of provisions, so that death should quickly take me to you, and thereby to gain for me nearness to you and the mercy of your Lord.

But instead I ponder, observe, and govern. I see for me no other way except patience and consideration, and that I claim your position and acquire your nobility, and so I endure. My Lord makes me patient and so I am patient. Conviction overcomes me and so I forbear.

Pilgrimage

Among the smaller details of individual *khuṭba*s, one with potential importance is al-Mu'izz's expressed intention to perform the pilgrimage to Mecca and Medina, which he makes public in the following passage, and which we can confirm from other reports. It is a hope he was never allowed to fulfil.

> O God! ... Provide me the means to visit his [Muḥammad's] tomb and mount his *minbar*, stay in his house, and perform the pilgrimage to Your sacred house, and with our banners halt at these majestic shrines.[170]

Miscellaneous themes

The surviving *khuṭba*s contain many other lesser details, elements of public policy, advice, comments, and good wishes. Some examples follow.

On the duties and rights of the imamate:

> God said: 'O you who believe, obey God and obey the Messenger and those with authority among you' [4: 59]. Thus He makes obedience a duty, attaching it to obedience to the regulators of His affairs. They are the ones who uphold, on behalf of God, His truth and those who summon to him whoever desires to obey Him. He singled them out by the imamate, which is the highest of the ranks below prophecy. He prescribed for the servants rights due them and ordered them to fulfil these. He stipulated that they are connected to obeying him, doubling their reward on the measure of how well they follow those whose authority is ordained. The imam has not the option to reduce the rights of his flock, nor is the flock to decrease the rights of their imam. Among the rights of the flock against their imam is the maintaining of the Book of God and the Sunna of His prophet, may God bless him and his family, and restitution from those who treat them unjustly for those so treated, and from the powerful among them for the weak, from the noble of them for the lowly, investigating their manner of life and the differing conditions of it, looking solicitously upon his dependants in his efforts, watching

170. *Khuṭba* of al-Mu'izz, 'Īd al-naḥr 341 (no. 9).

> over them with his eye. For He, great and glorious is He, concerning what He praised of the character of His prophet and His messenger said: 'There has come to you a messenger from among yourselves; a sorrow that befalls you grieves him; he is anxious concerning you; with the believers he is kind and compassionate' [9:128]. When he does that, the flock should revere him, honour him and extend assistance to him, standing prepared and ready, on behalf of what is right according to the book of God and the Sunna of His prophet, may God bless him and his family.[171]

On taxes:

> ...there will not be collected from you in the years to come other than the tenth and the alms tax: food stuffs for food stuffs, sheep from small cattle, oxen from bovines, mature camels from camels (*al-baʿīr min al-ibil*), in accord with the laws of God, may He be exalted, and the practice of my grandfather, the messenger of God.[172]

On the end of Ramaḍān alms (*zakāt al-fiṭr*):

> God has imposed on you an alms tax in your breaking the fast and it follows the practice of your Prophet, the lord of the prophets. So let each man among you contribute on behalf of his dependants, the males among them and the females, the young and the old, a *ṣāʿ*[173] of wheat or a *ṣāʿ* of barley, or a *ṣāʿ* of dates, all these of his own food, not of anything not eaten or contributed from something else. Truly, that is forbidden him and there is no reward for it.[174]
>
> So draw close to God in this day of yours by rendering the fast-breaking alms, which is the *zakāt* of your fast, and is the Sunna of your prophet, the lord of the prophets. Each man of you for himself and for each individual of his household, males and females, young and old, [contributes] half a *ṣā* of wheat, or a *ṣāʿ* of barley, or a *ṣāʿ*

---

171. *Khuṭba* of al-Qā'im, 302 (no. 1).

172. *Khuṭba* by al-Manṣūr, 335 (no. 4).

173. A *ṣāʿ* is a dry measure of four *mudd*, each *mudd* weighing a *riṭl* and one-third; a measure of five pints (*arṭāl*) and a third. F. Steingass, *A Comprehensive Persian-English Dictionary* (Beirut, 1982).

174. From the *khuṭba* by al-Manṣūr on the ʿĪd al-fiṭr 335 (no. 5).

of dates,[175] from the food of your own household and not from elsewhere. Otherwise it is unacceptable. Pray frequently and be consciously alert and expectant.[176]

On the sacrifices for the ʿĪd al-naḥr:

Most truly this day of yours is a sacred day during a sacred month, made more significant than other days, a day of the greater pilgrimage, in which God tested Abraham, His friend. He was redeemed in it from slaughtering his son, and God imposed the obligation on the whole people of Islam of pilgrimage to His sacred house, which He made a refuge for the people and a place of safety. So draw closer to God in it by means of what He has commanded you to do. The most worthy of what brings you to Him is the female of the camel, and the female of cattle, and the ram of sheep. Steer clear of sick animals and those with defects in the eyes or ears, and those of them deformed by excess in its creation or missing something. They will not be accepted on your part. That is in accord with the practice of your Prophet, and the imams among his pure progeny.[177]

Servants of God! Truly, this day of yours is a day of the feast God enjoins for the glorification and honouring of Him.... He made it a marker of the time for the pilgrimage to His sacred house and venerable ancient place. The gates of heaven open during it to receive prayers. So pray to God most sincerely and implore Him wishfully, approaching with what He commands you to do or restrained you from. From livestock of small cattle—and the most excellent of them is the female of the camel, the female of bovines, the ram of sheep—and he who sacrifices the young of a goat, for that he will not be rewarded, but for a young ram he will be. All animals slaughtered prior to the prayer are permissible meat, and after the prayer are acceptable sacrifice. The perfection of the sacrificed animal is soundness of eyes and ears. Avoid the sick one and the deformed, either in having extra limbs or not having some. Sharpen the blade for this purpose and treat the animal gently while slaughtering. 'So when they are down slaughtered on their sides, eat of them and feed he who is readily satisfied and the indigent' [22: 36]. Preserve

175. The text in the *Sīrat Jawdhar* here reads, instead of 'dates' (*tamr*), 'raisins' (*zabīb*).

176. From the *khuṭba* by al-Manṣūr, ʿĪd al-fiṭr in the year 336 (no. 7).

177. *Khuṭba* of al-Manṣūr, ʿĪd al-aḍḥā in the year 335 (no. 6).

> and praise God. 'Their meat does not reach God or their blood but the God-fearing piety of yours reaches Him' [22: 37], 'In that way have We made animals subject to you that you may render thanks' [22: 36].[178]

On the sword Dhu'l-Fiqār:

According to Fatimid accounts the fabled sword Dhu'l-Fiqār that the Prophet had given ʿAlī, and the possession of which the Shiʿa regard as an important sign of legitimacy, was restored to them during the reign of al-Qā'im after it was liberated from the Abbasids in Baghdad. Al-Manṣūr would later carry it into his battles with Abū Yazīd.[179] Here in a *khuṭba* he characterizes his father as the 'heir of the sword of his grandfather Dhu'l-Fiqār'.

> O God, bless Muḥammad Abu'l-Qāsim, the Imam al-Qā'im bi-Amr Allāh, son of al-Mahdī bi-llāh, Commander of the Believers, bearer of the proof of the Almighty, patron of the pious, the sharp sword of God and heir of the sword of his grandfather Dhu'l-Fiqār, a blessing bestowing the prayer of those who pray, hoisted into the heights of heaven, enduring forever among those who have passed before, abiding endlessly until the day of judgment.[180]

On *jihād* and the exile of war:

Having been forced away from his home in pursuit of the rebels, al-Manṣūr comments on the hardship his *jihād* has imposed on him:

> O God, You have sent me out of the land, an emigrant from the place of rest, in order to accomplish the duty of holy war that You imposed on me, on Your behalf and in support of Your religion, and the fortification of the community of Your apostle.[181]

178. From the *khuṭba* by al-Manṣūr, ʿĪd al-naḥr in the year 336 (no. 8).

179. For details and references see Paul E. Walker, 'Purloined Symbols of the Past: The Theft of Souvenirs and Sacred Relics in the Rivalry between the Abbasids and Fatimids', in F. Daftary and J. Meri, eds., *Culture and Memory in Medieval Islam: Essays in Honour of Wilferd Madelung* (London, 2003), pp. 364–367.

180. *Khuṭba* by al-Manṣūr, ʿĪd al-fiṭr in the year 335 (no. 5).

181. *Khuṭba* by al-Manṣūr, ʿĪd al-fiṭr in the year 335 (no. 5).

On the Kutāma:

The Kutāma tribesmen formed the backbone of the army for many years after the establishment of the caliphate. Most of them, moreover, were Ismaili, having been fully converted long before at the hands of Abū ʿAbdallāh al-Shīʿī. They were thus not just Muslims but quite loyal Ismailis as well. Even when the Fatimids benefited from the support of additional Berber groups, such as the Ṣanhāja who were behind the Zīrids but who were themselves never Ismaili, the Kutāma continued to provide a critically important element both in the military and the general population. In the following passage, as in another noted earlier, the Imam voices his gratitude to them and asks for God's special blessings on them in particular:

> O people of our *daʿwa*, O supporters of our dynasty, O Kutāma!
>
> Praise God and thank Him for that of His favours with which He singles you out, and the vastness of His beneficence. He gives preference in that over all of humans in the west and the east. He, the Mighty and Glorious, puts you first with the greatest favour, and then He attaches to you a magnificent beneficence, and He follows those two with such an abundance of grace to you that they cannot be counted. He made you see while the people were blind, and He informed you while the populace was ignorant. While servants were led astray, He guided you to His religion, to the triumph of His truth and obedience to His friend, the way-marker of guidance, the lamp in the darkness, the pole of religion, His firm rope. In precedence He raised you to His help, in pursuit of obeying Him, seeking shade in the shadow of His dynasty, being illuminated in the light of His wisdom, to the point that should God decree the convulsion of the county, the servants put to the test, darkness enveloping the earth, feet trembling, calamities magnifying, distress growing stronger, hearts aggrieved, God renders you immune. And He guides your hearts, firms up your feet, … those of you alive are happy and your dead are martyrs 'finding their sustenance with their Lord' [3: 169]. Congratulations to you; rejoice! …
>
> O God, truly have I come to be pleased with the Kutāma because of their holding firmly to Your rope and, in devotion to us, their having patience through misery and adversity for Your sake, acknowledging our precedence, carrying out that which God

> imposed on the servants because of us in order to reach You by obedience to us.
>
> O God! Approve them, multiply their goodness, erase their wickedness, gather them up among the group of Your prophet to whom they are indebted, and Your friend to whom they are loyal. Leave unchanged Your favour upon them, nay complete it for them. Perfect Your charity to them, and keep their posterity in power. Give their reward liberally and guide them. Purify their hearts.[182]

The next section of this book contains the full text of the sermons from which these few excerpts come, with more details and a greater opportunity to see how each *khuṭba* develops, what rhetorical devices and strategies operate in them, and how each of the speakers makes his case both to God and to his public. Ultimately, of course, the translations fail to convey the effect of the original Arabic. Qur'anic allusions and skilful use of rhyme, for example, heightened the thrust and flow of the words, adding meaning and resonance no rendering in another language can quite match. It should be remembered that these sermons were meant to be heard, not read; they are pieces of oral literature, not unlike poetry. But, in contrast to verse, as the speech of the imams, the divinely inspired leader of the community, for that same community they carried a spiritual consequence of far greater significance.

182. From the *khuṭba* by al-Manṣūr, ʿĪd al-fiṭr in the year 336 (no. 7).

PART TWO

The *Khuṭbas*

1

Khuṭba of al-Qā'im

On the 'Īd al-fiṭr, 302 (19 April 915) at Alexandria

['And when it was the feast of fast-breaking and al-Qā'im, who was then staying in Alexandria, he, God bless him, went out and prayed the prayer of the feast with the people for the year just mentioned; and he delivered the *khuṭba* of the feast at Alexandria. He said:'][183]

In the name of God, the Merciful, the Compassionate; in Him is our recourse. God is great; God is great; there is no god but God.

God is great; God is great. There is no authority other than His; there can be no obedience to anyone who disobeys Him. 'Is not the curse of God on the evildoers who block the path of God, wishing to make it crooked' [11: 18–19], and 'who kill those of the people who uphold justice' [3: 21]?

Praise God, the All-knowing Creator, the All-wise Regulator, 'who possesses the keys of the heavens and the earth' [39: 63],[184] 'He who has power over all things' [5: 120].[185] 'There is no intimate discourse among three but that He is the fourth of them; no five but He is the sixth of them; nor fewer than that or more but He is with them wherever they are' [58: 7]. His power and His knowledge encompasses them and 'they comprehend nothing of His knowledge except what He allows' [2: 255]. 'And faces will be humbled before the Living, the Self-sustaining, and those who tolerate injustice will despair' [20: 111]. He is the first prior to all time and season, place, limit and extent. He is the Kind One, the Expert, who 'created the heavens absent of pillars

183. *'Uyūn* (ed. Ya'lāwī), p. 198.

184. Also Qur'an (hereafter cited as Q) 42: 11.

185. And several other verses.

you can see' [31: 10]. Then He separated its lights, illuminating its sun, brightening its moon, unleashing its wellsprings, 'and the earth after that spread out; He brought out of it its water and its pastures' [79: 30–31]. So glory be to Him who is not indicated other than by His signs and what flows from His earth and in His heavens; He makes clear to His creation His governance and the complete perfection of His messengers sent to the nations, to the whole body of those who serve Him, when He said to them: Truly God is 'the Creator of the heavens and the earth; it is He who summons you in order to forgive you your sins and defer you to a term defined' [14: 10].

O people, I reach out to this community of yours just as the Messenger of God, may God bless and keep him, reached out to the Jews and the Christians, who had with them the Torah and the Gospels, churches and synagogues. He, may God bless and keep him, summoned them to the fulfilment of the knowledge that was in the Torah and the Gospels but they would not believe it. So he imposed on them the sword and the poll-tax and captivity, plunder and exile. In the same way I reach out to this community of yours which has taken your Qur'an in vain. You have thrown it behind your backs and sold it for a paltry price.[186] And so I say to you:

'O people of the book, you stand on nothing unless you uphold the Torah and the Gospels and what has come down to you from your Lord' [5: 68]. 'O people of the book, come to common terms between us and you that we not worship any but God and not associate with Him anything and not take some of us as lords over others except God Himself' [3: 64]. You accuse me of being a rebel bent on spreading heresy. You witnessed my effort and fighting and that God is my supporter and helper. I observe the inhabitants of the cities; they pray against me in their mosques. God, the Great and Glorious, is the One who questions their words: 'they think they stand on something but they are instead liars' [58: 18]. The lying apostate community, reneging on its intentions,[187] deviating from the command of their Lord, suppose that it has been correct in what it claims about its caliphs whom they insist are the caliphs of the Lord of the worlds, such as a

186. These words paraphrase Q. 15: 91 and 2: 187.

187. Q. 23: 66.

youth not yet mature, or like the boy lacking knowledge, or like the child who, according to their claim, governs Islam.[188] And yet among them a woman brings them wine from every valley and region on the backs of horses and in the bottoms of ships. As God the Exalted said: 'They take their priests and monks as lords besides God' [9: 31]. They spend the funds of orphans and the poor, wrongly on their part and unjustly, for singing lute players, skilled *ṭunbūr*ists and *miʿzafān*ists,[189] and talented drummers. You have seen their governors of cities, how one of them mounts the wooden planks of the Prophet's *minbar* to preach to the people but he does not preach to himself. Instead, he descends from that position and inquires of those in that land for male and female singers, *ṭunbūr*ists, *ʿūd* players, thieves, short change artists, and shavers of weights so that those can be brought to serve him. God curses the unjust and prepares for them a blazing fire.[190] That man is someone who neither commands the good nor prohibits the bad.

It is so bad that when the weak and poor servant of God stood up to summon them to God, 'they formed around him a swarm' [72: 19], 'from every side slipping away' [211: 96], and from every hard ground flowing in torrents. Are the servants of God thereby going forward to what God the Exalted summons in His book? Certainly not! God is He whom there is no god but He; 'Rather, We strike with the truth against the false, which causes it to shatter, and it disappears; woe to you for what you describe' [21: 18].

O people, truly you have fallen into an iniquitous blindness and a dark blackness, overwhelmed by a calamity that carries you into another calamity; it has led you astray by its heretical delusions and overcome you with its pernicious atmosphere. You are floating in its misfortune, drowning in its ideology, its doors locked against you, its reasons become obscure, the guide-markers of your religion obliterated, the works of your prophet effaced, the abomination among you obvious. And the acceptable is with you extinct. Where is it you are headed? To the hellfire from which you cannot withdraw? Will you

188. He refers to the Abbasid caliph of the time, al-Muqtadir, who had ascended to the throne in 295/908 at the age of thirteen, the youngest to do so.

189. Players of the long—(*ṭunbūr*) and short—(*miʿzaf*) necked lutes.

190. Borrowed from Q. 33: 64.

therefore be among those rewarded or those punished? Will you give thanks to God for His favour, because it is His proof on you? In the matter of His religion what protects and defends the sanctity of His prophet, may God bless him and his family? And who saves you from destruction? God said: 'O you who believe, obey God and obey the Messenger and those with authority among you' [4: 59]. Thus He makes obedience a duty, attaching it to obedience to the regulators of His affairs. They are the ones who uphold, on behalf of God, His truth and those who summon to him whoever desires to obey Him. He singled them out by the imamate, which is the highest of the ranks below prophecy. He prescribed for the servants rights due them and ordered them to fulfil these. He stipulated that they are connected to obeying him, doubling their reward on the measure of how well they follow those whose authority is ordained. The imam has not the option to reduce the rights of his flock, nor is the flock to decrease the rights of their imam. Among the rights of the flock against their imam is the maintenance of the Book of God and the Sunna of His prophet, may God bless him and his family, and restitution from those who treat them unjustly for those so treated, and from the powerful among them for the weak, from the noble of them for the lowly, investigating their manner of life and the differing conditions of it, looking solicitously upon his dependants in his efforts, watching over them with his eye. For He, great and glorious is He, concerning what He praised of the character of His prophet and His messenger said: 'There has come to you a messenger from among yourselves; a sorrow that befalls you grieves him; he is anxious concerning you; with the believers he is kind and compassionate' [9:128]. When he does that, the flock should revere him, honour him, and extend assistance to him, standing prepared and ready, on behalf of what is right according to the Book of God and the Sunna of His prophet, may God bless him and his family.

'O God, Creator of the heavens and the earth, of the world of the unseen and the visible, You judge among Your servants in matters about which they disagree' [39: 46]. O God, bless al-Mahdī bi-llāh Abū Muḥammad, the Commander of the Believers, just as You blessed and favoured the rightly guided *mahdī*-ist successors who upheld the truth and dispensed justice in accord with it. O God, just as You made them the succour for religion, and for the servants a sanctuary and a comfort, gladden the believers through him. Support him against Your insubordinately hypocritical, unbelieving, apostate, iniquitous enemies, God of creation, Lord of the worlds.

O God, grant victory to our troops and armies, in the eastern regions of the earth and in the western, on its land and its sea, its plains and its mountains. O God, curse Your enemies, the people who disobey You among the ancients and the later comers: the nation of Noah in the two worlds[191]—truly they were an impious group[192]—and ʿĀd and Thamūd, and the Associates of al-Rass,[193] and the tyrants of the tribe of Umayya and tribe of Marwān,[194] and Muʿāwiya b. Abī Sufyān,[195] who took from Your servants the rightful share[196] of dinars and dirhams, and waged war with them against the Emigrants and Helpers. Curse ʿAmr b. al-ʿĀṣ, ʿUtba b. Abī Sufyān,[197] al-Walīd b. ʿUtba,[198] al-Walīd b. Abī Muʿayṭ,[199] and that lizard son of a lizard—namely Marwān b. al-Ḥakam[200]—and al-Mughīra b. Shuʿba,[201] Ziyād

191. This is a reference to Q. 37: 79.

192. Q. 51: 46.

193. For the meaning and significance of the groups just named see Q. 50: 12–13, 'Before them the people of Noah, the Associates of the Rass, and the Thamūd denied, as did ʿĀd....', and Q. 25: 37–38 'And the people of Noah We had drowned them when they had accused the apostle of lies....ʿĀd and Thamūd and the Associates of the Rass...We administered warning to each of them and then destroyed them completely.'

194. The Marwānids were a branch of the Umayyad clan.

195. Founder of the Umayyad dynasty; on him see 'Muʿāwiya I' by M. Hinds in the *EI2*.

196. Q. 4: 128.

197. Brother of Muʿāwiya, who was on the side of ʿĀʾisha at the Battle of the Camel and of his brother at Ṣiffīn.

198. Governor of Medina on behalf of his uncle Muʿāwiya; he used to harass al-Ḥusayn b. ʿAlī.

199. al-Walīd b. ʿUtba b. Abī Muʿayṭ, half brother of ʿUthmān via his mother, he was one of those who sought to avenge the blood of ʿUthmān and blame ʿAlī.

200. He was the first caliph of the Marwānid branch of the Umayyad dynasty. He died in 65/685. For more details see C. E. Bosworth, 'Marwān I b. al-Ḥakam' in the *EI2*.

201. One of Muʿāwiya's governors of Kūfa but not an Umayyad; see 'al-Mughīra b. Shʿba' by H. Lammens in the *EI2*.

b. Summayya,[202] ʿUbaydallāh b. Ziyād,[203] al-Sulamī,[204] Dhu'l-Kalāʿ,[205] Ḥawshabā,[206] al-Ashʿath b. Qays,[207] ʿAbd al-Malik b. Marwān,[208] al-Ḥajjāj b. Yūsuf,[209] ʿAbd al-Raḥmān b. Muljam,[210] and those who were faithless and deviant, the apostates, transgressors, and heretics, and those who put off [acknowledging ʿAlī's succession] and those who refrained from going to war under the Commander of the Believers [i.e. ʿAlī]. O God, let the truth and those who seek it triumph; subdue the false and its partisans. 'Truly You are the All-mighty and All-wise' [2: 129 and others].

[Source: *ʿUyūn al-akhbār* (ed. Yaʿlāwī), pp. 198–202]

---

202. Ziyād b. Abīhi, the Umayyad commander in Iraq and killer of the Shiʿi hero Ḥujr b. ʿAdī.

203. Son of the previous man. He was governor of Iraq on behalf of the Umayyads.

204. Abu'l-Aʿwar ʿAmr b. Sufyān al-Sulamī, a close ally of Muʿāwiya and a general in his army, he was excoriated by ʿAlī accordingly.

205. Abū Sharāḥīl al-Ḥumayrī, a supporter of Muʿāwiya at Ṣiffīn.

206. Ḥawshab b. Ṭakhma al-Alhānī Dhū Ẓulaym was also on Muʿāwiya's side at Ṣiffīn.

207. Al-Ashʿath b. Qays al-Kindī was blamed by the Shiʿa for having forced ʿAlī into arbitration at Ṣiffīn. See 'al-Ashʿath' by H. Reckendorf in the *EI2*.

208. He was the fifth Umayyad caliph (r. 65/685 to 86/705).

209. On him see 'al-Ḥadjdjādj b. Yūsuf' in the *EI2* by A. Dietrich.

210. The murderer of ʿAlī; see 'Ibn Muldjam' in the *EI2* by L. Veccia Vaglieri.

2

Khuṭba of al-Qā'im

Rajab 333 (March 945). During the siege of al-Mahdiyya.
Read by al-Marwadhī

['And the Imam al-Qā'im bi-Amr Allāh, Commander of the Believers, may God bless him, dictated a sermon in which he exhorted the believers, and he ordered al-Marwadhī, his qadi in al-Mahdiyya, to read it to them. He said in it, following the praising of God the Exalted and honouring Him and the blessing for the Prophet Muḥammad, may the blessings of God be upon him and his family, the pure ones:'][211]

O people! Truly this accursed Nukkārī[212] has exacerbated his wickedness and his disease has infested the land. Deceptive hopes sustain him, and the soul that urges to evil[213] prompts him to esteem lightly the favour of God the Exalted to him; and the devil, who is his associate, intimates to him[214] that he has no conqueror. But it is merely that the Commander of the Believers loosens for him his reins in order to cause him to stumble in the abundance of his halter. So may God curse him with a calamitous curse and humiliate him with lengthy ignominy and make of him a blazing fire:[215] 'None shall burn in it but the most wretched' [92: 15].[216]

You have done, O men of Kutāma, what your fathers and veterans among your forbearers did as required for obedience and adhering to its bonds and taking shade in its shadow. And fighting for God

211. *'Uyūn* (ed. Ya'lāwī), p. 311.

212. See n. 166 above.

213. Q. 12: 53.

214. Q. 47: 25.

215. Q. 92: 14.

216. 'Therefore I warn you of a blazing fire; none shall burn in it but the most wretched, who denied the truth and turned away' (Q. 92: 14–16).

with the effort due Him. You were the cache where God placed this Muḥammadan, Fāṭimid, *mahdī*-ist right until He caused it to triumph, raising it high again. He made of you its pride and its glory. You are like the Apostles of Jesus and the Anṣār of Muḥammad, may God bless them both.

O sons of the Emigrants and the Anṣār, those who came first[217] and before, who were most intimate, was it not through you that God ended the dynasties of the tyrants, which had passed its long period of years, until He made them into a crop that withers away?[218] 'Did He not cause you to inherit their land and estates' [33: 27]; and thus it was that you commenced to conquer after having been conquered?

The accursed arch-deceiver has settled in front of you with a misled, erring party that does not draw on the light of true guidance. They are like startled [and heedless] cattle, figures that merely imitate the real, planks of wood propped up,[219] frightened donkeys.[220] If they stand in place, they are destroyed, and if they are called back, they are overtaken. Do not recoil after advancing! You are the party of God; they are the party of Satan.[221] Your dead are in paradise; their dead are in hellfire. So which truth other than this truth would you seek? With which imam other than your imam would you fight?

Fight, may God have mercy on you, the partisans of error, jackals of greed, moths of the fire, and pursue them to the ends of the earth, the extremities of the land, on every horizon, until God makes right the truth and wrong the false, even though the polytheists abhor it.[222]

[Sources: al-Jawdharī, *Sīrat Jawdhar*, pp. 53–55 (French trans. pp. 78–80), and Idrīs, *'Uyūn al-akhbār* (ed. Ya'lāwī), pp. 311–312]

---

217. Q. 9: 100.

218. Q. 21:15.

219. Q. 63: 4.

220. Q. 74:50.

221. 'party of God' (Q. 58: 22) and 'party of Satan' (Q. 58: 19).

222. The phrase 'makes right the truth and wrong the false, even though the polytheists hate it' echoes Q. 8: 8.

3

Khuṭba of al-Manṣūr

As *walī li'l-'ahd* (Heir-apparent) on the 'Īd al-fiṭr, 334 (6 May 946) at al-Mahdiyya

['When the day of fast-breaking arrived, al-Manṣūr bi-llāh Abu'l-Ṭāhir Ismā'īl b. Abi'l-Qāsim al-Qā'im bi-Amr Allāh, peace be upon him, went out from his palace surrounded by his sons, his brothers, his followers, his loyal friends, the adherents of his government, and his servants. The people raised their voices in supplication to him and asked God that He turn against his enemy and forsake him. Banners were unfurled and drums beaten. Happiness filled hearts and delighted breast. The stars of good fortune had risen indicating, by their appearing, the fate of the friends of God. When he reached the *muṣallā*, he prayed the festival prayer and then rose up as the preacher and said:'][223]

In the name of God, the Merciful, the Compassionate.

Praise be to God who is so good to us in His provisions and grants bountifully in His giving. I praise Him with the praise of one who is grateful for His goodness, and who follows in all matters what pleases Him. I seek His help with the resort of he who expects nothing from any one else and does not put faith in anything other than Him, who is answerable to Him alone from start to finish.

I bear witness that there is no god but God, alone, without associate, and I testify that Muḥammad was His servant and His messenger, chosen by Him for His revelation, selected by Him to convey His messages. He was for that purpose sent as the summoner to the truth, a witness for creation. Thus did he transmit the message of his Lord and advise His servants, exerting himself on His behalf.

223. *'Uyūn* (ed. Ya'lāwī), p. 339.

May the blessings of God be upon the Prophet, the chosen one, the approved messenger. And on his family be His peace, His mercy and His benediction.

Servants of God! This day of yours is a day of festival. God honours it and makes it important; He gives preference to it and exalts it; by it He closes the month of Ramaḍān and opens through it the pilgrimage to His noble house. Be faithful in it to your intentions and in it submit your requests to God. Seek forgiveness for your sins. Truly He whose praise is glorious and His names are sacred, says: 'Ask your Lord to forgive you; most certainly He is most forgiving' [71: 10]. Fear God, you servants of God! In fearing Him lies the success of those who seek and the triumph of those who win. And that is the counsel of God to those who came before and those who come after. Persist in obeying Him. Be heedful of what God the Exalted entrusted to you as His religion and His book, and has you observe of His rights and His penalties. What He causes you to desire of the bounty of His rewards and the nobility of His place of return, or He causes you to dread of His penalties and the pain of His punishment, '[for that] toil as the strivers should' [37: 61].

God inspires us and you with our guidance, and make us and you be resolved on fearing Him, following His guidance and attaining His approval.

[He, on whom be peace, sat briefly and then stood up and said:]

In the name of God, the Merciful, the Compassionate.

Praise be to God who bestows favours liberally, who crushes enemies, who deserves thanks and praise. God blesses with the most excellent of His blessings the most excellent of His prophets, Muḥammad, the seal of the prophets and lord of the messengers. [Bless] his pure family. O God, bless Muḥammad and the family of Muḥammad; have mercy on Muḥammad and the family of Muḥammad. Bless Muḥammad and the family of Muḥammad just as the most excellent of Your blessings, Your sanction, and Your mercy, fell on Abraham and the family of Abraham, 'Truly You are worthy of praise and glory' [11: 73].[224]

224. The content of Q. 11: 73 and adjacent verses concern the family of Abraham.

O God! bless also the sun of guidance by whose radiance Islam is made to shine, dispelling the darkness, empowering religion, completing favours for the believers, the servant of God, Abū Muḥammad, the Imam, the Commander of the Believers, al-Mahdī bi-llāh, son of the Rightly Guided Ones (*al-Mahdiyyīn*), the noble son of the most noble. May God and His angels bless him; may God honour his dwelling place near to Him, in noble mansions[225] and gardens of enduring bliss.[226]

O God, bless as well the one who holds power, the heir to glory and honour, through whom You increased Your benevolence, and bestowed Your favours profusely. You clothed him in the vestments of high nobility and crowned him with regal splendour and the caliphate. You combined in him the succession to those prophets who were sent as messengers with the inheritance of his fathers, the imams who succeeded, the rightly guiding guides, the chosen legatees, Muḥammad al-Qā'im bi-Amr Allāh, the Commander of the Believers.

O God, appraise him about what You have appointed him to do and have put him in charge of. Safeguard him in it and have confidence in him, with the most excellent of that which You have appraised any before him among Your deputies, the imams of guidance, his fathers, the rightly guided ones, by way of support, empowerment, inspiration, and the achievement of victory. Bring down upon his enemies, in the east and the west, on land and on the sea, the most severe assaults and retributions that You have done or caused to occur with any of those who were enemies of Yours, a destructive misfortune, dishonouring exemplary punishments. Destroy them by annihilation and burn them in the fire of hell.

O God, make religion victorious through him, and validate him with dominion and authority, grandeur and power, conquest and victory. Make his word lofty,[227] his hand far reaching, his army dominant,[228] and his partisans those who triumph.[229] Grant him a manifest

225. Q. 44: 26.
226. Q. 9: 21.
227. Q. 9: 40.
228. Q. 37: 173.
229. Q. 37: 172.

victory,[230] empower religion through him, and through him restore to good health the breasts of the believers,[231] God of creation, Lord of the worlds. 'Truly, You are He who hears prayers' [3: 38] and You do as You will;[232] 'You do not go back on promises made' [3: 194].

[Source: Idrīs, *'Uyūn al-akhbār* (ed. Ya'lāwī), pp. 339–341]

230. Q. 48: 1.
231. Q. 9: 14.
232. Q. 85: 16. *Fa''ālun limā turīdu.*

4

Khuṭba of al-Manṣūr

On Friday, 14 Muḥarram 335 (16 August 946). Read by Ja'far b. 'Alī, the Chamberlain, in the Mosque of Qayrawān

['The Imam, peace be upon him, ordered Ja'far b. 'Alī, the servant of his grandfather al-Mahdī bi-llāh, to the congregational mosque of Qayrawān. There he performed the Friday prayer and then rose for the *khuṭba*. He praised God and extolled Him; and asked for blessings on the Prophet and on his family, and on his legatee and the pure imams among his offspring. He thanked God profusely for the victory He had granted to His friends and the degradation and subjugation He had visited on His enemies, what trials and tribulation God had thereby removed from the people of Islam, both from the elite and the masses, the townsfolk and the bedouin, and what had now come to them in the way of peace and security. Then he said:'][233]

O people assembled! Our lord and master, the Amir Ismā'īl [al-Manṣūr bi-llāh], may God prolong his duration, cause his power to persist, and strengthen his dominion, extends greetings and says to you: God, may He be hallowed, has known the goodness of my intentions toward you, what fine thoughts I harbour for you, and what benefits for your affairs I wish, what I find in myself of sadness when affliction befalls you, what comes upon you of want and the loss of selves and property. Most surely I have many splendid hopes I hold out in expectation for you that nothing prevents from being revealed but this enemy before me, and my fight with him, and these

233. This version of the statement comes from Idrīs, *'Uyūn* (ed. Ya'lāwī), p. 378. Al-Maqrīzī (*al-Muqaffā*, 2: 138) offers another with slight differences indicating that he must have used the same source as Idrīs. His version of the *khuṭba* is similarly close to that of Idrīs but not exact.

events that have transpired between him and me. So if we reveal what we had hoped for you in the way of good things prior to victory, the ignorant would say: he does that in an attempt to generate sympathy in the hearts of the flock and out of fear for the enemy. Given that God has bestowed on us the favour you know about, and the support of His for us that you have seen, and granted victory to us against His enemies by His gifts and His power, I want to match the gifts of God, the Glorious and All-high, to us by thanks to Him and by good deeds to His servants and kindness to His creatures, and to announce some of what we intend in regard to you even though announcing it at the moment of victory is preferable and before that is more open to doubts, for the reason which I mentioned.

So the Commander, may God give him strength, has relinquished the dues incumbent on you in the coming year—that is, the year 335[234]—and the alms taxes, and all the obligations, and he does that for all of the people, Muslims among them as well as the protected peoples, out of kindness to them, and to aid them in refurbishing their land and steppes. So let those who witness this convey it to those who are absent. Let each bedouin among you return to his steppe without suffering heavy loss or expenditure. Subsequently, there will not be collected from you in the years to come other than the tenth and the alms tax: food stuffs for food stuffs, sheep from small livestock, oxen from bovines, mature camels from camels (*al-baʿīr min al-ibil*), in accord with the laws of God, may He be exalted, and the practice of my grandfather, the Messenger of God, may God bless him and keep him. Subsequently, those things by which the gifts of God enhance you will be conveyed to you though acts of beneficence, the emerging of justice, the resurgence of the truth, the defeat of falsehood, and you will come to recognize thereby the blessedness of our days and the prosperity of our dynasty, should God so will.

[Sources: Idrīs, *ʿUyūn al-akhbār* (ed. Yaʿlāwī), pp. 378–380; and al-Maqrīzī, *al-Muqaffā*, biography of al-Manṣūr, 2: 138–139 (with a slightly different text)]

---

234. The year 335 commenced in August of 946.

5

Khuṭba of al-Manṣūr

On the ʿĪd al-fiṭr, 335 (25 April 947). During the siege of Abū Yazīd at Kiyāna

[ʿAnd when it was Sunday the first day of the month of Shawwāl of the year 335, he (al-Manṣūr), peace be upon him, rode to the *muṣallā* that he had constructed, and he prayed with the people the *ʿīd* prayer and mounted the *minbar* and delivered the *khuṭba*. He said:'][235]

In the name of God, the Merciful, the Compassionate.

'Praise be to God who created the heavens and the earth, and made the darkness and the light; yet those who do not believe regard others as equal' [6: 1], a god worshipped and a lord praised. We take none other than Him as God and we do not associate with Him anything.

Praise be to God who 'holds up the heaven that it not fall to the earth other than by His leave; truly God is kind and compassionate with the people' [22: 65].

God is great! God is great! There is no god but God. And God is great! Praise be to God! 'Glory be to our Lord; indeed the promise of our Lord has been fulfilled' [17: 108]. 'Glory be to God when the evening falls and when the day dawns; His praise is in the heavens and the earth, at nightfall and when it is noontime' [30: 17–18]. 'Glory be to your Lord, the Lord of power, over what they ascribe to Him; peace be on the messengers and praise be to God, the Lord of the worlds' [37: 180–182].

Praise be to God, the First, the Eternal, who never ceases to be, the Last, perpetual, who never changes, the all-wise knower who never does not know, the munificent benefactor who is never stingy

235. *ʿUyūn* (ed. Yaʿlāwī), p. 417.

His mercy encompasses all things[236] so that none despair of obtaining it except those who go astray;[237] He brings into being His creation for the worship of Him such that no one refuses to do it except the depraved. Proof of Him is established by the wonderful indications of Him which are such that they cannot be denied except by the infidels. Souls are submissive before Him in their glorification and hearts yield willingly to Him in their humility. Vision turns away from what it desires short of Him and, in its impotence, surrenders to His all-mighty power. Intellects testify to Him through their innate character that He, as He describes Himself, is the Alive, the Everlasting: 'drowsiness does not overtake Him nor sleep' [2: 255],[238] 'nothing is like him' [42: 11], 'no vision apprehends Him yet He apprehends all visions, and He is the Kind and All-knowing' [6: 103]. His praise is glory; His names sacred; His brilliance powerful; His splendour exalted.

I bear witness that there is no god but God, alone, without associate, and I testify that Muḥammad was His servant and His chosen messenger, His approved trustee. He sent him with the radiant light and decisive proof to the whole of His creation, bearing witness to those of the messengers who came before him and asserting the truth of the books in his hands, an indication of God, a summons to Him, of the intermission in the time between messengers and the interruption in the revelation, the obliteration of the truth, and the going astray of the people, so that he then conveys on behalf of God His message, complies with His command,[239] and summons to the way of his Lord with wisdom and fine exhortation,[240] striving for God with the true striving due Him. Providing security to His servants, he served his Lord until the certainty[241] overtook him, God bless him among those who were first and those who were later. [Bless also] his family, the pure and the chaste, the chosen legatees, the most distinguished rightly guided ones.

236. Q. 7: 156.

237. Q. 15: 56.

238. This verse begins 'God there is no god but Him, the Alive, the Everlasting, drowsiness does not overtake Him nor sleep....'

239. Q. 15: 99.

240. Q. 16: 125.

241. *al-yaqīn*, i.e. death. Q. 15: 94.

I urge upon you the worship of God by fearing God, He whom you cannot do without, nor is there a refuge for you other than with Him, in dying or in living, not in the afterlife nor in this world. Sacrifice yourselves in what He wants and approves. It brings you nearer to Him.

Truly, this is a day God made for you as a festival and ceremony, in which the fasting comes to an end and the months of pilgrimage commence. So make your souls answerable, may God have mercy on you! He who speaks of good let him praise God and let him increase it; he who speaks of shortcomings let him ask for censure, or of shame, and let him repent. Verily God the Exalted 'Accepts repentance from His servants and forgives sins; and He knows what you do' [42: 25].

God has imposed on you an alms tax in your breaking the fast and it follows the practice of your Prophet, the lord of the prophets, may God bless him and his family. So let each man among you contribute on behalf of his dependants, the males among them and the females, the young and the old, a *ṣāʿ* of wheat or a *ṣāʿ* of barley, or a *ṣāʿ* of dates,[242] all these of his own food, not of anything not eaten or contributed from something else. Truly, that is forbidden him and there is no reward for it.

May God protect us and you through devotion and employ us and you in doing what He wants and is pleasing to Him. Make our next life better for us and for you than the first.[243]

[The second *khuṭba*:][244]

In the name of God, the Merciful, the Compassionate.

Praise be to God, the one who unifies by His overlordship, the one who is alone in His absolute unity, the First, eternal, the Living, everlasting. I praise Him with His praises, all of them for the least of His favours and for the great, a praise requiring praise for praise, for the good fortune from Him and the guidance.

---

242. See note 173 above. On these rules for the *zakāt al-fiṭr*, see the *Daʿā'im*, 1: 266–267, trans. 1: 331–332.

243. Q. 93: 4.

244. Addition by the editor. According to al-Yaʿlāwī, Idrīs himself gives no indication of the break between *khuṭbas*.

And I testify that there is no god but God, alone, without associate, in fidelity to His absolute oneness and in acknowledgement of His lordship.

I bear witness that Muḥammad was His servant, chosen by Him, and His messenger whom He sent. His prophecy is complete with revelation and the announcement of the proof is in the truth of his message, may God bless him and keep him, and raise high his renown, give him peace and honour.

O you people! Truly God orders you in a command in which He begins with Himself, then makes a doublet of it with His angels. He said: 'Truly God and His angels give their blessings to the Prophet, O you who believe, bless him and greet him with a greeting' [33: 56]. O God, bless Your servant and Your messenger with a perpetually perfect blessing; increase him with an honour to his honour and a nobility to his nobility. Bless also all of the Companions of the Cloak (*aṣḥāb al-kisāʾ*), the pure ones, the immaculates: ʿAlī, the Commander of the Believers, Fāṭima the Radiant, mistress of the women of the two worlds, and al-Ḥasan and al-Ḥusayn, the two most noble and most righteous, and [bless] the rightly guided imams among the progeny of al-Ḥusayn, the luminaries of guidance, the full moons of the darkness, the masters of mankind, friends of the Most Merciful, the proofs of times, and pillars of the faith.

O God, bless the heir of every glory and praise, excellence and nobility, Your approved servant, Your chosen friend, and Your accepted upright deputy (*khalīfa*), the servant of God, Abū Muḥammad, the Imam al-Mahdī bi-llāh, Commander of the Believers, by whose light the horizons radiate, through whom brightness pervades, the sun of mankind and the full moon of the darkness, revealer of the light, and the revivifier of what was obliterated of the waymarkers of guidance, with the most excellent of Your perfect blessings, Your increasing benedictions, Your everlasting munificence.

O God, bless the holder of his appointment during his lifetime and his successor after his death, the chosen and selected, the venerable and sanctioned, Muḥammad Abu'l-Qāsim the Imam al-Qāʾim bi-Amr Allāh, son of al-Mahdī bi-llāh, Commander of the Believers, bearer of the proof of the Almighty, patron of the pious, the sharp sword of God and heir of the sword of his grandfather Dhu'l-Fiqār, a blessing bestowing the prayer of those who pray, hoisted into the heights of heaven, enduring forever among those who have passed before, abiding endlessly until the Day of Judgment.

O God, most certainly I am Your servant and Your friend. On me You have bestowed such favours that I am by You made mighty; You made me superior and thus You made me most generous. You have raised me and made me honoured by what You had me attain of the deputyship (*khilāfa*) from esteemed forefathers, the imams of right guidance, and You appointed me the flag of religion. You raised me to the imamate of the believers.

O God, complete Your favour to me, just as You completed it previously for those of the forefathers and grandfathers, the highly esteemed and celebrated, the bearers of Your banner, the keepers of Your inspiration, Your guardians of Your people, Your elite among Your servants, those chosen by You from the family of Your prophet for whom You combine the nobility of both abodes and the excellence of both residences.

O God, I am anxious about custody of their covenant and fulfilment of their promise, and the discharge of their obligations, completing their orders, keeping their memory alive, empowering those who were friends of theirs, humbling those who were enemies to them. Unite me and them, O God, in the seat of Your mercy, the residence of Your paradise, the neighbourhood of Your prophet, with the prophets and true friends, and the martyrs and the righteous, those who are faithful,[245] O Lord of the worlds.

O God, You have sent me out of the land, an emigrant from the place of rest, in order to accomplish the duty of holy war that You imposed on me, on Your behalf and in support of Your religion, and the fortification of the community of Your apostle.

O God, grant me a clear and swift victory.[246] Make me on Your behalf the defending dominant power against my enemy who is Your enemy.[247] Truly You are over all things omnipotent.

O God, forgive the believers, male and female, and the Muslims,

245 Q. 4: 69.

246 Q. 48: 1.

247 A borrowing of Q. 17: 80.

men and women, the living among them and the dead, and those who join them coming later except for he who renounces Your names or he who is inimical to Your friends, or he who takes as friend Your enemies. Complete their recompense, and keep safe for them their religions, until they meet You having fulfilled their oath, being then worthy of Your reward. Truly You are forgiving and compassionate. 'Verily God commands justice and good deeds and giving to relatives and prohibiting indecent acts, the reprehensible and oppressive, and He admonishes you that you may remember' [16: 90]. Praise be to God, the Lord of the worlds.

[Source: Idrīs, *'Uyūn al-akhbār* (ed. Ya'lāwī), pp. 417–421.]

6

Khuṭba of al-Manṣūr

On the ʿĪd al-aḍḥā, 335 (2 July 947). During the siege of Abū Yazīd at Kiyāna

[ʻAnd when it was the day of sacrifice, Friday the 10th of Dhu'l-Ḥijja, the Imam, peace be upon him, rode a roan red horse with golden fringes on the side. He was dressed in a garment of yellow, turbaned with a saffron turban, its tail hanging loose. He was surrounded by his supporters, his army, his loyal friends and servants. Arriving at the *muṣallā* that had been put up for him prior to that, he dismounted and prayed the festival prayer. He climbed up the *minbar* that had been constructed of stones and he gave the sermon. He said:'][248]

In the name of God, the Merciful, the Compassionate.

Praise be to God who unites through divine lordship, who is unique in oneness, who is almighty in ability and endurance, all-powerful in majesty and grandeur, the first without limit, the last without end, transcending the comparisons of the ignorant and the definitions of the describers, the conditions of the attributers, and the comprehension in visions of those who speculate.

I bear witness that there is no god but God, alone, without associate, and I testify that Muḥammad is His servant and His messenger. He honoured him with prophecy and chose him for the message; He awarded him with excellence. He sent him with a light for him to shine and with the truth for him to proclaim, with guidance for him to command, against unbelief to hold back, over the prophets to keep watch, and for that which they had brought to

248. This account comes from Idrīs, *ʻUyūn* (ed. Yaʻlāwī), p. 427. Al-Maqrīzī (*al-Muqaffā*, 2: 146) provides a similar account, adding to it the display of lances, banners and drums in sections of the army.

confirm its truth. So he conveyed the message and guided the way out of error. He led away from destruction successfully and made clear the waymarkers of religion and its obligations. He explained its terms and its statutes. He waged war on behalf of God with an effort worthy of Him[249] until the certainty overcame him.[250] May God bless him among those who came first and those who come later. And [bless also] his family, the pure, the chaste, the noble, the imams of right guidance, the esteemed and revered. Upon them have mercy and deference.

I prescribe for you, the servants of God, what I previously prescribed for myself as to fearing God and His surveillance, and doing what will please Him and bring us and you closer to Him. So, in fearing Him, there is His approval and, in His being pleased, success in paradise and salvation from the fire. And 'whoever is saved from the fire and admitted to paradise has been granted success; and the life of this world is but the merchandise of delusion' [3: 185].

Most truly this day of yours is a sacred day during a sacred month, made more significant than other days, a day of the greater pilgrimage, in which God, the hallowed and exalted, tested Abraham His friend. He was redeemed in it from slaughtering his son, may God bless them both, and God imposed on the whole people of Islam the obligation of pilgrimage to His sacred house, which He made a refuge for the people and a place of safety.[251] So draw closer to God the Exalted in it by means of what He has commanded you to do. The most worthy of what brings you to Him is the female of the camel, and the female of cattle, and the ram of sheep. Steer clear of sick animals and those with defects in the eyes or ears, and those of them deformed by excess in its creation or missing something. They will not be accepted on your part. That is in accord with the practice of your Prophet, may God bless him and keep him and his family, the imams among his pure progeny, the righteous and highly esteemed, on them the most excellent of salutation. 'It is not their flesh or blood that reaches God, but the God-fearing piety that reaches Him' [22: 37].

---

249. Reference to Q. 22: 78.

250. i.e. death. Q. 15: 99.

251. Q. 2: 125.

God accepts from us and from you, and He prescribes for us and for you, a pilgrimage to His sacred house, reaching His place of great assembly and His revered stations, by empowering our victory, completing our affair, and implementing the advancement of His promise to us. Truly He does not go back on His promise[252]; what He wants is never impossible for Him.[253]

[The second *khuṭba:*]

In the name of God, the Merciful, the Compassionate.

Praise be to God, He who starts things and brings them back, the most efficient benefactor, the One who effects what He wants,[254] Creator of creation, Bestower of sustenance, the One who causes the rain to descend, the Arranger of affairs, the One who survives the heavens and the earth and what is in them, and to Him do they return.

God is great! God is great! There is no god but God!

And God is great! God is great! Praise be to God!

I bear witness that there is no god but God, alone, without associate, and I testify that Muḥammad is His chosen servant, and His approved messenger, His confidant for what He reveals, the deliverer from error and destruction, may God bless him and his revered family, the rightly guided ones, the imams of righteous guidance: ʿAlī, the Commander of the Believers and master of the legatees and best of Muslims; Fāṭima the Radiant, mistress of the women of the two worlds; and al-Ḥasan and al-Ḥusayn, the two lords of the youth among the people of paradise; and the imams from the progeny of al-Ḥusayn, the chaste ones, the remainder of the messenger of God and his fruit, his two heirs, his proof to the servants, the mountains of religion, lords of the believers and saints of the worlds. And [bless] the approved imam, the chosen guardian, the servant of God, Abū Muḥammad, the Imam al-Mahdī bi-llāh, Commander of the Believers, inheritor of the excellence of the rightly guiding imams from his forefathers, the rightly guiding caliphs, the choicest of the choice

252. Echoing Q. 3: 9 and several other verses.
253. Echoing Q. 35: 44.
254. Q. 85: 16.

among the earliest of them and the latest, through whom the nation of believers rose and by whose sword the necks of the hypocrites were humbled, so that Islam was reestablished fresh and flourishing and religion made splendid and radiant, the truth luminous and resplendent. Through him God revived what had been obliterated of religion and, of the truth, what had become obscure. God combined for him the nobility of this world and its glory, and brought him the excellence of the next and its treasures, may the blessings of God be upon him and His approval, His mercy, and His affection.

O God, bless the holder of his covenant and heir of his glory, his successor after him, appointed to the imamate, crowned with high honour, the servant of God, Abu'l-Qāsim, the Imam al-Qā'im bi-Amr Allāh, Commander of the Believers, the son of al-Mahdī billāh, Commander of the Believers, scion of the elite of the prophets and remnant of those who went before, distinguished offspring of the rightly guiding imams. [Bless them] with a blessing by which You increase him in honour and esteem, nobility and majesty, sublime in ability, exalted in glory, growing in renown, enduring through the ages.

O God, just as You made me Your deputy whom You treat with deference and whom You honour, whom You hold in check and proscribe, curse those who claim it but who have no right to it and put to shame those who are hostile to it, cutting short thereby the hands of those who arrogate to it. You chose for it one after another my forefathers, the rightly guided ones, the chosen and revered, the rightly guided caliphs. Next You have me inherit their position, and You revived through me remembrance of them. You made complete through me their command. You had me follow in their tracks; You appointed me to what You appointed them, as the argument made through us to Your creation, the upholding of Your command, support of Your religion, empowering of the community of Your messenger. You made me victorious, triumphant, and dominant. You empowered through me the community after it had been humiliated and You multiplied them after they had been few. You brought them together after separation. You removed from them the shadows of discord, the gloom of darkness, and the black night of affliction, through our dynasty which You have made powerful and victorious, by our days which

You honour and thus chose, and our swords which You execute on the arch-deceiver and his party, the hypocrite and his like. You made them by it the harvest of the dying. The truth became radiant and falsehood comes to nothing,[255] a bounty from You to us and a favour You renew with us. Upon the favours before it, You bestow it amply on us and bountifully. O God, inspire us with gratitude for Your favours; have us take up the task that has us please You and brings us closer to where You are and draws us nearer to You. For truly there is no might or power except through You. On You we depend; to You we turn.[256] My affairs I entrust to You; in You I take refuge.

'My prayers and my devotions, my living and my dying, are for God, Lord of the worlds' [6: 162]. O God, forgive me and the believers, male and female, Muslims, man and woman, the living among them and the dead. Accept their deeds and attest to the validity of their efforts. Guide them and show mercy to them. Truly You are most gracious and merciful.

[Sources: Idrīs, *'Uyūn al-akhbār* (ed. Ya'lāwī), pp. 428–431; al-Maqrīzī, *al-Muqaffā*, 2: 146–148, biography of al-Manṣūr]

255. Q. 17: 81.
256. Q. 42: 10 and 11: 88.

7

Khuṭba of al-Manṣūr[257]

On the ʿĪd al-fiṭr, 336 (14 April 948), at al-Mahdiyya

[ʻThe festival of fast-breaking was on Thursday at the onset of Shawwāl of the year 366. The Commander of the Believers al-Manṣūr bi-llāh, may the blessings of God be upon him, went out to the *muṣallā* that the Imam al-Mahdī bi-llāh had built outside of al-Mahdiyya. His heir apparent al-Muʿizz li-Dīn Allāh Abū Tamīm was behind him. His paternal uncles, the sons of al-Mahdī bi-llāh, and his brothers, the sons of al-Qāʾim bi-Amr Allāh, and his own sons came after al-Muʿizz li-Dīn Allāh. He proceeded along with his troops with solemn dignity, reverence, praising God, until he reached the *muṣallā*. There he completed the festival prayer and mounted the *minbar* to deliver the sermon. He said:ʼ][258]

In the name of God, the Merciful, the Compassionate.

Praise be to God, in gratitude for His favours which no number can possibly count, extending to the superabundance of His bounty, which is inexhaustible. There is no god but God, in keeping with His absolute oneness. And God is great, in deference to any mentioning of God, the highest and most glorious. Hallowed is God, He whose

---

257. This *khuṭba* is one of two that al-Manṣūr deposited with Ustadh Jawdhar and which the latter copied for his own records. Along with the documents, the caliph sent him a note of explanation and that read in part: ʻThis, the second [of the two *khuṭbas*], is of my own composition. It is the one in which I preached to the people in the year [3]36 after having returned from the Maghrib, announcing in it publicly the death of al-Qāʾim bi-Amr Allāh, may the blessings of God be upon him. We recalled in it the enormous misfortune of losing him.ʼ al-Jawdharī, *Sīrat Jawdhar*, p. 53.

258. From *ʿUyūn* (ed. Yaʿlāwī), p. 480.

signs bear witness to His power. His essence refuses the association with it of attributes, the vision of Him by sight, the definition of Him by intellects, being most grand and almighty, glorious and powerful, splendid and magnificent. His is the highest heavens and the lowest earth and what falls between them and what is beneath the soil.[259] All submit to His majesty, humble before His might, acting in accord with His will, falling under His power.

I bear witness that there is no god but God, alone and without associate. And I testify that Muḥammad is His servant and messenger, selected and approved by Him, picked and chosen by Him, ennobled and purified by Him. He sent him with guidance and the religion of truth,[260] by which those of the nearest angels in the heavens and those of the men and jinn on the earth express devotion. Thus he, on him be peace, was fully conversant with what had been made suitable, and he imparted what he was sent with, complying with the command of his Lord, patiently enduring sufferings and adversities on his part, until God caused His to prevail over all religions, and by His truth to destroy the vanities of the graven images. May the blessings of God be upon him and his family, and keep, exalt, and honour them.

Servants of God! I urge upon you the fear of God and obedience to Him. Dread God and His surveillance; draw near to God by that of which He approves. Most certainly He is fully acquainted with what is in your hearts and sees your deeds. No secret is hidden from Him;[261] the weight of a single atom in the heavens and earth escapes Him not.[262] There is no such thing as being saved from His displeasure, or a deliverance into His mercy other than by obeying Him; 'and those who obey God and His messenger will succeed greatly' [33: 71].

Indeed, most truly, did God, the Mighty and Glorious, make this day of yours a feast of greater importance than other days. He seals with it a month more excellent than other months. With it He commenced the days of the month of pilgrimage to the Ancient House, which He ennobled and sanctified. He made it the direction of prayers, the centre of blessings, the place of compassion, a rendezvous for the people and

259. Q. 20: 6.
260. Q. 9: 33.
261. Q. 69: 18.
262. Q. 34: 3.

a safe retreat,[263] a lighthouse of religion and a guidepost. So draw close to God in this day of yours by rendering the fast-breaking alms, which is the *zakāt* of your fast, and is the Sunna of your prophet, the lord of the prophets, may God bless him and his family and keep him. Each man of you for himself and for each individual of his household, males and females, young and old, [contributes] half a *ṣāʿ*[264] of wheat, or a *ṣāʿ* of barley, or a *ṣāʿ* of dates,[265] from the food of your own household and not from elsewhere. Otherwise it is unacceptable. Pray frequently and be consciously alert and expectant. 'O you who believe, have fear of God and let each soul consider what it has set ahead for the morrow' [59: 18]. For it is near at hand, by God, as if already here.

Truly He, the Mighty and Glorious, would not have you be heedless in overlooking hunger and yet He does not impose a hardship in religion,[266] but there is no excuse after having made the programme clear and confirmed by proofs, through His Messenger and the imams of guidance among his descendants, on him and on them the most excellent peace of God and His mercy.

Make us and you appropriate for His approval and brought near to Him. Draw us to Him. Truly we are His and by Him. And may the blessings of God, the first and last, be on Muḥammad, the seal of the prophets and lord of the messengers, and on his righteous and chaste family, the rightly guided (*mahdī*-ist) imams, the most noble overlords who have determined and will enjoin the truth and on the basis of it have and will rule justly.

[*The second khuṭba*. And he sat briefly and then stood and said:]

In the name of God, the Merciful, the Compassionate.

Praise be to God, Lord of the universe, the ultimate end for that which would be perfect. And blessings, those coming and those going, growing, thriving, and enduring, be upon Muḥammad and his righteous and chaste family, the rightly guided (*mahdī*-ist) imams, noblest lords, the

263. *mathābatan lil-nās wa amnan*, Q. 2: 125.

264. See note 173 above.

265. The text in the *Sīrat Jawdhar* here reads, instead of 'dates' (*tamr*), 'raisins' (*zabīb*).

266. Q. 22: 78.

pure and most pious. Praise! Praise! Thanks! Thanks! You carried out Your promise; You made Your servant victorious, against the hatred of the unbelievers, the minions of the cunning, depraved, profligates, the partisans of the lying arch deceiver, the misguiding object of anger, the filthy and unclean, the contemptible and wretched, the damned and infamous, those accursed throughout the earth and heaven.

Praise! Praise! And thanks to You! Thanks! Over and over again. There is no equivalent for Your favours; no repayment for Your kindnesses, confessing thus to the inability to express thanks even though it were to be attempted in every language throughout the whole of time.

May the peace of God and His blessings, benedictions, salutations, and charity (*zakiyyāt*) be on you both, O Commanders of the Believers, O you two caliphs of the Lord of the universe, O you two sons of the *mahdī*-ists' guidance, O father, O grandfather, O sons of Muḥammad, the messenger of God! The peace is that of the one who submits to God in regard to what He imposed on me in losing you both, and the patience concerning what He tries me with after you. May it be so throughout the misfortune and flow of tears over me, O father, O Muḥammad, O Abu'l-Qāsim, O mountain, O what longing, O what agony!

And Creator of the earth and heaven, Resurrector of those who are dead, Exterminator of those who are alive, I am not in doubt as to the choice of God, the Blessed and Glorious, for you and His transporting you to the abode of His favour and residence of His mercy, which provides accommodations for Muḥammad, His messenger, upon him be peace, your grandfather, as well as the Commander of the Believers, ʿAlī b. Abī Ṭālib, your father, and Fāṭima, the radiant virgin, your mother, and your pure righteous *mahdī*-ist forefathers. But the grief of the grief-stricken is a spur to sorrows, causing tears in the eyes. So I am God's and to Him I will return.[267] His are those who submit; for whatever happens to us we are grateful, and for His favours thankful.

God, the Mighty and Glorious, has enhanced the favour and multiplied the benevolence with the patience He has attached to my heart. Subsequently, He honoured me by might and victory, by means of which He spread the foundations of Islam, and with which He

267. Q. 2: 156.

illuminated the hearts of the believers following upon the darkness, and the cessation of hope due to the length of the period of tribulation with the great sedition and its horrors, and its chaos and its convulsions, black darknesses, deaf blindnesses, ignorant barbarism, due to the hypocritical arch deceiver and his apostate partisans, the enemies of religion and supporters of the accursed Iblīs. May God grant them a delay[268] to bring them around bit by bit, and offer them a respite.[269] So they increase in transgression as in an abyss. 'In order for God to separate the impure from the pure' [8: 37] and to show those with minds the confirmation of the promise of God in the book: '*alif lam mim*; Do the people suppose that they will be left alone who say "We believe"; and that they will not be tested? We tried those who came before, and God will certainly know those who are true from those who are false' [29: 1–3], a promise from God not subject to breaking and a determination unchanging, in respect to those of His servant who came before and those of later, until the Day of Judgement. There was, thanks to God and His favour against our enemies, a trial that blinded them, made them deaf, led them astray, caused their apostasy, ruined them, made them degenerate, debased, dishonoured, while we and our friends had an ordeal that secured for us recompense and treasure, and brought about might and glory. Its means were vile but its results noble. Since God, the Mighty and Glorious, wanted the renewal of our dynasty and our might and to show His favour to us, His being burdened with our victory, and the testing of our friends, and the destruction of our enemies, so that when the end of it arrived and it had reached the furthermost degree, the satan came out hopeless, uttering rants, his fire blazing, his persistence continuing. Having been aroused to anger over his transgressors, God allowed retribution[270] among them by giving control to His servant and appointing him to the task. Thus did God clear up its darkness and cast light on its blackness, open its denseness, and avert the distress of it, through me and by my hand, as a mark of esteem by which God singled me out, an excellence whose nobility He bestowed on me, a favour for

268. *amhalhum*, Q. 86: 17.

269. '*wa amlī lahum*', Q. 7: 183 and 68: 45.

270. See Q. 43: 55.

me to store up. It is up to me to restrict it and connect its newness to the older favour to my pure forefathers and the previous beneficence of His to my grandfathers, the rightly guided imams.

Prior to that, swords were unsheathed, so He broke them; soldiers advanced toward me, so He defeated them; the armies of unbelief made common cause against me, so He left them in the lurch; eyes aspired after me, so He effaced them; heads were raised, so He made them bow down; noses were turned up in disdain, so He abased them; cheeks became contemptuous, so He made them humble. God, glorious is His glory, willed the realization of my promise and my command, the consolidation of my triumph, my coming out on top, my being victorious, my being supported and raised high, in fulfilment of His promising Muḥammad, upon whom be peace, to make his community triumph, elevating his proof and the victory of the imams of guidance from his offspring. His decree comes out having mastery; His enemies have been suppressed by force. There is no gainsaying His rule[271] and no going against His command; no partner in praise does He have.

O people of our *daʿwa*, O supporters of our dynasty, O Kutāma!

Praise God and thank Him for that of His favours with which He singles you out, and the vastness of His beneficence. He gives preference in that over all of humans in the west and the east. He, the Mighty and Glorious, puts you first with the greatest favour, and then He attaches to you a magnificent beneficence, and He follows those two with such an abundance of grace to you that it cannot be counted. He made you see while the people were blind, and He informed you while the populace was ignorant. When servants were led astray, He guided you to His religion, to the triumph of His truth and obedience to His friend, the way-marker of guidance, the lamp in the darkness, the pole of religion, His firm rope. In precedence He raised you to His help, in pursuit of obeying Him, seeking shade in the shadow of His dynasty, being illuminated in the light of His wisdom, to the point that should God decree the convulsion of the county, the servants put to the test, darkness enveloping the earth, feet trembling, calamities magnifying, distress growing stronger, hearts aggrieved, God renders you immune. And He guides your hearts, firms up your feet until

271. Q. 13: 41.

God removes it from you in particular and from the servants as a whole, through us and by our hands. So there is on you a favour and on the servants a proof, so that it is removed from you and God, and you appear in a favourable light,[272] satisfying the promise of God,[273] clinging to the rope of God, fighters on behalf of God; those of you alive are happy and your dead are martyrs 'finding their sustenance with their Lord' [3: 169]. Congratulations to you; rejoice!

O God! Truly I am Your servant. You have chosen and approved me; You have honoured me with what You have caused me to inherit of the position of Your most pure, the caliphate of Your friends. You have made me rich and the people poor in their religion and their worldly affairs in need of me. You have shown me mercy. You gave no one strength over me save Yourself; You set me up to give life to Your truth, and to be a testament to Your creatures. Most certainly I speak nothing but the truth, utter only what is correct. There has reached me on the authority of my fathers from our grandfather Muḥammad, the messenger of God, may God bless him and keep him, that he said: 'There is no preacher who preaches but that God stops him on the day of resurrection and questions him about every word and what he meant by it.' So by Your majesty, and Your glory, the highness of Your position and greatness, I do not stand in awe of any enemy, nor do I speak a falsehood, nor thank anyone for favours other than You.[274]

O God, truly have I come to be pleased with the Kutāma because of their holding firmly to Your rope and, in devotion to us, their having patience through misery and adversity for Your sake, acknowledging our precedence, carrying out that which God imposed on the servants because of us in order to reach You by obedience to us.

O God! Approve them, multiply their goodness, erase their wickedness, gather them up among the group of Your prophet to whom they are indebted, and Your friend to whom they are loyal. Leave unchanged Your favour upon them, nay complete it for them.

272. Q. 3: 107.

273. Q. 2: 177.

274. This paragraph and the final phrases of the preceding passage are found only in al-Maqrīzī, yet they appear to belong to the text and so have been retained.

Perfect Your charity to them, and keep their posterity in power. Give their reward liberally and guide them. Purify their hearts. Truly You are the One close by and listening who hears all prayer.

[Sources: al-Jawdharī, *Sīrat Jawdhar*, pp. 55–60, French trans. pp. 80–87; Idrīs, *'Uyūn al-akhbār* (ed. Ya'lāwī), pp. 480–486; al-Maqrīzī, *al-Muqaffā*, biography of al-Manṣūr, 2: 163–168]

8

Khuṭba of al-Manṣūr

On the 'Īd al-naḥr, 336 (21 June 948) at al-Mahdiyya

['Al-Manṣūr rode from his palace in al-Mahdiyya for the prayer of the 'Īd al-naḥr according to the ceremony used previously for the 'Īd al-fiṭr. He prayed with the people and then mounted the *minbar* and said:'][275]

In the name of God, the Merciful, the Compassionate.

God is great! God is great! There is no god but God. And God is great! God is great! And to God belong praise and dominion and creation.

May God be praised, the Lord of the worlds, Governor of affairs, and Resurrector of those in the graves.

I bear witness that there is no god but God, alone, without associate, who is adorned with might, dressed with majesty, stands alone in omnipotence and eternity, who is absolutely one in sovereignty and lordship, the Almighty, the Forgiving, the All-great, the Most powerful, transcending attributes, known by clear signs, worshipped in the earths and the heavens.

I testify that Muḥammad is His servant and His messenger, the seal of His prophets and master of His chosen, the most noble of His friends. He sent him with guidance, providing sight to the blind, rescue from error and ruin, and through him He completed His favour and benefaction to the servants, made clear through him His displeasure and His approval. Thus he, may peace be upon him, conveyed the message and announced the good tidings, proclaimed the warning. God shed light through him on the darkness and cancelled

275. From al-Maqrīzī, *al-Muqaffā*, 2: 168.

the Period of the Ignorance of the ignorant, so much so that those averse became reconciled, unbelievers believed, infidels worshipped, and the obdurate submitted. The truth became clear after having suffered extinction, radiant after eradication in idols worshipped and infidel hearts, hands joined in alliance against it, until God permitted His religion victory over all religions.[276]

The blessings of God be upon Muḥammad, the master of the prophets, he who was well acquainted with burdens, patient through distress and adversity, spending himself for God, strengthening souls in worth and honouring them in importance with God, raising them among the heavenly host in remembrance. Servants do not ask about that as recompense except for love of kin,[277] as his Lord commanded him so that the love for the imams of guidance from his offspring be the cause for his intercession and being assembled within his group.

God is great! God is great! There is no god but God.

And God is great! God is great! To God belong praise, majesty, and glory.

Servants of God! Truly this day of yours is a day of the feast God enjoins for the glorification and honouring of Him, and by it He commences the counted days[278] and seals by it the appointed days.[279] He made it a marker of the time for the pilgrimage to His sacred and revered house, the ancient sanctuary. The gates of heaven open during it to receive prayers. So pray to God most sincerely and implore Him wishfully, approaching with what He commands you to do or restrained you from. From livestock of the smaller animals—the most excellent of all livestock being the female of the camel, the female of bovines, and the ram of sheep—he who sacrifices the young of a goat, for that he will not be rewarded, but for a young ram he will be. All animals slaughtered prior to the prayer are permissible meat, and after the prayer are an acceptable sacrifice. The perfection of the sacrificed animal is soundness of eyes and ears. Avoid the sick one and the deformed, either in having extra limbs or not having some. Sharpen the blade for this purpose and treat the animal gently while

276. Q. 9: 33, 48: 28, and 61: 9.

277. Q. 42: 33.

278. Q. 2: 203.

279. Q. 22: 28. See *Daʿāʾim*, trans. 1: 410.

slaughtering. 'So when they are down slaughtered on their sides, eat of them and feed he who is readily satisfied and the indigent; in that way have We made animals subject to you that you may render thanks' [22: 36].

May God accept from us and from you our sacrifice, and answer our prayers and witness the validity of our actions, for truly He is a noble benefactor, a merciful provider.

[The second *khuṭba:*]

God is great! God is great! There is no god but God.
And God is great! God is great! God is great! Praise belongs to God always, and dominion without end, might overpowering, religion everlasting.[280] So hallowed be He who is unique in perpetuity, absolutely one in sublimity, most glorious in majesty, who overwhelms creation by annihilation and yet bestows favours and benefits, makes it begin through His goodness and provides rewards in His justice. God bears witness and those who glorify Him that there is no god but Him; and likewise [say] the closest angels and believers possessed of minds, that He is equitable, unique in dominion, one in lordship. There is no god but He, the Almighty and Omniscient.[281]

[He bears witness also] that Muḥammad is His servant and His messenger, the seal of the prophets and master of the messengers, the most noble of those chosen, most excellent of those selected. May the blessings of God be upon him and on those who preceded him of the prophets and messengers, and on his successor among the rightly guided imams from his noble progeny, the chaste, the tongues of the truth, the banners of right, guides of the people, summoners to guidance, and the indication of the goal.

O God, among them bless the one who manifested his light, the shiner of his brilliance, the sea of knowledge obscuring the summits, the moon of the heaven, the radiance of the planets, the illumination for the darkness, the uncoverer of the blackness, revivifier of laws, destroyer of seditions. That one is the servant of God and His chosen,

280. 'Religion everlasting', Q. 16: 52.

281. Q. 3: 18.

most sincere friend, Abū Muḥammad, the Imam al-Mahdī bi-llāh, Commander of the Believers, the one approved for the religion, the guide to the plain truth, the sword of God unsheathed against the unbelievers. O God, bless him with the most perfect of Your blessings, connect to him Your salutations, renew for him Your honours, and increase him in Your favours and the bounties of Your benefits and the amplitude of Your gifts.

O God, and bless the one who inherited his position, who was connected to his times, the brilliant banner, the shining lamp, Muḥammad Abu'l-Qāsim al-Qā'im bi-Amr Allāh, Commander of the Believers, whom You chose and honoured, whom You selected and approved, whom You tested and tried, so that, for Your favours, he was thankful and, in the trials, he was patient, unblemished because of the salutation of Your most honoured prophets and chosen saints, to uphold their affairs and their honour, not their shame.

Truly, he was tried by the most serious of sedition and the most severe tribulation, by the nations most deserving of ignominy and execration, for their insolence toward You, their pursuit of rebellion against You, and their repudiation of Your revelation, their declaring Your messenger a liar, their conspiring to extinguish Your light,[282] and their joining forces for the demolition of Your religion. He was not to a likeness of You beseeching and not to other than You submitting and, not in regard to Your support, doubting. He announced it plainly, and he explained it most clearly, a confirmation for the believers, an argument against the unbelievers. But his days were cut short and his death arrived prior to the cure of his rage and the grasping of his revenge, the attainment of his hope. He departed this world agreeable to You, laughing and happy at meeting You, confident of Your reward. O God, bless him with a blessing hopes never reach and deeds ultimately do not result in. Single him out among them by the most sublime of bounty and closest of means. Increase him in good deeds and approval, mercy and affection, of Your bounty of which the giving is never lacking and Your goodness in which there is neither benefit nor harm. Truly we are, because of Your provisions provided through him, kept unblemished, and, because of Your preference for him, we

282. Q. 9: 32 and 61: 8.

are approved. Because of Your reward to him, we are staunch in faith. Our prayers for him and our salutations on him are an obligation from You that we fulfil, a right You impose on us that we carry out.

O God, for You there is praise both before and after for Your favours to me and for Your having made come to me the imamate of rightly guiding forefathers and the caliphate of the righteous imams. You having appointed me to revive religion by upholding the practice of the master of the messengers, empowering the believers and humiliating the unbelievers, during the time of the tyranny of satan, and when falsehood kneeled down on the truth its breast and neck, and You completed my command and You empowered my victory, bestowing amply Your favours upon me. You brought back Your generosity to me and You did not allow to any creature against me power or trouble in that.

To You is the loftiest of my wishes, the most eminent of my desires in allotting gratitude for Your favours, the execution of Your rights, the fulfilment of Your duties, the good fortune of what pleases You, draws nearer to You, brings us closer to You.

O God, most assuredly, I am Your servant and Your friend. You give preference to me and thus I am superior, and You empower me and so I am powerful. I am the mighty because of You, but submissive to You; the noble because of Your ennobling, but modest due to Your vast regard; made glorious due to Your might, but submissive to Your authority, caring out of fear of You. There is no one who desires or dreads but for You and from You. Complete for me Your favour through the good fortune by which Your goodness is extracted and Your mercy and approval are made deserved.

O God, forgive the believers, male and female, the living among them and the dead, those on whom Your favours fall because of us and so they are thankful, and fight on behalf of our dynasty and so have patience, pondering our religion, fulfilling their covenant,[283] submitting to the warden of their affairs,[284] asserting the truth of the right when it comes to them, hastening to the treasures,[285] struggling

283. Q. 2: 177, 13: 20 and others.

284. Q. 4: 59.

285. Q. 3: 114 and 22: 61.

to do righteous deeds. O God, double their reward and strengthen their support, subdue through them the hearts of Your enemies and those who deny the rights of Your saints.

And bless, O God, Muḥammad, Your prophet, the chosen one and Your approved messenger. [Bless also] his pure family and the rightly guided imams. Praise be to God, the Lord of the worlds, as the First and the Last, the Inner and the Outer.

[Source: al-Maqrīzī, *al-Muqaffā*, 2: 168–172 (biography of al-Manṣūr)]

9

Khuṭba of al-Mu'izz

On the 'Īd al-naḥr, 341 (28 April 953) at al-Manṣūriyya

['The Commander of the Believers al-Mu'izz li-Dīn Allāh, may the blessings of God be upon him, hid the passing of his father the Commander of the Believers from the end of the month of Shawwāl, the day of his death, until the tenth of Dhu'l-Ḥijja, the day of the sacrifices. Then he went out for the prayer of the festival wearing solemn attire and the emblems of the imamate. He prayed the festival prayer and then mounted the *minbar*. He delivered his sermon in which he revealed publicly the death of the Commander of the Believers al-Manṣūr bi-llāh. He said:'][286]

In the name of God, the Merciful, the Compassionate.

God is great! God is great! There is no god but God!

And God is great, the mightiest, the most powerful, the Creator, the Governor, possessor of all strength and majesty, of might and sovereignty, the One, the Eternal, the matchless and unique, the highest master, the Inner and the Outer, the First and the Last,[287] instigator of the heavens and the earth with force, master of them with might, governor of them with wisdom, and creator of them with all the wonders of nature they contain and the marvels of their composition and making; He to whom every thing alive and inert speaks a prayer and is evidence for Him, testifying that He is absolutely one, great, and glorious. His causing things to come into being from nothing all at once and altogether is evidence that nothing came before Him and their end at a term indicates that there is no limit to Him. That they are

286. *'Uyūn* (ed. Ya'lāwī), p. 541.

287. Q. 57: 3.

apprehended by definitions establishes that He has no definition. The weakness, impotence, poverty, and want of which created beings are not free is the most eloquent admission and most truthful evidence for the Creator, who is alone, glorious is His praise, in divinity and singularity, in power and lordship, in completeness and perfection, in eternity and perpetuity. God be praised, Lord of the universe, 'who made all things He created excellent' [32: 7]. And He assigned for each living thing its sustenance, and then, next, the guidance of intellect, which established the proof of Him and the necessity of obeying Him, and the scriptures and the messenger though which His word reached fruition.[288] Therefore God bless them all, and Muḥammad, the lord of the messengers who upholds His mention, and the most powerful of them; highest is his powers. He bestowed on him the most noble means and singled him out by every sort of excellence, sending him as the guide for the servants and a light in the land, through him providing knowledge against ignorance, guidance away from error, increasing from little, empowering from lowliness, thereby to bring harmony out of dissonance, lightning through him the murky blackness of gloom. May the blessings of God be upon him and on his rightly guiding (*mahdī*-ist) family, the chosen, the good.

O people, God created you not in jest,[289] nor will He overlook you without purpose. He does not impose on you a hardship in religion,[290] and yet He does not disregard being remembered but rather He created you for worship, obeying Him, and He ordered you to obey His messenger. For obedience He made fixed signs and written decrees, and the most excellent of these signs and the most noble of days for that is the day of the great pilgrimage to the ancient house of God, the dwelling place of Abraham, the friend of God, and the prayer-direction of Muḥammad, the messenger of God, may God bless and keep him. So draw near to God through what He commanded you to do. He provides you the means for it from livestock animals, following the model of Muḥammad's Sunna, he who was the prophet of mercy and guidance, he being conscious of God with proper piety. For truly

288. Q. 6: 115.
289. Q. 23: 115.
290. Q. 22: 78.

God, the Almighty and Glorious, said: 'Their meat and blood do not reach God, but rather it is your piety that reaches Him' [22: 37]. So it is through piety that deeds are accepted and hopes realized. Praise God for His having guided you;[291] thank Him for what He has given you.

Indeed, certainly the best offering is the camel and the best camel is its female. Likewise with bovines. Next the ram among sheep. The soundness of the sacrifices means sound eyes and ears and that it be lawfully owned.

We ask God for our sakes and yours that the reception of this act pleases Him and attains the hoped aim of His approval, and His mercy and beneficence.

[The second *khuṭba*:]

God is great! God is great! There is no god but God!
And God is great! God is great in terms of significance, the mightiest in authority, too manifest in signs and proofs for minds to deny His absolute oneness or wish to define Him. Creator of the heavens and the earth, ruler and governor of them both, the Unique, the Eternal, the One, the Only, who has neither partner nor peer, Creator almighty, the merciful forgiver, He whose judgment effects. What He wants comes to be with perfect mastery of every thing in production, bestowing everything abundantly supported, comprehending all things in knowledge.[292] I praise Him, I beg His assistance, I ask His forgiveness, I seek His guidance; and I defer to Him and I rely on Him in all matters.

I bear witness that there is no god but God, alone, without partner, and I testify that Muḥammad was His choice from among His servants, noblest of His creation, most pure of the chaste, and His messenger to the whole of the world, the one sent by Him with the imamate to men and jinn, to convey the proof of the Lord, to explain the way to the truth. Thus he brought the message of God, was merciful and gracious to the servants of God, patient with the great against the cunning of the unbelievers, until God granted the upper

291. Q. 22: 37.

292. Q. 65: 12.

hand to the truth over falsity, guidance over errors, kindling in him a light in the unknown, in Muḥammad, on whom the most excellent of blessings and their most pure, most complete, copious, enduring, and perpetual. And on the rightly guided (*mahdī*-ist) imams among his noble and chaste progeny who have been chosen for the caliphate and approved for the imamate, confirming their proof in the testament of the Messenger, making obedience to them necessary in the revelation, after His conferring excellence on them over the world through the parentage of Muḥammad, the lord of the messengers, and ʿAlī, the most excellent of the legatees, those whose mother was the mistress of women, the fifth of the Companions of the Cloak. The blessing of God be upon them all. And on the two Commanders of the Believers, al-Mahdī bi-llāh and al-Qāʾim bi-amr Allāh, the two lords of all mortals and imams of right guidance, through whom God raised high the appeal to the truth, and by whom He caused the faith and the faithful to speak, and on whom He established the pillars of religion. By means of their truth, He annihilated the falseness of the pretenders and the lies of the prevaricators,[293] and cut out with their swords the roots of transgressors.[294]

O God, single out the excellent imam, the just successor, the completely pious, the showering rain, he of the splendid marvels, penetrating miracles, the spender of his noble self in times of hardship and troubles, the man patient in misery and loss, until the land was cleared of the tyranny of enemies, Your servant, advocate, chosen one, and friend Abu'l-Ṭāhir al-Manṣūr bika ['the One Victorious through You'], he who relied on You, who committed to You, he who did what pleased You, who drew near to You, coming close to You, he whom You have made us miserable by his loss and left us alone after him. You have separated us from him and made us grieve. So accept his prayer and answer his call; bring together him and his dear ones in the abode of Your paradise and the abundance of Your mercy.

Truly the distress and severe agony due to you O my father, O master, O Ismāʿīl, O Abu'l-Ṭāhir, O sea of the knowledge of the

293. Q. 17: 81.

294. Q. 6: 45.

chaste imams, of *mahdī*-ist guidance, O remnant of the sons of the Messenger and sons of the legatee and the immaculate lady, O imam of the community and key of the door to mercy, O lamp of right guidance, sun of mankind, he who casts light in the deep darkness, O he whom God made special by swift favours, what God has inflicted on you affects us grievously. The misfortune is great; because of losing you, consolation does not exist; and tongues fail in enumerating your excellences or counting your virtues. So, by Him who singled you out with His mark of honour and presented you with the abundance of His gifts, ennobled you with the parentage of His messenger, were it not for what You inspire in me because of him and confirm for me as to upholding the truth of God and defending the community of your forefather, the messenger of God, rescuing them from the flood of ignorance, the sea of error, abysses of disorder, and the wreckage of misfortunes, and what was resolved for me and what sank into my breast of the reward for fidelity to God and His messenger, and to the imams of right guidance, if it were not for that I would strike my face as a traveller in the land, loathing a place of rest, being content with a bag full of provisions, so that death should quickly take me to you, and thereby gain for me nearness to you and the mercy of your Lord.

But instead I ponder, observe and govern. I see for me no other way except patience and consideration, and that I claim your position and acquire your nobility, and so I endure. My Lord makes me patient and so I am patient. Conviction overcomes me and so I forbear. Thus do I say: We belong to God and to God we will return.[295] There is no might or power except through God, the Most High and Mighty, the Merciful and Compassionate, for Him thanks for what afflicts and gratitude for what is done.

Companions of our friends, those who confess their loyalty to us and those who hold fast to our rule! These, by God, are grievously severe trials, which ripen the liver; this convulsion so great that feet cannot be firmly planted, these processions that your imams never cease explaining and, when it comes upon you and the trials in it fall upon you, constantly request of God to plant your feet firmly and

295. Q. 2: 156.

keep your hearts unblemished. So be resolute and safe. Do not go astray and then have to repent! God will never leave His land and His age, through all of time, without someone who upholds the truth on behalf of God, a witness for creation in whom the believers rest assured and through whom the deviant deceiving unbelievers are repudiated.

Indeed God, with praise to Him, created creatures without need on His part for them but rather for worship of Him and the manifesting of His excellence and generosity to them. He made life in them a productive power and death a round cup, and what is after death a reward for work. He explained to you that between these two is the path well trod by His chosen messengers and by the chosen imams of right guidance. He fashioned their reward and share in accord with the value of their communication and effectiveness, and their proficiency with His commandments, and the guiding of His creatures. He created among them degrees of excellence in rank. Thus He, glorious is praise of Him, said: 'Then We made inherit the book those of our servants that We have chosen; among them some were unjust to themselves, some follow a middle course, and some excel in good deeds with the permission of God; that is a great blessing' [35: 32]. God, the blessed, Lord of the universe, He who sanctioned the worldly realm not as a reward for the believers, nor as a punishment for the unbelievers.

O people, there is no living thing that is not subject to death, and no deceased but that after it there is resurrection, and no resurrection except with the accounting, and hence either reward or punishment. So blessedness for he who meets God holding fast to the near relations of His friends, keeping safe by means of their infallibility, upholding the requirements of the loyalty imposed on them by His proofs and His chosen ones, seeking shade in the shadow of the banners of the family of our lord Muḥammad, the messenger of God, lord of the messengers, a day on which nothing will avail but religion and nothing will save except the authenticity of certitude. 'A day on which each soul will find before it what good it has done and what evil it has done; it will wish that there were a great separation between it and them, but God cautioned you about Himself, and God is kind to those who serve' [3: 30].

O people! Actions are in how they end, and the reward from God is commensurate with fidelity to God and to His messenger, and to the imams of right guidance among the offspring of the Messenger. You have seen the lord of the imams, the shepherd of the community and the lamp in the darkness. In residences and shrines he fulfilled there the obligation his Lord imposed on him and carried out the charge given him by his grandfather, Muḥammad. He made clear to you that, if you follow his law, you will never go astray, nor will you be cut off from the mercy of God. Your vision will never grow too dim to follow the straightest path and adhere to great proof. There is no prior guardian but that after him there is a succeeding legatee, who upholds on behalf of God His rights in expectation of realizing his reward, doing what will please Him in accord with his own capacity and the ultimate limit of what he is able to accomplish. 'God burdens no soul beyond its capability' [2: 286]. And, for the maintenance of His religion and for the guiding of His creatures and the care of the community of His prophet, He approves only those most excellent and praiseworthy, unique individuals, of the highest high-mindedness, exemplary character, proud souls, of the purest lineage. God's law runs through His creatures and His wisdom brings about what is impossible to reject, or for speech to refute, such connection of the messengers to the explanation of the path from one time to another, and to proclaim His religion to the extent possible. So He grants to the servants reward according to their obedience and their response to the appeal and acceptance of the guidance, and punishment according to their displeasure, rejection, and repudiation. Rejection of the last of them is not for a believer in the first of them; nor does accepting the truth of the last of them avail the rejecter of the first of them, in regard to the reward and mercy against the painful punishment and abiding shame. God has connected obedience to the imams of right guidance with obedience to the Messenger, and obedience to the Messenger with obedience to Himself. Thus He said: 'Obey God and obey the Messenger and those with command among you' [4: 59]. And that is His practice concerning prophets and messengers. 'You will find no alteration in the law of God, and you will find no deviation in the law of God' [35: 43]. Is there for he who affirms the prophethood of Moses and the messengership of Jesus, on both of whom be peace, a need to state the superiority of our lord Muḥammad, the seal of the prophets and lord of the messengers, if that person rejects his prophethood? Is there any benefit to his acts or a reward for his devotion?

The light, O people, is in us well protected; the gift of your Lord to us is undiminished. So where do you go and in what land do you lose you way? 'Far, very far, is what you are promised' [23: 36]. So obey us and be guided; cling to our rope and be led on the right path. Do that which will have you succeed in your afterlife and be happy! Do not make the greatest of your concerns your present life. The Commander of the Believers, ʿAlī b. Abī Ṭālib, father of the rightly guided (*mahdī*-ist) imams, may the blessing of God be on them altogether, said: 'God makes licit what is permitted and provides assistance for it, and He makes illicit the forbidden and how to guard against it.' So call for what is little when it is plentiful, and what is narrow when it is extended! Thus he commands for you an action and burdens you with the means to live. So the search for what is guaranteed you is not more important for you than seeking what you are supposed to do.

O God! Prompt in us thankfulness for Your blessings, adapt us to what meets Your approval and draws us near to You, and makes necessary a high degree of Your bounty and stored up treasures with You by the completion of Your favour upon me in this world and the next, God of creation, Lord of the universe.

O God! Support me with Your aid; conquer for me Your enemies with a victory that revives religion and by which the community of Muḥammad, lord of the messengers, grows mighty. Provide me the means to visit his tomb and mount his *minbar*, stay in his house, and perform the pilgrimage to Your sacred house, and with our banners halt at these majestic shrines. You have restored our might and that of our friends; You have supported us and them with victory; You have honoured us with triumph and made us prevail over the oppressors, subjugating for us the necks of the rebellious opposition. The times appointed to approach You have gone for fathers and grandfathers. Your promise has no variance; there is no gainsaying Your command. Acceptance and being safe lie in what You have decreed, or have arrived quickly or come slowly.

O God! Make what You bestow a portion of Your beneficence, and what You restore in us a part of Your bounty, and Your favour to us and to the servants, a mercy from You.

O God! And connect to all of the might You restore for us a humility that reassures my heart in the face of Your majesty, glory, and awesome dignity. There is no power except through submission and worship of You; no riches other than in needing You; no security but in apprehension of You; no felicity in this world or the next without Your approval, O Lord of the universe.

O God! Watch over the believers, both men and women, and the Muslims, both male and female, those of them living as well as the dead. Single out the friends of our dynasty and supporters of our *daʿwa*, the fighters, the steadfast, the grateful, with Your mercy, with which they are obligated by obedience to You, to carry out Your orders and maintain friendship with Your friends and enmity to Your enemies.

May God bless Muḥammad, lord of the messengers in former times and later. Remember God, the Mighty, in your invocation;[296] seek His protection both for me and for you. Praise be to God and may His blessings and peace be on our lord Muḥammad and his family in its entirety.

[Sources: al-Jawdharī, *Sīrat Jawdhar*, pp. 76–84; Idrīs, *ʿUyūn al-akhbār* (ed. Yaʿlāwī), pp. 541–548]

296. Q. 2: 152.

10

Khuṭba of al-Muʿizz

[‘We will mention a part of what has come down from the imams of truth, on whom be peace, explaining thereby the loftiness of their positions, the eminence of their ranks, and what is required in regard to them, which is to believe about them what our lord al-Muʿizz li-dīn Allāh, the blessings of God be upon him, said in one of his *khuṭbas*:’][297]

Praise be to God, He who unifies the ones that indicate His oneness, He who makes splendid splendours by the splendour of His lordship, He who makes eternal eternity by the eternity of His divine being, who connects perpetuity with time through the innovating of His divine lordship, who causes that which His causation causes, above that which moves and its mover in its motion, raised high over both of them by the supreme degree of the power of His omnipotence. He was before there was motion and stillness, appearance and concealment, He who makes the ages revolve and eras come around, determiner of night and day, the inner meaning produced by the intellect and the senses, the outer meaning in the picturing of forms and individuals. I thank Him for that in which He singles us out, makes particular to us, chooses us by the letter *lam* in *al-ẓilāl*,[298] gives us prominence without equal among persons, makes us the means to the majesty of His awesomely overwhelming power so that we are its gateways

297. Ḥātim b. Ibrāhīm al-Ḥāmidī, *Kitāb tuḥfat al-qulūb wa farjat al-makrūb*, ed. Abbas Hamdani (forthcoming), ch. 15. Unfortunately we have no other information on this *khuṭba*.

298. I have been unable to determine the meaning of this reference; *al-ẓilāl* ordinarily implies anything that provides shade, or a shadow, or trace.

and its treasurers, its face, its side, its two outstretched hands[299] in His servants. We are the gateway of relief of which whoever enters his sins are pardoned and his torments removed. We are the doorway to His house inhabited, His ceiling raised high,[300] the straight path,[301] and the splendid tidings.[302]

O people! We have shown you a remembrance, so recollect the fullness of the favours to you through us, the perfection of religion that God approved for you as religion, the religion of Islam,[303] no other than that should be sought, or accepted. 'Whoever seeks a religion other than Islam, will find it unacceptable and he will be in the next life among the losers' [3: 85]. Abraham was the first in it; Muḥammad was the end of it. We are its completion, its perfection, and its end. 'Truly Satan is an enemy to you; treat him as an enemy; he calls upon his party only to become the companions of the inferno' [35: 6]. God never ceases to have appear with our appearance a satan in each time and age, in order to show, by his imperfection, our excellence and, in his corruption, our benefit. The Prophet, may God bless him and his family, said: 'There is associated with each prophet a satan and with us there are two satans.' Do not purchase error for guidance[304] by following someone who is insolent and tyrannical, who issues lies, and seizes control, who shed blood in the sacred month,[305] he and those of his forbearers who came earlier, while the people were in an inviolable state. That is disbelief in God and is to declare false what God promised would be secure to His friends. These people 'God cursed for their disbelief' [2: 88][306] and made their hearts remorseless in their inequity.[307] 'Most surely, the curse of God falls on the iniquitous' [11: 18].

O God, grant a pardon to me and to the believers, the men and the women, 'and do not increase the iniquitous except in ruination'

---

299. Q. 5: 64.

300. *al-bayt al-maʿmūr wa'l-saqf al-marfūʿ*, Q. 52: 4 and 5.

301. Q. 1: 6 and other verses.

302. *al-naba' al-ʿaẓīm*, Q. 38: 67 and 78: 2.

303. Q. 5: 3.

304. Q. 2: 16 and 2; 175.

305. al-Muḥarram.

306. Also Q. 4: 46.

307. Echoing Q. 22: 53, 39: 22 and 5: 13.

[71: 28].[308] 'And peace was upon me the day I was born, and the day that I will die, and on the day I will be restored to life' [19: 33]. In existing, there is sublime joy and, in the return, the grace of divine light; from Him it began and to Him it returns.

[Source: Ḥātim b. Ibrāhīm al-Ḥāmidī, *Kitāb tuḥfat al-qulūb wa farjat al-makrūb*, ed. Abbas Hamdani, (forthcoming), ch. 15]

---

308. The whole of this verse is relevant here: 'O Lord, grant a pardon to me and to my parents and to whoever enters my house as a believer and to the believers, the men and women, and do not increase the iniquitous except in ruination'.

11

Khuṭba of Qirwāsh

On 4 Muḥarram 401 (18 August 1010) at Mawṣil

['Among the events of that year came the news that Abu'l-Manīʿ Qirwāsh b. al-Muqallad had assembled the people of Mawṣil and revealed to them his allegiance to the ruler of Egypt. He announced to them his intention to establish a *daʿwa* for him and he invited them to accept that. They responded with the answer of an enslaved flock restrained in aversion and repugnance. The one to give the *khuṭba* was present on that Friday the 4th of Muḥarram; he received a robe of honour and was given a copy of the sermon he was to deliver. It went as follows:'][309]

God is great, God is great; there is no god but God.

For Him is the praise of those who are, by His light, above the floods of fury, who, by His power, burst asunder the pillars supporting idols, who, by His light, cause the rising of the sun of truth from the west, who, by His justice, blot out the tyranny of injustice and break, by His might, the back of inequity so that matters revert to their original state and truth returns to its owners. Distinct in His essence, alone in His attributes, manifest in His signs, solitary in His indications, time passes by Him not so that the seasons preceded Him and forms do not resemble Him so that places contain Him. Eyes do not see Him so that tongues can describe Him. His existence is prior to all existences; His goodness surpasses all goodness. His oneness is fixed in every intellect; His presence exists in every vision. I praise Him with what is required of His grateful friends, the highest of praise for

309. Ibn al-Jawzī, *al-Muntaẓam*, 7: 248–249. On Qirwāsh, see the Introduction, Chapter One, above.

Him. I implore Him to do as He wills and wants. I acknowledge about Him what His most sincere friends and His witnesses acknowledge. I bear witness that there is no god but God, alone, no partner does He have; this is testimony unadulterated with the filth of idolatry or afflicted with delusions of doubt. It is free of deceit; it consists solely of obedience and submission.

I bear witness that Muḥammad is His servant and His messenger, may God bless him. He chose him and selected him for the guidance of the people and for the upholding of the truth so that the message and guidance away from error arrives. The populace was at that time heedless and astray from the path of truth because of following personal whims. He saved them from the worship of idols and commanded them to obey the most Merciful so that the proofs of God and His signs were upheld. He brought to perfection his words by the delivery of them,[310] may God bless him, and bless the first to respond to him, 'Alī, the Commander of the Faithful and lord of the legatees, the establisher of excellence and mercy, the pillar of knowledge and wisdom, the root of the noble and righteous tree generated from the sacred and pure trunk. And [blessings be] on his successors, the lofty branches of that same tree, and on what comes from it: the fruit that grows there.

O people, 'fear God with the piety He is due' [3: 102]; seek His reward: beware of His punishment. You have seen what was recited to you in His book. God the Exalted said: 'the day We summon all the people by their imam' [17: 71], and He said: 'O you who believe, obey God and obey the Messenger and obey those with command among you' [4: 59]. So beware, beware, O people, it is as if the present world were leading you to the next. Its conditions have become clear, the pathway looms up, interrogation is its reckoning and entry is according to its book: 'thus whosoever does an atom's weight of good he will see it; whosoever does an atom's weight of bad he will see it' [99: 7–8]. Climb aboard the ship of your salvation before you founder; 'hold fast to the rope of God altogether, do not scatter' [3: 103]. Know that He knows what is in your souls, so beware of Him.[311] Return to God with

310. Q. 6: 115.

311. Q. 2: 235.

the best of returns, respond to the summoner[312] who is the gateway of compliance, before 'you yourself should say, "Ah, woe is me, I neglected my duty to God and am now among those who scoffed"; or should say, "Alas, if God had guided me I would have been among the God-fearing"; or should say, upon seeing the punishment, "O that I could have another chance that I might be among those who do good"' [39: 56–58]. Be on your guard against heedlessness and indifference before that remorse, and the sorrow, the hoping for another chance, the begging for redemption, and 'it is too late to escape' [38: 3]. Obey your imam and you will be well guided; cling to the holder of the covenant and you will be led on the right way. He has shown you knowledge by which you are led rightly and the path by which you are guided. May God make us and you those who follow His wish; He makes faith his provision. He inspires him with his piety and good sense. May God the most magnificent grant us and you forgiveness, and for all Muslims the same.

[Then he sat and rose again and said:]

Praise be to God who is the Most Glorious and who is the Creator of mankind, who determines the divisions though He is [Himself] matchless in eternity and perpetuity, who causes the dawns to break, who creates phantoms and makes spirits. I praise Him as the First and the Last. I testify that He is the Outward and the Inner. I seek His aid as the divine power. I request His support as the victorious guardian. And I testify that there is no god but God, alone, who has no associate, and that Muḥammad is His servant and His messenger, this testimony from one who affirms His absolute oneness in true faith and who confesses to His divinity willingly, knowing the demonstration of what He summons to and understanding the truth of the proofs for Him. O God, bless your radiant guardian and your greatest friend, 'Alī b. Abī Ṭālib, the father of the rightly guided imams. O God, bless the two pure grandsons al-Ḥasan and al-Ḥusayn and the righteous imams, the best and most excellent, those of them that stood forth

312. Q. 46: 31.

and appeared and those of them that were concealed and hidden.[313] O God, bless the imam who is 'The One rightly guided by You' [*al-Mahdī bi-llāh*], and who conveyed Your commandments and made manifest Your proofs and who took up the cause of justice in Your lands as the guide for Your servants. O God, bless 'The one who takes charge by Your order' [*al-Qā'im bi-amr Allāh*] and 'The one who is victorious through Your support' [*al-Manṣūr bi-naṣr Allāh*], these two who expended themselves for Your satisfaction and waged holy war on Your enemies. O God, bless 'The one who makes strong Your religion' [*al-Mu'izz li-dīn Allāh*], warrior in Your cause who revealed Your authentic signs and prominent proofs. O God, bless 'The one who is mighty because of You' [*al-'Azīz bi-llāh*], by whom the land is cleared and by whom the servants are guided. O God, extend all of Your blessings and the most perfect of Your favours to our lord and master, the imam of the age, fortress of the faith, head of the 'Alid *da'wa* and prophetic religion, Your servant and guardian on Your behalf, al-Manṣūr Abū 'Alī al-Ḥākim bi-Amr Allāh, Commander of the Believers, just as You blessed his rightly guided forefathers and as You ennobled Your saints who were rightly guided. O God, bear in mind what You have appointed him to do and safeguard him in what You observe of him. Favour him in what You bring to him; support his armies; raise high his banners in the east of the land and its west, for indeed You are capable of all things.

[Sources: Ibn al-Jawzī, *al-Muntaẓam*, 7: 248–251; Ibn Taghrī Birdī, *al-Nujūm*, 4: 224–227]

---

313. This is a reference to those imams in the Ismaili line—usually said to be three between Muḥammad b. Ismā'īl b. Ja'far al-Ṣādiq and al-Mahdī—who went into concealment to avoid Abbasid persecution.

12

Khuṭba of al-Āmir

On a Friday, during Ramaḍān

['I quote from some *khuṭbas* of his that I found on a piece of silk on which it had been transcribed for the Lady al-Ḥurra, the Ṣulayḥid queen; applied to it was the noble signature of the Commander of the Believers. It is word for word what follows here:'][314]

In the name of God, the Merciful, the Compassionate.

Praise be to God, He whom the intelligent fall short of understanding the true nature of His essence, and tongues are unable to enumerate His attributes. Those in His earth and His heavens yield to His might; and the splendour of His signs indicates the oneness of His majestic dominion. No one gainsays His decrees; 'nor alters His words' [6: 115].[315] We thank Him for His favours that never cease to make us flow along the good favour of His customary way. We bear witness that there is no god but God, alone, without associate, a testimony that effaces from the one who says it the greatest of his sins, and entails the doubling of his goodnesses. We bear witness also that our grandfather Muḥammad was His servant and messenger whom He sent, the one most excellent of character among His signs. May God bless him and our father, the Commander of the Believers, ʿAlī b. Abī Ṭālib, he who gave alms upon completing his prayers. And bless the chaste imams from the offspring of them both, the demonstrations of guidance and its markers. Peace unconditioned.

O people, until when will you be 'in the flood of forgetfulness' [51; 11], heedless of what is before you in the way of the horror that

---

314. *'Uyūn* (ed. Sayyid), 7: 223.

315. Also Q. 18: 27.

dawns, for perceptions you can not use, for what they summon to and you cannot do, 'On the contrary, you will know; most certainly you will come to know' [102: 3–4]. Then God has mercy for the man who directs his attention to his imam, and who is guided by the straight road of his imam, who satisfies his creator in his rejection and in his confirmation, avoiding obscenity in his speech and words.

Servants of God! This is the month of Ramaḍān, the blessed, which has descended upon you as does the arrival of a guest. So go to utmost length to honour it. Increase its prayers and fasting. Strive to pass its days in sacrifice and piety, and its nights prostrate and bent in prayer, and to fast in it for offences and sins, your fast without drink and food.

Truly, the most decisive is that read on the tops of the *minbar*s, and the hearing of the bedouin and the settled heed; it is the speech of the one completely familiar with the unseen, the one who knows the secrets. God, the Exalted, said in His well-concealed book: 'When the Qurʾan is read, listen to it and hearken well, perhaps you may be treated with mercy' [7: 102]. Seek the protection of God and His power against Satan and his tendency. In the name of God, the Merciful, the Compassionate: 'Ramaḍān is the month in which the Qurʾan was sent down, a guide for the people, explanations of guidance and a criterion; so those of you present during the month, let them fast during it; and those who are sick or travelling should make it up on other days' [2: 185].

God blessed us and you in the magnificent Qur'an, and benefited us and you in the verses and the wise remembrance. We ask the forgiveness of God for us and whoever of the believers who submit to us in unconditional acceptance.

[The second *khuṭba:*]

In the name of God, the Merciful, the Compassionate.

Praise be to God, creator of creation, and knower of the unknown, too high for companions and offspring. God bless our grandfather, Muḥammad, the guide to the shinning path, and our father, the Commander of the Believers, 'Alī b. Abī Ṭālib, his brother and son of his paternal uncle, whom he sanctioned for the position of executor, and the chaste imams among the descendants of both, the clear evident proofs of God to His creatures, peace unconditioned.

O people, truly did God, the Exalted, raise our grandfather Muḥammad to the highest rank and caused him to obtain such nobility as the utmost of hope and desire have never achieved. He, may He be hallowed, issued an order, in which He began with Himself and then included His angels, to revere him in celebration and glorification of his honour. He who is greater than the sayer said: 'Truly, God and His angels blessed the Prophet; O you who believe, bless him and wish him peace unconditionally' [33: 56]. O God, bless our grandfather Muḥammad, Your noble messenger, the guide to Your straight path, he upon whom was revealed: 'Truly, you it was on whom the Qur'an was bestowed coming from the All-wise, All-knowing' [27: 6], and bless, O Lord, the family of Muḥammad.

O God, bless our grandfather Muḥammad, who caused the face of blackish time to shine by his having been sent and to bring by his appearance the good news of all the noble prophets, and for whom was revealed to describe him: 'Truly you are of sublime character' [68: 4]. And bless, O Lord, the family of Muḥammad. And bless, O God, our father, the Commander of the Believers, ʿAlī b. Abī Ṭālib, who held the place with respect to him that had Aaron with Moses, the one who spoke to God. And [bless] our mother Fāṭima, the radiant and chaste, and her two sons the imams Abū Muḥammad al-Ḥasan and Abū ʿAbd Allāh al-Ḥusayn, the best of creatures, and ʿAlī b. al-Ḥusayn Zayn al-ʿĀbidīn, and Muḥammad b. ʿAlī Bākir ʿUlūm al-Dīn, and Jaʿfar b. Muḥammad al-Ṣādiq al-Amīn, and the true imam Ismāʿīl, and Muḥammad his son, possessors of the nobility of the authentic caliphate and they who had all excellences and superiority, and [bless] the imams who were concealed from their enemy all of whose actions consistently opposed them, and on the piercing stars of truth, the suns rising from the places of setting, al-Mahdī bika, al-Qāʾim bi-Amrika, al-Manṣūr bi-Naṣrika, al-Muʿizz li-Dīnika, al-ʿAzīz bika, al-Ḥākim bi-Amrika, al-Ẓāhir fi-Izāz Dīnika, al-Mustanṣir bika, and al-Mustaʿlī bika, who have been taken to Your secure presence, residing there among the companions of the right hand.[316]

316. 'Companions of the right hand', Q. 56: 27.

O God, and I am Your servant al-Āmir bi-Aḥkāmika, he who is thankful for Your favour. You put in proper order for me by Your grace the contracts of good fortune, and You crowned me with the highest crown, adorned with pearls of well-ordered success. You made me inherit the position of caliph which was transferred to me from noble forefathers and grandfathers, and You have made my days the advantages of existence. You have had submit to me the necks of lions, and You have joined in obeying me the hearts of both lords and subjects.

O God, so just as You have singled me out by this clear favour, and made of me Your far-reaching proof to the two worlds, bless me and my offspring with the rope of the imamate until the Day of Judgement, as You promised. Make those who follow me be among those who are safe and successful.

O God, be pleased with the Illustrious Excellency, al-Afḍal, the son of the Lord Commander of the Armies, may he please You with what are the best of deeds.[317] Extend the support of Your mercy to them both without interruption.

Grant victory, O God, to our armies and battalions wherever they are or will be, on land or sea, and extirpate by their swords the root of Your enemies who rebel tyrannically and heretically, and protect the Muslims from them in triumph and victory.

Forgive, O God, the Muslims, men and women, believers, male and female, the alive among them and the deceased. Truly You are the benefactor of good deeds and the forgiver of sins.

'Truly, God has ordained justice, the doing of good deeds, giving to one's relatives, and He has forbidden indecency, evil acts, and oppression; He admonishes you so that you will remember' [16: 90]. Be mindful of the exalted God that He might remember you, and offer thanks that He will advance you.

Praise be to God, the Lord of the universe, and may His blessings be on His messenger, our lord Muḥammad, and his family, the chaste ones.

[Source: Idrīs, *'Uyūn al-akhbār* (ed. Sayyid), pp. 223–227]

---

317. Q. 18: 30.

13

Khuṭba of al-Āmir

On the ʿĪd al-fiṭr

[ʻAnd another among his *khuṭbas* that I found written on a piece of silk and on which was the noble signature: *al-ḥamdu li-lahi rabbu'l-ʿālamīn*, and this is what it said:'][318]

God is great, God is great! And there is no god but God, and praise be to God, and God is great! God is great! And to God thanks, God is great, for that which He guides us, and for Him gratitude for that which He entrusts to us.

In the name of God, the Merciful, the Compassionate.

Praise be to God, who supports through us, who are the body of imams from the family of His prophet, the religion of Islam, which is indispensable, and who hurls at our enemy, the adversaries, perpetual torture and burning incendiaries of piercing flames,[319] and who enforces among those who oppose us the judgments of our sharp swords, the piercing of fencers, which spreads though us the markers of justice, the renown of which is exalted in the easts and wests. We thank Him for His favours, which rainstorms generously grant us by the spraying shower of good deeds poured out, and the realization of our hopes all that is both near and distant. We testify that there is no god but God, alone, without associate, a testimony that produces certainty from its wholesome, most agreeable beverages, and which establish the absolute oneness of the Almighty and the ennobling to the highest degree. We bear witness that our grandfather Muḥammad was His servant and His

318. *ʿUyūn* (ed. Sayyid), 7: 228.

319. 'perpetual torture' and 'piercing flames' Q. 37: 9 and 10 respectively.

messenger by means of whom He guided to the Ḥanīfite religion[320] and the most excellent of the laws and ways of conduct. He inspired him with the Qur'an, so brilliant in its signs and wonders, and He aided him through our father, the Commander of the Believers, ʿAlī b. Abī Ṭālib, his brother and his legatee and the spokesman of his law who explained its peculiar intricacies. May God bless both of them, and the imams from their progeny, a blessing that causes them to attain by it the noblest of return to the ultimate of ranks.

O people, adhere to the mighty Book of God and to the Sunna of His messenger. Act in accord with what we have understood as its command and example. Rely on them both in the practical applications of religion and in its root principles. Do not pass beyond that to what God forbids, plunging thus into the discourse of heresy and its vanities. Truly, that is one of the snares of Satan and his errors. Accordingly, you have heard the words of the exalted God: 'This is my straight path; follow it and do not follow the roads that will separate you from His way' [6: 153]. Obey our exhortation, which issues from the purity of sincere advice and solicitude. 'Do not be dissuaded by Satan' [43: 62] and his supporters, the people of aberration and hypocrisy, from the laws and what they make clear about the way to proper worship. Indeed God, the Exalted, supports it with His books, His messengers, and their miracles with the most potent of argumentation. He makes minds serve these and does not make minds a judge of the laws. The laws emanate from Him and He is the Creator, unique in knowing the unseen and the perfect. He created intellects, like other attributes of created beings, imperfect. Any imperfection that applies to the perfect cannot be attributed to the Almighty. Be thus fully engaged in what God ordered you to do, and shun what He forbade your doing. Submit to Him to be happy and safe; do not seek salvation by disputation and be thus led to error and regret.

Servants of God! This day of yours is a festival in which God honours the religion of Islam, and closes with it the month of

320. The reference to Ḥanīfite religion appears to point to the Qur'anic use of the term which is normally taken as meaning the pure original monotheism of Abraham. Exactly why and how it was used by the Fatimids in this period is, however, not known for certain.

fasting, which distinguishes it over the other months, and gives it preference. He imposes the fasting of it in commemoration of His favours in His Book, which He revealed during it, and promised all of those who do good deeds in it and repent, a hope of realizing a doubling of the good deeds and forgiveness for evil deeds. In it He turns his face toward the months of pilgrimage to His sacred house, which guarantees to each of its pilgrims and those who perform its *ʿumra*, a wiping away of his sins, bringing him to the preciousness of his portion of it. So unsheathe, may God have mercy on you, resolutions that have been accomplished; mount those efforts that will be fulfilled; put first the blessings of those way-markers. Seek refuge in the sanctuary of God, the most all-inclusive of compassions, overcome by His having forgiven crimes, and become successful in the perpetual pleasure of being with Him. Be, for the sanctity of this festival, one who preserves it, doing and saying in it what pleases God. Return to your poor, as assistance, of your funds and kindness. Be safe from a present enemy and a future fear. May God make abundant your share of the lights of certitude. Do for yourself what will be pleasing for you in terms of religion and guard you from the deception of the accursed Satan.

Truly, the most complete of offerings and the clearest of them as guides and means is the words of God and what comprises His statement: 'The word of your Lord is perfect in truth and justice' [6: 115], and He says, may He be exalted: 'When the Qur'an is read, listen to it and hearken to it, perhaps you will be shown mercy' [7: 204]. I seek refuge in God and the guidance and the light those with Him have, away from Satan and the heresy and delusion he summons to. In the name of God, the Merciful, the Compassionate, 'they were ordered to serve God alone, sincere in faith to Him, Ḥanīfs, and to observe prayers and offer alms; that is the proper religion' [98: 5]. God's blessing for us and you in the noble Qur'an; He avails us and you in the verses and wise remembrance. We seek God's forgiveness for us and for those believers who submit to us with true submission.

[The second *khuṭba:*]

In the name of God, the Merciful, the Compassionate.

Praise be to God who makes strong through us, the company of imams from the family of His prophet, the partisans of faith, and causes it to be victorious, and puts in order its affairs. God bless our grandfather, Muḥammad, His messenger who perfected His religion, His miracle, and His proof; and [bless] our father, ʿAlī b. Abī Ṭālib, his brother and legatee, through whom he supported, confirmed and upheld it. And [bless] the imams from the progeny of both with a blessing that multiples for each his eminence and beneficence in the abode of His honour.

O people! He ordered you to bless His prophet, the one sent to all creatures, the most perfect of His messengers in principle and in practice. Accordingly, He, hallowed is He, said in a munificent bestowing of favours: 'Verily, God and His angels extend blessings to the Prophet; O you who believe, bless him and wish him peace without reservation' [33: 56]. O God, bless Muḥammad by means of whose law You provide creation with considerable guidance and direction. You guide them to salvation and the straight path to it. And [bless] the family of Muḥammad. O God, bless Muḥammad through whom You summon to the abode of Islam and its abiding happiness. By it You bring safety from the fire of hell and its most painful chastisement. And [bless] the family of Muḥammad. O God, bless our father, the Commander of the Believers, his brother and his legatee, brother of his *naqʿatihi*[321] companion, truthful advisor, his prudent wazir, dispeller of his troubles in critical life threatening battle situations. [Bless] our mother Fāṭima, the radiant, nurturer of the revelation and the nobility of character and honour that was particular to prophecy. [Bless] al-Ḥasan and al-Ḥusayn two imams of the community and shining lights of the sphere of religion and its perfection in assemblies and festivals. [Bless] the imams from the progeny of al-Ḥusayn proceeding in accord with the Sunna of their prophet in traditions and duties, they who hold fast to the signpost of his law, requiring for the

321. The meaning of this term, and the precise reading of it, is unclear. Perhaps there is an error in the text.

knowledge of any of those who know the imams of right guidance, the chosen of God among the servants, those for every group of whom a guiding imam was appointed.[322] They are the most excellent of the servants and ascetics, and the people of good fortune in establishing orthodox religion and due diligence. A group that adopts anyone else as guardian goes astray; they are ignorant concerning their excellence clearly and conspicuously. They reject the truth by casting it behind them, paying it no attention, perpetrating a false thing by their pertinacity and their splitting off.

O God, most certainly I am Your servant, the one who summons to Your path, the fighter against the enemies of Your messenger, the explainer of Your signs, the indication of that which You promised to Your friends of Your paradise, the clarifier of Your demonstrations and proofs, and the seeker of Your forgiveness and approval. O God, grant me victory over the unbelievers and infidels; make through me appear justice and empower religion, support the warriors and fighters, protect the territory of the believers, defend Islam and the Muslims, guide to the distinct path of the truth those who want guidance. Be for me the best guardian and defender through Your mercy, O most Merciful of the merciful. And praise be to God, the Lord of the worlds. God bless our lord Muḥammad and his family the chaste.

[Source: Idrīs, *ʿUyūn al-akhbār* (ed. Sayyid), pp. 228–231.]

322. Possible reference to Q. 32: 24.

Glossary

Anṣār:	those in and from Medina who assisted and supported the Prophet.
Buyids:	a dynasty of Daylamite origin which ruled the eastern Islamic lands from the middle of the 4th/10th to the middle of the 5th/11th centuries.
dāʿī:	the person who summons or appeals on behalf of the true faith, hence an agent or missionary for the imam and his *daʿwa*.
daʿwa:	the invitation or appeal issued by God and the imam for men to believe in and accept the true religion, Islam.
Dhu'l-Fiqār:	the legendary sword acquired by the Prophet and then given by him to ʿAlī.
duʿāʾ:	prayer or invocation.
ḥāfiẓ:	a person who knows the Qurʾan by heart.
hawdaj:	a camel litter.
Ibādīs:	the Khārijite sect to which the rebel Abū Yazīd belonged.
ʿĪd al-aḍḥā:	the festival of the feast of sacrifice on the 10th of Dhu'l-Ḥijja. Also called ʿĪd al-naḥr.
ʿĪd al-fiṭr:	the festival of the breaking of the fast following the close of Ramaḍān.
ʿĪd al-naḥr:	See ʿĪd al-aḍḥā.
iḥrām:	entering a state of ritual purity, of consecration, particularly as in putting on the clothes worn for the pilgrimage.
iqāma:	the call to stand for prayer.

jihād: the waging of holy war, especially against infidels.

Khārijites: a Muslim sect noted for its opposition to both Sunnis and Shiʿis.

khaṭīb: the preacher attached to a mosque who delivers the Friday sermon.

Kiyāna: a high fortress in the Ḥoḍna mountains of what is now Algeria and the last refuge of the Khārijite rebel Abū Yazīd.

Kutāma: the Berber tribe that were the first to support the mission in North Africa of the *dāʿī* Abū ʿAbdallāh al-Shīʿī and then of the Fatimid imams.

Legatee: Arabic *waṣī*, the executor or administrator of an estate or legacy, also its guardian.

Mahdiyya: the North African coastal town founded by the caliph al-Mahdī to serve as the capital of the Fatimid empire.

manḥar: a place where animals are slaughtered for sacrifice.

maqṣūra: box or stall in a mosque near the *miḥrāb* reserved for the ruler.

miḥrāb: the principal place or niche in a mosque pointing out the direction of Mecca.

minbar: the pulpit of a mosque.

mu'adhdhin: the one who calls to prayer.

Muḥājirūn: those Companions of the Prophet who left Mecca and joined him in Medina.

muḥannak: a class of court eunuchs distinguished by wrapping the tail of their turbans under the chin.

muṣallā: the place for prayer, especially the open ground of a festival square used for *ʿīd* prayers and sermons.

maṣṭaba: a raised bench on the outside of homes and buildings for people to sit on.

najwā: a confidential discourse.

rakʿa: an inclination of the head during prayer so that the palms of the hands rest on the knees.

Raqqāda: a suburb of Qayrawān that became, for a time, the administrative capital under the Aghlabids and earliest Fatimids.

ṣāʿ:	a dry measure of four *mudd*, each *mudd* weighing a *riṭl* and one-third.
Ṣanhāja:	the Berber tribal group from which came the Zīrids.
Seljuks:	a Turkish dynasty which dominated the Islamic east beginning in the mid-11th century.
takbīr:	declaring the greatness of God by saying *Allāhu akbar*.
tashahhud:	making a profession of religion by testifying to the unity of God and the apostleship of Muḥammad.
ʿumra:	the sacred, lesser visitation (as distinct from the *ḥajj* or ritual pilgrimage) to the holy cities of Mecca and Medina.
ʿUqaylids:	an Arab dynasty of northern Iraq which flourished from about 380/990 until 564/1169.
Zīrids:	a Berber dynasty of North Africa who began as the appointed successors of the Fatimids.
ẓuhr prayer:	the afternoon prayer.

Bibliography

al-Amīnī, Muḥammad Hādī. *'Īd al-Ghadīr fī 'ahd al-Fāṭimiyīn*. Najaf, 1962; Tehran, 1997.

'Arīb b. Sa'd al-Qurṭubī. *Ṣilat ta'rīkh al-Ṭabarī*, ed. M. J. De Goeje. Leiden, 1897.

Bosworth, C. E. 'Marwān I b. al-Ḥakam', *EI2*.

Dietrich, A. 'al-Ḥadjdjādj b. Yūsuf', *EI2*.

Fierro, Maribel. 'On al-Fāṭimī and al-Fāṭimiyyūn', *JSAI*, 20 (1996), pp. 130–161.

Goldziher, I., C. van Arendonk and A. S. Tritton, 'Ahl al-bayt', *EI2*.

Golmohammadi, J. 'Minbar. 2', *EI2*.

Halldén, Philip. 'What is Arab Islamic Rhetoric? Rethinking the History of Muslim Oratory Art and Homiletics', *International Journal of Middle East Studies*, 37 (2005), pp. 19–38.

Halm, Heinz. *Das Reich des Mahdi: Der Aufstieg der Fatimiden*. Munich, 1991; English trans. M. Bonner, *The Empire of the Mahdi: The Rise of the Fatimids*. Leiden, 1996.

—— *Die Kalifen von Kairo: Die Fatimiden in Ägypten, 973–1074*. Munich, 2003.

al-Ḥāmidī, Ḥātim b. Ibrāhīm. *Kitāb tuḥfat al-qulūb wa farjat al-makrūb*, ed. Abbas Hamdani (forthcoming).

Heinrichs, W. P. and Afif Ben Abdesselem. 'Sadj'' (parts 1–3), *EI2*.

Ibn 'Abd al-Ẓāhir. *al-Rawḍa al-bahiyya al-zāhira fī khiṭaṭ al-mu'izziyya al-qāhira*, ed. Ayman Fu'ād Sayyid. Cairo, 1996.

Ibn al-Athīr, 'Izz al-Dīn Abu'l-Ḥasan 'Alī. *al-Kāmil fi'l-ta'rīkh*, ed. C. J. Tornberg. Leiden, 1867; reprinted Beirut, 1965–1967.

Ibn al-Dawādārī, Abū Bakr b. 'Abdallāh b. Aybak. *Kanz al-durar wa jāmi' al-ghurar*, Pt. 6, *al-Durra al-muḍiyya fī akhbār al-dawla al-Fāṭimiyya*, ed. S. al-Munajjid. Cairo, 1961.

Ibn Ḥajar al-ʿAsqalānī. *Rafʿ al-iṣr ʿan quḍāt Miṣr*, ed. ʿAlī Muḥammad ʿUmar. Cairo, 1998.

Ibn Ḥammād, Abū ʿAbdallāh Muḥammad b. ʿAlī al-Ṣanhājī (also Ibn Ḥamādu). *Histoire des Rois ʿObaïdides* (*Akhbār mulūk banī ʿUbayd wa sīratihum*), ed. and tr. M. Vonderheyden. Algiers and Paris, 1927; ed. ʿAbd al-Ḥalīm ʿUways. Cairo, 1980.

Ibn ʿIdhārī, Abu'l-ʿAbbās Aḥmad b. Muḥammad al-Marrākushī. *al-Bayān al-mughrib fī akhbār al-Andalus wa'l-Maghrib*, vol. 1, ed. G. S. Colin and É. Lévi-Provençal. Beirut, 1948.

Ibn al-Jawzī, Abu'l-Faraj ʿAbd al-Raḥmān. *al-Muntaẓam fī ta'rīkh al-mulūk wa'l-umam*. Hayderabad, 1939.

Ibn Khallikān, Aḥmad b. Muḥammad. *Wafayāt al-aʿyān*, ed. Iḥsān ʿAbbās. 8 vols. Beirut, 1968. Eng. trans. M. de Slane. 4 vols. Paris, 1842–1871.

Ibn al-Ma'mūn, Jamāl al-Dīn Abū ʿAlī Mūsā. *Nuṣūṣ min Akhbār Miṣr*, ed. Ayman Fu'ād Sayyid. Cairo, 1983.

Ibn Muyassar, Tāj al-Dīn Muḥammad. *al-Muntaqā min Akhbār Miṣr*, ed. Ayman Fu'ād Sayyid. Cairo, 1981.

Ibn Saʿīd, ʿAlī b. Mūsā al-Maghribī. *al-Nujūm al-zāhira fī ḥulā ḥaḍrat al-Qāhira, al-qism al-khāṣṣ bi'l-Qāhira min Kitāb al-Mughrib fī ḥulā al-Maghrib*, ed. Ḥusayn Naṣṣār. Cairo, 1970.

Ibn al-Ṣayrafī, Abu'l-Qāsim ʿAlī. *al-Ishāra ilā man nāla al-wizāra*, ed. Ayman Fu'ād Sayyid. Cairo, 1990.

Ibn Taghrī Birdī, Jamāl al-Dīn Abu'l-Maḥāsin. *al-Nujūm al-zāhira fī mulūk Miṣr wa'l-Qāhira*. Cairo, 1929–1949; Cairo, 1963–1971.

Ibn al-Ṭuwayr, Abū Muḥammad ʿAbd al-Salām. *Nuzhat al-muqlatayn fī akhbār al-dawlatayn*, ed. Ayman Fu'ād Sayyid. Beirut, 1992.

Ibn Ẓāfir, Jamāl al-Dīn ʿAlī. *Akhbār al-duwal al-munqaṭiʿa*, ed. André Ferré. Cairo, 1972.

Idrīs ʿImād al-Dīn. *ʿUyūn al-akhbār*, ed. M. al-Yaʿlāwī as *Ta'rīkh al-khulafā' al-Fāṭimiyyīn bi'l-maghrib: al-qism al-khāṣṣ min Kitāb ʿuyūn al-akhbār*. Beirut, 1985.

—— *ʿUyūn al-akhbār, al-sabʿ al-sādis* (vol. 6), ed. Muṣṭafā Ghālib. Beirut, 1984.

—— *ʿUyūn al-akhbār, al-sabʿ al-sābiʿ* (vol. 7), ed. A. F. Sayyid in his *The Fatimids and Their Successors in Yaman: The History of an Islamic Community*. London, 2002. Manuscript copy, Fyzee, Hayderabad.

al-Jawdharī, Abū ʿAlī al-Manṣūr. *Sīrat Ustādh Jawdhar*, ed. M. K. Ḥusayn and M. ʿAbd al-Hādī Shaʿīra. Cairo, 1954; French trans. M. Canard, *Vie de l'ustadh Jaudhar*. Algiers, 1958.

Lammens, H. 'al-Mughīra b. Sh'ba', *EI2*.

Lewicki, T. 'al-Nukkār', *EI2*.

Madelung, Wilferd. 'al-Mahdī', *EI2*.

al-Mālikī, Abū Bakr. *Kitāb riyāḍ al-nufūs fī ṭabaqāt ʿulamāʾ al-Qayrawān wa Ifrīqiya*, ed. Bashīr al-Bakkūsh. Beirut, 1981–1983.

al-Maqrīzī, Taqī al-Dīn Abu'l-ʿAbbās Aḥmad. *Ittiʿāẓ al-ḥunafāʾ bi-akhbār al-aʾimma al-Fāṭimiyyīn al-khulafāʾ*, vol. 1, ed. Jamāl al-Dīn al-Shayyāl, and vols. 2–3 ed. Muḥammad Ḥilmī Muḥammad Aḥmad. Cairo, 1967–1973.

—— *al-Khiṭaṭ (al-maʿrūf bi'l-mawāʿiẓ wa'l-iʿtibār bi'dhikr al-khiṭaṭ wa'l-āthār)*, ed. of *musawwada*, A. F. Sayyid. London, 1995. Complete text, 2 vols. Bulāq, 1853. New edition by A. F. Sayyid, 5 vols, London, 2002–2004 (unless otherwise noted all references are to this edition).

——*Kitāb al-muqaffā al-kabīr*, ed. M. al-Yaʿlāwī. 8 vols. Beirut, 1991.

Metz, Adam. *The Renaissance of Islam*, tr. S. Kh. Bukhsh and D. S. Margoliouth. London, 1937. 'Sermons', pp. 317–332.

al-Musabbiḥī, al-Mukhtār 'Izz al-Mulk Muḥammad. *al-Juz al-arbaʿūn min Akhbār Miṣr*. Pt. 1 (historical section), ed. Ayman Fuʾād Sayyid and Th. Bianquis. Cairo, 1978.

al-Mustanṣir. see *Sijillāt*.

al-Nuwayrī, Shihāb al-Dīn Aḥmad. *Nihāyat al-arab fī funūn al-adab: al-Juz al-thāmin wa'l-ʿishrūn*, ed. Muḥammad Muḥammad Amīn and Muḥammad Ḥilmī Muḥammad Aḥmad. Cairo, 1992.

Pedersen, J. 'Minbar. 1' and 'Khaṭīb', *EI2*.

Pellat, Ch. 'Ibn Sharaf al-Ḳayrawānī', *EI2*.

Poonawala, Ismail K. *Biobliography of Ismāʿīlī Literature*. Malibu, CA, 1977.

Qāḍī al-Nuʿmān, *Daʿāʾim al-Islām*, ed. A. A. A. Fyzee. Cairo, 1951–1961; tr. Fyzee, revised by Ismail K. Poonawala, *The Pillars of Islam*, 2 vols. New Delhi, 2002–2004.

——*Iftitāḥ al-daʿwa wa ibtidāʾ al-dawla*, ed. Farhat Dachraoui. Tunis, 1975; tr. Hamid Haji as *Founding the Fatimid State: The Rise of an Early Islamic Empire*. London, 2006.

——*Kitāb al-majālis wa'l-musāyarāt*, ed. al-Ḥabīb al-Faqī, Ibrāhīm Shabbūḥ, and Muḥammad al-Yaʿlāwī. Tunis, 1978.

——*Sharḥ al-akhbār fī faḍāil al-aʾimma al-aṭhār*. 3 vols. Beirut, 1994.

al-Qalqashandī, Shihāb al-Dīn Aḥmad. *Ṣubḥ al-aʿshā fī ṣināʿat al-inshāʾ*. Cairo, 1912–1938.

Reckendorf, H. 'al-Ashʿath', *EI2*.

Sanders, Paula. *Ritual, Politics, and the City in Fatimid Cairo*. Albany, NY, 1994.

——'Claiming the Past: Ghadīr Khumm and the Rise of Ḥāfiẓī Historiography in Late Fātimid Egypt,' *Studia Islamica*, 75 (1992), pp. 81–104.

Sayyid, Ayman Fu'ād. *al-Dawla al-Fāṭimiyya fī Miṣr: Tafsīr jadīd*, 2nd ed. Cairo, 2000.

Steingass, F. *A Comprehensive Persian-English Dictionary.* Beirut, 1982.

Sijillāt al-Mustanṣiriyya, ed. 'Abd al-Mun'im Mājid. Cairo, 1954.

Schmucker, W. 'Mubāhala,' *EI2*.

Stern, S. M. *Studies in Early Ismā'īlism.* Jerusalem and Leiden, 1983.

—— 'Abū Yazīd al-Nukkārī,' *EI2*.

al-Suyūtī, Jalāl al-Dīn. *Ḥusn al-muḥāḍara fī akhbār Miṣr wa'l-Qāhira.* 2 vols. Beirut, 1997.

Tamīm b. al-Mu'izz. *Dīwān Tamīm b. al-Mu'izz li-Dīn Allāh al-Fāṭimī*, ed. M. Ḥ. al-A'ẓamī et al. Cairo, 1957.

Tritton, A. S. 'Ahl al-kisā',' *EI2*.

Vaglieri, L. Veccia. 'Ibn Muldjam,' *EI2*.

Walker, Paul E. *Early Philosophical Shiism: The Ismaili Neoplatonism of Abū Ya'qūb al-Sijistānī.* Cambridge, 1993.

——*Abū Ya'qūb al-Sijistānī: Intellectual Missionary.* London, 1996.

—— *Ḥamīd al-Dīn al-Kirmānī: Ismaili Thought in the Age of al-Ḥākim.* London, 1999.

——*Exploring an Islamic Empire: Fatimid History and its Sources.* London, 2002.

——'Purloined Symbols of the Past: The Theft of Souvenirs and Sacred Relics in the Rivalry between the Abbasids and Fatimids,' in F. Daftary and J. Meri, eds. *Culture and Memory in Medieval Islam: Essays in Honour of Wilferd Madelung.* London, pp. 364–367.

Wensinck, A. J. 'Khuṭba,' *EI2*.

al-Ya'lāwī (Yalaoui), Muḥammad. *al-Adab bi-Ifrīqiya fi'l-'ahd al-Fāṭimīyya.* Beirut, 1986.

Index

الخطب الفاطمية

١

خطبة القائم

في عيد الفطر سنة ٣٠٢ بالإسكندرية

[ولما كان عيد الفطر والقائم بأمر الله عليه سلام مقيم بالإسكندرية خرج صلى الله عليه فصلى بالناس صلاة العيد في السنة المذكورة وخطب خطبة العيد بالإسكنردية فقال:[١]]

بسم الله الرحمن الرحيم، وبه نستعين.

الله أكبر الله أكبر لا إله إلا الله.

والله أكبر، الله أكبر، لا حكم إلا لله، لا طاعة لمن عصى الله. «ألاَ لَعْنَةُ الله عَلَى الظَّالمِينَ الذينَ يَصَدُّونَ عَن سَبِيلِ الله وَيَبْغُونَهَا عِوَجًا» [١١: ١٨-١٩]، «وَيَقْتُلُونَ الذينَ يَأْمُرُونَ بِالقِسْطِ مِنَ النَّاسِ» [٣: ٢١].

الحمد لله الخلاّق العليم، المدبر الحكيم، الذي «لَهُ مَقَالِيدُ السَّمَاوَاتِ وَالأَرْضِ» [٣٩: ٦٣[٢]] «وَهُوَ عَلَى كُلِ شَيءٍ قَدِيرٌ» [٥: ١٢٠[٣]] «مَا يَكُونَ مِن نَجْوَى ثَلاَثَةٍ إلاَ هُوَ رَابِعُهُم وَلاَ خَمْسَةٍ إلاَ هُوَ سَادِسُهُم وَلاَ أَدْنَى مِن ذَلِكَ

[١] إدريس، عيون الأخبار، تحقيق اليعلاوي، ص ١٩٨.
[٢] أيضا آية ٤٢: ١١.
[٣] وغيرها.

وَلاَ أَكْثَرَ إِلاَ هُوَ مَعَهُم أَيْنَ مَا كَانُوا» [٥٨: ٧]، أحاطت بهم قدرته وعلمه «ولاَ يُحيطُونَ بشَيْءٍ من علْمه إلاَ بما شَاءَ» [٢: ٢٥٥]، «وَعَنَت الوُجُوهُ للحَيِّ القَيُّومِ وَقَدْ خَابَ مَن حَمَلَ ظُلْمًا» [٢٠: ١١١]. هو الأول قبل كل أوان وزمان ومكان وغاية ونهاية، وهو اللطيف الخبير الذي «خَلَقَ السَمَاوَاتِ بغَيرِ عَمَدٍ تَرَونَهَا» [٣١: ١٠] ففلق مصابيحها وأضاء شمسها وأنار قمرها وفجّر ينابيعها «وَالأَرْضَ بَعْدَ ذَلكَ دَحَاهَا أَخْرَجَ منهَا مَاءَهَا وَمَرْعَاهَا» [٧٩: ٣٠-٣١]. فسبحان الذي لا يدل عليه إلا بآياته وما فطر من أرضه وسماواته وبان لخليقته من تدبيره وتكامل رسله إلى الأمم كافّة من عباده إذ قال لهم: إنّ الله فاطر «السَمَاوَاتِ وَالأَرْضِ يَدْعُوكُم لِيَغْفِرَ لَكُم مِن ذُنُوبِكُم وَيُؤَخِّرَكُم إِلَى أَجَلٍ مُسَمًّى» [١٤: ١٠].

معاشر الناس، إني أصبتُ أمتكم هذه كما أصاب رسول الله صلى الله عليه وسلم اليهود والنصارى معهم التوراة والإنجيل ومعهم كنائس وبيع، فدعاهم صلى الله عليه وسلم إلى كمال العلم بما في التوراة والإنجيل فما آمنوا به[١] فحكم عليهم صلى الله عليه وسلم بالسيف والجزية والسبي والنهب والجلاء. وكذا أصبتُ أمتكم هذه قد اتّخذت قرآنكم عِضِين[٢] ونبذتموه وراء ظهوركم واشتريتم به ثمنًا قليلاً[٣] فقلت لكم:

«يَا أَهْلَ الكتَاب، لَسْتُم عَلَى شَيْءٍ حَتَّى تُقيمُوا التَوراةَ وَالإِنْجِيلَ وَمَا أُنزِلَ إِلَيكُم من رَبِّكُم» [٥: ٦٨]. «يَا أَهْلَ الكتَاب، تعَالَوا إلَى كَلمَةٍ سَوَاءٍ بَيْنَنَا وَبَيْنَكُم أَلاَ نَعْبُدَ إِلاَ اللهَ وَلاَ نُشْرِكَ به شَيئًا وَلاَ يَتَّخذ بَعْضُنَا بَعْضًا أَرْبَابًا مِن دُونِ الله» [٣: ٦٤]. فرميتموني بأني خارجيٌّ مبتدع، ورأيتم جهادي وقتالي والله ناصري ومعيني ورأيت أهل الأمصار وقد دعوا عليّ في مساجدهم والله عز وجل سائلهم عن كلامهم «يَحْسَبُونَ أَنَّهُم عَلَى شَيْءٍ

[١] آمنوا به: قاموا به، Stern
[٢] اقتباس من القرآن ١٥: ٩١
[٣] اقتباس من القرآن ٣: ١٨٧

ألاَ إنَّهُم هُمُ الكَاذِبُونَ» [٥٨: ١٨]، فظنت[١] الأمة الكاذبة المرتدّة الناكصة على عقبها[٢]، المغيرة لأمر ربها أنها قد أصابت فيما ادّعته لخلفائها الذين يزعمون أنهم خلفاء رب العالمين مثل صبيّ لم يبلغ ومثل غلام لم يعقل، ومثل طفل يدبر الإسلام بزعمهم ومعهم[٣] امرأة تحمل إليهم الخمور من كل واد وكل قطر على ظهور الخيل وبطون السفن، كما قال الله تعالى: «اتَّخَذُوا أحْبَارَهُم وَرَهْبَانَهُم أرْبَابًا مِن دُونِ الله» [٩: ٣١] فأنفقوا أموال اليَتامى والمساكين ظلمًا منهم وعدوانًا لمغنٍّ عوّادٍ، وطنبراني حاذق ومعزفاني وطبّال مجيد، ورأت ولاتها في الأمصار يصعد أحدهم أعواد منبر رسول الله صلى الله عليه وسلم فيعظ الأنام وهو غير واعظ لنفسه، وينزل عن ذلك الموضع فيسألهم[٤] في البلد عن[٥] مغن ومغنية وطنبراني وعوّاد وسارق وباخس مكيال وناقص ميزان، فيجيء ذلك إليه، لعن الله الظالمين وأعدّ لهم سعيراً[٦]، فلا آمرٌ بمعروف ولا ناهٍ عن منكر.

حتى إذا قام عبد الله الضعيف المسكين يدعوهم إلى الله «كَادُوا يَكُونُونَ عَلَيهِ لِبَداً» [٧٢: ١٩] «مِنّ كُلِ حَدَبٍ يَنسلُون» [٢١: ٩٦]، ومن كل حزن يهطلون. فهلمّوا عباد الله إلى ما دعا الله تعالى في كتابه! كلاّ فالله الذي لا إله إلا هو «بَلْ نَقْذِفُ بِالحَقِّ عَلَى البَاطِلِ فَيَدْمَغُهُ فَإذَا هُوَ زَاهِقٌ وَلَكُمُ الوَيْلُ مِمَّا تَصِفُونَ» [٢١: ١٨].

يا أيها الناس، إنكم أصبحتم في عمياء مظلمة وسوداء مدلهمة، غامرة بفتنة تنقلكم إلى فتنة. قد أضلتكم بأضاليلها المبتدعة وشملتكم بأكنافها المهلكة. فأنتم عائمون في غواشيها مغرقون في مباديها، قد

---

[١] فتظن: فظنت، Stern
[٢] اقتباس من ٢٣: ٦٦.
[٣] ومعهم: ومعه، Stern
[٤] فيسألهم: فيسألكم، Stern
[٥] عن: من، Stern
[٦] اقتباس من القرآن ٣٣: ٦٤

غُلّقت عليكم أبوابها، وعميت عليكم أسبابها، فأعلام دينكم طامسة، وآثار نبيكم دارسة، والمنكر فيكم ظاهر، والمعروف فيكم داثر، فأين تذهبون؟ إلى الجحيم لا محالة تُسحبون، أفمثابون أنتم أم معذبون؟ أشكرتم لله نعمته، لأنها حجته عليكم، ما استحفظكم من أمر دينه والذب عن حرم نبيه صلى الله عليه وعلى آله، الذي استنقذكم من الهلكة؟ قال الله عز وجل: «يَا أَيُّهَا الذينَ آمَنُوا أَطِيعُوا اللهَ وَأَطِيعُوا الرَسُولَ وَأولِي الأمْرِ مِنْكُم» [٤: ٥٩]، فجعل الطاعة فريضة وصل[١] بها طاعة ولاة أمره، فهم القائمون لله بحقه والداعون إليه مَن رغب إلى طاعته، واستخصّهم بالإمامة التي هي أعظم الدرجات بعد النبوة، وفرض على العباد حقوقها، وأمرهم بأدائها، وجعلها موصولة بطاعته، وضاعف لهم الثواب بقدر ما والَوا من أمروا بولايته. وليس للإمام أن ينقُص الرعية حقها، ولا للرعية أن تنقص حق إمامها. فمن حق الرعية على إمامها: إقامة كتاب الله جل ثناؤه، وسنة نبيه، صلى الله عليه وعلى آله، والأخذ لمظلومها من ظالمها. ولضعيفها من قويها، ولوضيعها من شريفها، والتفقد لمعاشها واختلاف حالاتها، نظر الشفيق على عياله بجهده، الكالئ لهم بعينه، فإنه عز وجل فيما حمد من أخلاق نبيه ورسوله قال: «لَقَدْ جَاءَكُم رَسُولٌ مِن أنْفُسِكُم عَزِيزٌ عَلَيهِ مَا عَنِتُّم حَرِيصٌ عَلَيكُم بِالمُؤْمِنِينَ رَؤُوفٌ رَحِيمٌ» [٩: ١٢٨]. فإذا فعل ذلك كان على الرعية إجلاله وإكرامه ومكانفته والاستعداد والاستقامة ما استقام على كتاب الله وسنة نبيه صلى الله عليه وسلم.

«اللهُمَّ، فَاطِرَ السَمَاوَاتِ وَالأرْضِ عَالِمَ الغَيْبِ وَالشَهَادَةِ أنْتَ تَحكُمُ بَيْنَ عِبَادِكَ فِيمَا كَانُوا فِيهِ يَخْتَلِفُونَ» [٣٩: ٤٦]. اللهم، وصلّ على المهدي بالله أبي محمد أمير المؤمنين كما صليتَ وباركتَ على الخلفاء الراشدين

---

[١] وصل: ووصل، Stern

المهديين الذين قاموا بالحق وبه يعدلون، اللهم كما جعلتهم للدين غياثًا، وللعباد ملجأ وملاذاً فأقرّ به أعين المؤمنين، وانصرْه على أعدائك العصاة الفاسقين الكفرة المارقين الظالمين، إله الخلق رب العالمين.

اللهم، انصر جيوشنا وسرايانا في مشارق الأرض والمغاربها، وبرها وبحرها، وسهلها وجبلها. اللهم، العن أعداءك وأهل معاصيك من الأولين والآخرين، وقوم نوح في العالمين[١]، «إِنَّهُم كَانُوا قَومًا فَاسِقِينَ» [٥١: ٤٦]، وعاداً وثمودا وأصحاب الرس[٢]، وجبابرة بني أمية وبني مروان[٣]، ومعاوية بن أبي صفيان الذي اتخذ من عبادك نصيبًا مفروضًا[٤] بالدنانير والدراهم وقاتل بهم المهاجرين والأنصار، والعن عمرو بن العاص وعتبة بن أبي سفيان[٥] والوليد بن عتبة[٦] والوليد بن أبي مُعَيط والوزغ ابن الوزغ - يعني مروان بن الحكم - والمغيرة بن شعبة وزياد بن سمية وعبيد الله بن زياد والسلمي وذا الكلاع وحوشبا والأشعث بن قيس وعبدالملك بن مروان والحجاج بن يوسف وعبد الرحمان بن ملجم والناكثين والقاسطين والمارقين والخالفين والمبتدعين والمرجئين والقاعدين عن الجهاد مع أمير المؤمنين، اللهم انصر الحق وطلابه وأذل الباطل وأحزابه، إنك أنت العزيز الحكيم.

[المصدر: إدريس، عيون الأخبار، ١٩٨-٢٠٢]

[١] اقتباس من آية ٣٧: ٧٩.

[٢] آية ٢٥: ٣٨. أصحاب الرس-الرس هو البئر- هم القوم الكافرون الذين كذبوا شعيبا

[٣] لمعرفة الأشخاص التالية اطلع على حاشية الترجمة الإنجليزية لهذه الخطبة.

[٤] اقتباس من ٤: ١٢٨.

[٥] هو ممن شهدوا يوم الجمل مع عائشة وصفين مع معاوية،وهو أخوه.

[٦] هو ولي المدينة لمعاوية عنه وليزيد بن معاوية

٢

خطبة القائم

أثناء حصار المهدية، قرأها المروزي رجب ٣٣٣

[«وأنشأ الإمام القائم بأمر الله أمير المؤمنين صلى الله عليه خطبة يحرّض فيها المؤمنين، وأمر المروزي قاضيه بالمهدية أن يقرأها عليهم. يقول فيها، بعد حمد الله تعالى والثناء عليه والصلاة على النبي محمد صلى الله عليه وعلى آله الطاهرين:»[١]]

أيها الناس، إن هذا اللعين النكاري قد استشرى شرُّه، واستوبأ مرتعُه، وحملتْه الأماني الغرّارة، والنفس التي هي بالسوء أمّارة، على أن غمط نعمة الله تعالى عليه، وسوّل له الشيطان الذي هو قرينُه[٢] أن لا غالب له. وإنما أرخى له أميرُ المؤمنين في زمامه. ليعثر في فضل خطامه فلعنه الله لعنًا وبيلاً، وأخزاه خزيًا طويلاً، وصيّره إلى نار تلظّى[٣] «لا يَصْلاَهَا إلاّ الأشْقَى» [٩٢: ١٥].

وقد عملتم يا معشر كتامة ما مضى عليه آباؤكم وقدماء أسلافكم من لزوم الطاعة والاعتصام بحبلها والتفيُّئ بظلّها، والمجاهدة في الله حقّ جهاده، وأنّكم خبيئةُ الله لهذا الحقّ المحمدي الفاطمي المهدي حتى أظهره وأعلاه، وجعل لكم فخره وسناه، فأنتم كحواريّي عيسى وأنصار محمد صلى الله عليهما.

---

[١] إدريس، عيون الأخبار، تحقيق اليعلاوي، ض ٣١١.
[٢] القرآن ٤٣: ٣٦.
[٣] القرآن ٩٢: ١٤.

يا أبناء المهاجرين والأنصار، والسابقين الأوّلين[١] المقرّبين! أليس بكم أزال الله دُوَلَ الظالمين، التي مضت لها أحقاب السنين، حتى جعلهم حصيداً خامدين؟[٢] «وَأَوْرَثَكُم أَرْضَهُم وَدِيَارَهُم» [٣٣: ٢٧]، فصرتم تَغزُونَ بعد أن كنتم تُغزَون؟

نزل بإزائكم دجّال لعين في شرذمة ضالّة مضلّة لم يستضيئوا بنور هداية: فهم كالأنعام المجفّلة[٣]، والصوَر المثّلة، والخشُب المُسنَدة، والحُمُر المستنفِرة[٤]. إن أقاموا هلكوا، وإن طولبوا أدركوا. فلا تنكصوا بعد الإقدام! وأنتم حزب الله وهم حزب الشيطان[٥]، وقَتيلُكم في الجّنة وقبيلُهم في النار، فأيّ حقّ بعد هذا الحق تطلبون، ومع أيّ إمام بعد إمامكم تقاتلون؟

فقاتلوا، رحمكم الله، أحزابَ الضلال، وذئابَ الطمع، وفراشَ النار، واطلبوهم في نواحي الأرض وأقاصي البلدان، وجميع الآفاق حتى يُحقّ الله الحقّ ويُبطل الباطلَ ولو كره المشركون[٦].

[المصدر: سيرة جوذر، ص ٥٤؛ إدريس، عيون الأخبار، ٣١١]

---

[١] القرآن ٩: ١٠٠
[٢] القرآن ٢١: ١٥.
[٣] المجفّلة: المهملة، سيرة جوذر
[٤] القرآن ٧٤: ٥٠.
[٥] حزب الله، القرآن ٥٨: ٢٢ و حزب الشيطان، ٥٨: ١٩.
[٦] اقتباس من بالقرآن ٨: ٨، «ليحق الحق ويبطل الباطل ولو كره المجرمون» مع الآيات القرينة.

٣

خطبة المنصور

وليًا للعهد في عيد الفطر ٣٣٤ بالمهديّة:

[«ولما كان يوم الفطر خرج المنصور بالله أبو الطاهر إسماعيل بن أبي القاسم القائم بأمر الله عليه السلام من قصره وقد حفّ به بنوه وإخوته وشيعته وأوليائه وأهل دولته وعبيده، والناس يرفعون أصواتهم بالدعاء له ويسألون الله تعالى أن يركس عدوّه ويخذله، والأعلام تنشّر والطبول تضرب، والمسرّة قد ملأت القلوب وأثلجت الصدور، ونجوم السعد قد طلعت قاضية لأولياء الله بالظهور. فحين انتهى إلى المصلى، صلّى صلاة العيد، وقام عليه السلام خطيبًا فقال: »[1]]

بسم الله الرحمن الرحيم.

الحمد لله الذي أحسن إلينا في قضائه، وأصفى الجزيل من عطائه، أحمده حمدَ مَن شكر حُسناه، وآثر في الأمور كلها رضاه، وأستعينه استعانة من لا يرجو غيره ولا يثق بسواه، ولا يتوكّل إلا عليه في أُولاه وأُخراه.

وأشهد أن لا إله إلاّ الله وحده لا شريك له، وأشهد أنّ محمداً عبده ورسوله، اصطفاه لوحيه، واختاره لتبليغ رسالاته، فابتعثه داعيًا إلى الحقّ، وشاهداً علي الخلق، فبلّغ رسالة ربّه، ونصح لعباده، وجاهد في سبيله، صلاة الله عليه نبيًا مصطفى ورسولاً مرتضى، وعلي آله، وسلامُه ورحمتُه وبركاته.

عباد الله! إنّ يومكم هذا يوم عيد، شرّفه الله وعظّمه، وفضّله وكرّمه،

[1] إدريس، عيون الأخبار، تحقيق اليعلاوي، ض ٣٣٩.

ختم به شهر رمضان، وافتتح به حجّ بيته الحرام، فأخلِصوا فيه نيّاتِكم، وارفعوا إلى الله فيه طلباتكم، واستغفروا لسيئاتكم، فإنّه يقول، جلّ ثناؤه، وتقدّست أسماؤه: و«اسْتَغْفِرُوا رَبَّكُم إنّهُ كانَ غَفَّاراً» [٧١: ١٠].
اتّقوا الله عباد الله! فبتقواه نجح الطالبون وفاز الفائزون، وهي وصيّة الله في الأوّلين والآخرين، وتمسّكوا بطاعته، وحافظوا على ما استحفظكم الله تعالى من دينه وكتابه، واسترعاكم من حقوقه وحدوده. فلمثل ما رغّبكم الله من جزيل ثوابه، وكريم مآبه، وخوّفكم من عقابه وأليم عذابه، «فَليَعْمَلِ العَامِلُونَ!» [٣٧: ٦١[1]].

ألهَمَنا اللهَ وإيّاكم رُشدَنا، وعزم لنا ولكم على تقواه، واتّباع هداه، وبلوغ رضاه.

[وجلس عليه السلام جلسة خفيفة، ثمّ قام فقال:]

بسم الله الرحمن الرحيم.

الحمد لله مُسبغ النعماء، وكابت الأعداء، ومستحقّ الشكر والثناء، وصلى الله أفضلَ صلاته على أفضل أنبيائه محمد خاتم النبيّين، وسيّد المرسلين، وعلى آله الطيّبين. اللهمّ صلّ على محمد وعلى آل محمد، وارحم محمداً وآل محمد، وبارك على محمد وآل محمد، كأفضل صلاتك وبركاتك ورحمتك على إبراهيم وعلى آل إبراهيم، إنّك حميد مجيد.

اللهمّ، وصلّ عل شمس الهدى، الذي بضيائه أشرق الإسلام، وانجاب الظلام، وعزّ الدين، وتمّت النعمَةُ على المؤمنين، عبد الله أبي محمد الإمام أمير المؤمنين، المهديّ بالله ابن المهديّين، الكريم ابن الأكرمين، صلى الله وملائكته عليه، وأكْرَمَ اللهُ مثواه لديه، في المقام الكريم، والنعيم المقيم!

اللهمّ، وصلّ على وليّ الأمر، ووارث المجد والفخر، الذي أعظمتَ

[1] القرآن ٣٧: ٦٠-٦١، «إنّ هذا لهو الفوز العظيم؛ لمثل هذا فليعمل العاملون».

عليه منّتك، وأسبغتَ عليه نعمتك، وألبستَه حلل الكرامة وتوجّتَه تاج البهاء والخلافة، وجمعتَ له خلافةَ الأنبياء المرسلين، وإرثَ آبائه الأئمة المستخلَفين، الهداةِ المهديّين، الأوصياء المنتَجَبين، محمد القائم بأمر الله أمير المؤمنين.

اللهمّ، عرّفه فيما ولّيتَه واسترعيتَه، واستحفظته عليه وائتمنته، أفضل ما عرّفت أحداً قبله من خلفائك الأئمة الراشدين، آبائه المهديّين، من النصر والإعزاز والتأييد والإظهار. وأوقِعْ بأعدائه، شرقًا وغربًا، براً وبحراً، أشدَّ ما أوقَعْتَ وأحلَلْتَ بأحدٍ من أعدائك من السطوات والنقمات، والقوارع المبيدات، والمَثُلات[1] المخزيات، ودمّرهم تدميراً وأصْلِهم سعيراً.

اللهمّ، انصر به الدين، وأيّده بالظهور والتمكين، والعلوّ والقهر، والنصر والظفر، واجعل كلمته العليا[2]، ويده الطولى، وجندَه الغالبين[3]، وحزبه المنصورين[4]، وافتح له فتحًا مبينًا، وتُعزّ به الدين، وتَشفي به صدور المؤمنين،[5] إلهَ الخلق ربَّ العالمين، إنّك سميع الدعاء، فعّال لما تشاء، «لاَ تُخْلِفُ المِيعَادَ» [٣: ١٩٤].

[المصدر: إدريس، عيون الأخبار، ٣٣٩-٣٤١]

---

[1] المثُلات: القرآن ١٣: ٦

[2] القرآن ٩: ٤٠

[3] القرآن ٣٧: ١٧٣

[4] القرآن ٣٧: ١٧٣

[5] القرآن ٩: ١٤

٤

خطبة المنصور

يقرؤها جعفر بن علي الحاجب يوم الجمعة ١٤ محرّم ٣٣٥ بجامع القيروان.

[«وأمر الإمام عليه السلام جعفر بن عليّ مولى جدّه المهدي بالله إلى جامع القيروان، فصلّى الجمعة وأقام الخطبة، فحمد الله وأثنى عليه وصلى على النبي وعلى آله وعلى وصيه والأئمة الطاهرين من ذريته، وأكثر من حمد الله وشكره على ما فتح لأوليائه من النصر، وأحلّ بأعدائه من الذلّة والقهر، وما كشف الله به عن أهل الإسلام الخاصّ منهم والعامّ، من البلاء والمحنة، وما صاروا إليه من السلامة والأمنة، ثم قال:»[١]]

معاشر الناس! مولانا وسيّدنا الأمير إسماعيل [المنصور بالله]، أطال الله بقاءه وأدام عزّه، وعظّم ملكه يقرأ عليكم السلام ويقول لكم: قد علم الله سبحانه حسنَ نيّتي فيكم، وما أُضمره من الخير لكم، وما أحبّه من صلاح أموركم، وما أجد في نفسي من الغمّ لما حلّ بكم من البلاء، وما نزل بكم من الفقر وذهاب الأنفس والأموال. وإنّ لي آمالاً كثيرة حسنة أؤمّلها فيكم ما منعني عن إظهارها إلاّ كونُ هذا العدوٍّ بحذائي، ومحاربتي له، وما كان من هذه الوقائع بيني وبينه. فلو كنّا أظهرنا ما كنّا نؤمّله من الإحسان إليكم قبل الظَفَر، لقال الجهّال: إنّما فعل ذلك استمالةً لقلوب الرعيّة وخوفًا من العدوّ. فلمّا كان مِن منّ الله علينا ما علمتموه، ومِن نصره لنا ما رأيتموه، وفتح لنا على عدوّه بمنّه وطَوله، أرَدنا أن نقابَل منّة الله، جل وعلا، علينا، بالشكر له والإحسان إلى

[١] إدريس، عيون الأخبار، تحقيق اليعلاوي، ض ٣٧٨.

عباده، والرفق بخَلقه، وأن نُظهر بعض ما نويناه فيكم إذ كان إظهاره في وقت الفتح أولى وأشبهَ منه قبل ذلك، للوجه الذي ذكرناه.

فقد ترك الأمير أعزّه الله، ما يجب عليكم في هذه السنة الآتية، وهي سنة خمس وثلاثين وثلاثمائة، من العُشُر، والصدقات، وجميع اللوازم. وفعل ذلك بجميع الناس مسلمهم وذِمّيهم، رفقًا بهم، وعونًا لهم على عمارة أرضهم وبواديهم. فليبلّغ الشاهد الغائب، وليرجعْ كل بدويّ منكم إلى باديته بلا مرزئةٍ عليه ولا كلفة. ثمّ إنّه لا يُؤخذ منكم في إقبال السنين، إلاّ العشر والصدقة، الطعام من الطعام، والشاة من الغنم، والثور من البقر، والبعير من الإبل، على فرائض الله سبحانه، وسنة جدّي رسول الله صلى الله عليه وسلم. ثمّ بعد ذلك يُساق إليكم من الإحسان، وإظهار العدل، وإحياء الحقّ، وإماتة الباطل ما تعظم به منّة الله عليكم، وتعرفون [به] بركة أيّامي ويُمن دولتي إن شاء الله.

[المصدر: إدريس، عيون الأخبار، ٣٧٨-٣٨٠؛ المقريزي، المقفى، ج ٢، ص ١٣٨-١٣٩، ترجمة المنصور]

٥

خطبة المنصور

في عيد الفطر سنة ٣٣٥، وهو يحاصر أبا يزيد بكيانة:

[«ولما كان يوم الأحد غرّة شهر شوّال من سنة خمس وثلاثين وثلاثمائة ركب عليه السلام إلى المصلّى الذي بناه، فصلى بالناس صلاة العيد ورقي إلى المنبر وخطب فقال:»[1]]

بسم الله الرحمن الرحيم.

«الحَمْدُ لله الذي خَلَقَ السَمَاوَاتِ وَالأرْضَ، وَجَعَلَ الظُلُمَاتِ وَالنُورَ ثُمَّ الذينَ كَفَرُوا بِرَبِّهِم يَعْدِلونَ» [٦: ١] إلهًا معبوداً، وربًا محموداً، لا نتّخذ من دونه إلهًا ولا نُشرك به شيئًا.

الحمد لله الذي «يُمْسِكُ السَمَاءَ أنْ تَقَعَ عَلَى الأرْضِ إلاّ بِإذْنِهِ إنَّ اللهَ بِالنَاسِ لَرَؤُوفٌ رَحِيم» [٢٢: ٦٥].

الله أكبر! الله أكبر! لا إله إلاّ الله. والله أكبر! ولله الحمد. «سُبْحَانَ رَبِّنَا إنْ كَانَ وَعْدُ رَبِّنَا لَمَفْعُولاً» [١٧: ١٠٨]، «سُبْحَانَ الله حِينَ تُمْسُونَ وَحِينَ تُصْبِحُونَ، وَلَهُ الحَمْدُ في السَمَاوَاتِ وَالأرْضِ وَعَشِيًّا وَحِينَ تُظْهِرُونَ» [٣٠: ١٧-١٨]، «سُبْحَانَ رَبِّكَ [رَبّ العِزَةِ] عَمَّا يَصِفُونَ وَسَلامٌ عَلَى المُرْسَلِينَ وَالحَمْدُ لله رَبِّ العَالَمِينَ» [٣٧: ١٨٠-١٨٢].

الحمد لله أوّلاً قديمًا لم يزَلْ، وآخراً باقيًا لم يَحُل، وعالمًا حكيمًا لم يجهَلْ، وجواداً كريمًا لم يبخَلْ، وسِعَت رحمتُه كل شيء[2] فلا يقنط منها إلاّ

[1] إدريس، عيون الأخبار، تحقيق اليعلاوي، ض ٤١٧.
[2] القرآن ٧: ١٥٦

الضالّون[١]، وفطر بريّته لعبادته لا يستنكفُ عنها إلاّ الخاسرون، وثبتت حجّتُه بحسن دلالته فلا يُنكرها إلاّ الجاحدون. خشعت له النفوس بتعظيمها، وأذعنت له القلوب بخشوعها، وانحسرت الأبصار دونه عن مرامها، وسلّمت لعزّه القُوى بعجزها، وشهدت له العقول بفطرتها أنّه كما وصف نفسه حيّ قيّوم «لا تَأْخُذُهُ سِنَةٌ وَلا نَوْمٌ» [٢: ٢٥٥[٢]]، «لَيسَ كَمِثْلِه شَيءٌ» [٤٢: ١١]، «لا تُدْرِكُهُ الأبْصَارُ وَهُوَ يُدْرِكُ الأبْصَارَ وَهُوَ اللَطِيفُ الخَبِيرُ» [٦: ١٠٣]، جل ثناؤه، وتقدّست أسماؤه وعزّ بهاؤه وعلا علاؤه.

وأشهد أنّ لا إله إلاّ الله وحده لا شريك له، وأشهد أنّ محمداً عبده ورسوله المصطفى، وأمينه المرتضى، أرسله بالنور الساطع، والبرهان القاطع، إلى جميع بريّته شاهداً لمن كان قبله من الرسل ومصدّقًا لما بين يديه من الكتب، ودليلاً على الله، وداعيًا إليه، على حين فَترة من الرسل، وانقطاعٍ من الوحي، وطموسٍ من الحقّ، وضلالٍ من الخلق، فبلّغَ عن الله رسالتَه، وصدع بأمره[٣]، ودعا إلى سبيل ربّه بالحكمة والموعظة الحسنة[٤]، وجاهد في الله حقّ جهاده، وأدّى الأمانة إلى عباده، وعَبَدَ ربّه حتى أتاه اليقين[٥]، صلى الله عليه في الأوّلين والاخرين، وعلى آله الطيّبين الطاهرين، الأوصياء المنتخبين، الكرام المهديّين.

أوصيكم عبادَ الله بتقوى الله الذي لا غَناء بكم عنه، ولا موئل لكم دونه في ممَات ولا محيى، ولا آخرةٍ ولا دنيا، وابتذال أنفسكم فيما يُحبّ ويرضى، ويقرّبكم إليه زلفى.

ألا إنّ هذا يومٌ جعله الله لكم عيداً ومنسكًا، انقضى فيه الصومُ ودخلت به أشهر الحجّ، فحاسِبوا أنفسكم رحمكم الله! فمَن ذكر خيراً

---

[١] القرآن ١٥: ٥٦

[٢] القرآن ٢: ٢٥٥، «لا إله إلاّ هو الحي القيوم لا تأخذه سنة ولا نوم».

[٣] القرآن ١٥: ٩٤

[٤] القرآن ١٦: ١٢٥

[٥] القرآن ١٥: ٩٩

فلْيحمد الله وليزدَدْ، ومن ذكر تقصيراً فليستعتبْ، أو سَوْءاً فلْيتب، فإنّ الله تعالى «يَقْبَلُ التَوْبَةَ عَنْ عِبَادِهِ وَيَعْفُو عَنِ السَيِّئَاتِ وَيَعْلَمُ مَا تَفْعَلُونَ» [٤٢: ٢٥].

وقد فرض الله عليكم زكاة فطرتكم، وجرت به سنّةُ نبيكم سيّد الأنبياء، صلى الله عليه وعلى آله. فَلْيُؤدِّ كل امرئ منكم عن عياله، ذكورهم وإناثهم، صغيرهم وكبيرهم، صاعًا من بُرّ أو صاعًا من شعير، أو صاعًا من تمر، من طعامه، لا يأكل من شيء ويُؤَدّي من آخر، فإنّ ذلك مُحرّمٌ عليه وغيرُ مُجزٍ عنه.

عَصَمنا الله وإيّاكم بالتقوى، واستعمَلَنا وإيّاكم فيما يُحبّه ويرضى، وجعل الآخرة خيراً لنا ولكم من الأولى[١].

[الخطبة الثانية:[٢]]

بسم الله الرحمن الرحيم.

الحمد لله المتوحّد بربوبيّته، المتفرّد بوحدانيّته، الأوّل القديم، الحيّ القيّوم، أحمدُه بمحامده كلها، على أصغر نعمه وأجلّها، حمداً يوجب حمداً على حمد، للتوفيق منه والرشد.

وأشهد أنّ لا إله إلا الله وحده لا شريك له، إخلاصًا لتوحيده، واعترافًا بربوبيته.

وأشهد أنّ محمداً عبده انتجبه، ورسوله ابتعثه، تمّت بالوحي نبوّته، ونطق البرهان بحقيقة رسالته، صلى الله عليه وسلم، وأعلى ذكره، وسلّم وكرّم.

---

[١] القرآن ٩٣: ٤

[٢] زيادة من المحقق

أيّها الناس، إنّ الله أمركم بأمر بدأ فيه بنفسه، ثمّ ثنّى بملائكته فقال: «إنّ اللهَ وَمَلائكَتَهُ يُصَلُّونَ عَلَى النبيِّ، يَا أيُّهَا الذينَ آمَنُوا صَلُّوا عَلَيْه وَسَلِّمُوا تَسْلِيمًا» [٣٣: ٥٦]. اللهمّ، صلّ على عبدك ورسولك صلاةً تامّةً باقيةً، تزيده كرامةً إلى كرامته وشرفًا إلى شرفه، وصلِّ على جميع أصحاب الكساء، الطاهرين الأزكياء: علي أمير المؤمنين، وفاطمة الزهراء، سيّدة نساء العالمين، والحسن والحسين، الأكرمَين الأبرَّين، وعلى الأئمّة المهديّين من ذرية الحسين، أعلام الهدى، وبدور الدجى، وسادات الورى، أولياء الرحمن، وحجج الأزمان، ودعائم الإيمان.

اللهمّ، صلّ على وارث كل مجدٍ وثناء، وفضل وعُلا، عبدك المرتضى، ووليّك المصطفى، وخليفتك العدل الرضى، عبد الله أبي محمد الإمام المهدي بالله أمير المؤمنين، الذي استضاءت بنوره الآفاق، وعمّ به الإشراق، شمس الورى، وبدر الدجى، وكاشف الضياء، والمحيي لما درس من معالم الهدى، بأفضل صلواتك التامّات، وبركاتك الناميات، وكراماتك الباقيات.

اللهمّ، وصلّ على وليّ عهده في حياته وخليفته بعد وفاته، المنتجب المجتبى، المكرّم المرتضى، محمد أبي القاسم الإمام القائم بأمر الله، ابن المهدي بالله أمير المؤمنين، حامل حجّة الجبّار، وليّ الأبرار، وسيف الله البتّار، ووارث سيف جدّه ذي الفقار، صلاةً تفضُل صلاة المصلّين، رافعة في علّيّين، خالدة في الغابرين، باقيةً إلى يوم الدين.

اللهمّ، إنّي عبدك ووليّك أنعمتَ عليّ فأعظمت وأفضلت فأجزلتَ، ورفعتني وكرّمت، بما أفضيتَ إليّ من خلافة الآباء الأكرمين، الأئمّة المهديّين، ونصبتني علمًا للدين، وأقمتني إمامًا للمؤمنين.

اللهمّ فأتمم عليّ نعمتَك، كما أتممْتَها من قبلُ على الآباء والأجداد، الأكارم الأمجاد، حمَلةِ علمك، وخُزّان وحيك، وأمنائك على خلقك،

وصفوتك من عبادك، وخيرتك من آل نبيّك الذين جمعتَ لهم شرفَ الدارَيْن، وفضلَ المقامَيْن.

اللهمّ، وأعنّي على رعاية عهدهم، وإنجاز وعدهم، وقضاء دَينهم، وتمام أمرهم، وإحياء ذكرهم، وإعزاز أوليائهم، وإذلال أعدائهم. واجمَعْ بيني وبينهم، اللهمّ، في مستقرّ رحمتك، وقرار جنّتك، ومجاورة نبيّك، مع النبيّين والصدّيقين، والشهداء والصالحين[١]، آمين يا ربّ العالمين.

اللهمّ، إنّ تغرّبي في البلاد، وهجري للمهاد، لقضاء ما فرضتَه عليّ من الجهاد، في سبيلك ونصرة دينك، وتحصين أمّة رسولك.

اللهمّ، وافتح لي فتحًا مبينًا يسيراً[٢]، واجعل لي من لدُنك على عدوّي الذي هو عدوّك سلطانًا نصيراً[٣]، إنّك على كل شيء قدير.

اللهمّ، اغفر للمؤمنين والمؤمنات، والمسلمين والمسلمات، الأحياء منهم والأموات، ولمن هو لاحق بهم من بعدهم غير ملحد في أسمائك، ولا معادٍ لأوليائك، ولا مُوالٍ لأعدائك. وأكمل أجرهم، وسلّم لهم أديانهم، حتى يَلْقَوك مُوفينَ بعهدهم، مستوجبين لثوابك، إنّك أنت الغفور الرحيم. «إنّ اللهَ يَأمُرُ بالعَدْلِ وَالإحْسَانِ وَإيتَاءِ ذِي القُرْبَى، وَيَنْهَى عَنِ الفَحْشَاءِ وَالمُنْكَرِ وَالبَغْيِ، يَعِظُكُمْ لَعَلّكُمْ تَذَكَّرُونَ» [١٦: ٩٠]، والحمد لله ربّ العالمين.

[المصدر: إدريس، عيون الأخبار، ٤١٧-٤٢١]

---

[١] القرآن ٤: ٦٩

[٢] القرآن ٤٨: ١

[٣] اقتباس من القرآن ١٧: ٨٠

٦

خطبة المنصور

في عيد الأضحى سنة ٣٣٥، بقلعة كيانة وهو يحاصر أبا يزيد:

[«ولما كان يوم النحر، يوم الجمعة لعشر خلون من ذي الحجة ركب الإمام عليه السلام فرسًا ورداً أحمر بحفافٍ مذهّب، وقد لبس قباء أصفر وتعمّم عمامة صفراء وأرخى ذؤابته، وحفّ به أنصاره وجنوده وأَولياؤه وعبيده، وانتهى إلى مصلّى كان عُمل له قبل ذلك فنزل وصلّى صلاة العيد، وارتقى منبراً كان بني له من الحجارة وخطب فقال: »[1]]

بسم الله الرحمن الرحيم.

الحمد لله المتوحّد بالربوبية، المتفرّد بالوحدانية، المتعزّز بالقدرة والبقاء، المتجبّر بالعظمة والكبرياء، الأوّل بلا غاية، والآخر بلا نهاية، المتعالي عن تشبيه الجاهلين وتحديد الواصفين وتكييف الناعتين ودرك أبصار الناظرين.

وأشهد أنّ لا إله إلا الله وحده لا شريك له، وأشهد أنّ محمداً عبده ورسوله، أكرمه بالنبوّة، واصطفاه بالرسالة، وحباه بالفضيلة، وابتعثه بالنور ساطعًا، وبالحقّ صادعًا، وبالهدى آمراً، وعن الكفر زاجراً، وعلى الأنبياء مهيمنًا، ولما جاؤوا به مصدّقًا. فبلّغ الرسالة وهدى من الضلالة، وأنقذ من الهلكة، وأَنْهَجَ معالم الدين وفرائضه، وبيّن حدوده وشرائعه، وجاهد في سبيل الله حقّ جهاده حتى أتاه اليقين[2]، صلى الله عليه في

[1] إدريس، عيون الأخبار، تحقيق اليعلاوي، ض ٤٢٧. قابل بالمقفى للمقريزي، ص ١٤٦: «وجاء عيد الأضحى يوم الجمعة، فركب المنصور إلى المصلى على فرس ورد بتجافيف مذهبة وعليه ثوب أصفر وعمامة صفراء، والمطارد والبنود والطبول في نواحي العسكر، فصلى بالناس ثم رقي المنبر فخطب»

[2] القرآن ١٥: ٩٩

الأولّين والآخرين، وعلى آله الطيّبين الطاهرين الأكرمين، الأئمّة المهديّين الكرام الأبرّين، ورحم وكرّم.

أوصيكم عبادَ الله بما أوصيتُ به نفسي قبلَكم من تقوى الله ومراقبَته، والعمل بما يُرضيه، ويقرّبنا وإيّاكم إليه، ففي تقواه رضاه، وبرضاه الفوز بالجنّة والنجاة من النار و«مَنْ زُحْزِحَ عَنِ النارِ وَأُدْخِلَ الجَنَّةَ فَقَدْ فَازَ وَمَا الحَيَاةُ الدُنْيَا إلاّ مَتَاعُ الغُرورِ» [٣: ١٨٥].

ألا وإنّ يومكم هذا يومٌ حرامٌ من شهرٍ حرام، مُعظَّمٌ على الأيّام: يوم الحجّ الأكبر، امتحن الله تبارك وتعالى فيه إبراهيم خليلَه، وفدى فيه من الذبح ولَدَه صلى الله عليهما، وافترض على كافّة أهل الإسلام، الحجّ إلى بيته الحرام، الذي جعله مثابةً للناس وأمنًا[١]. فتقرّبوا إلى الله تعالى فيه بما أمركم به. وأفضلُ ما أنتم مقرّبوه إناث الإبل، وإناثُ البقر، وفحولُ الضأن. واجتنبوا المريض من الحيوان ومعايب العُيُون والآذان، والمشوّهَ منها بالزيادة في خلقه والنقصان، فإنّها غير مقبولة منكم. بذلك جرت سنّة نبيّكم، صلى الله عليه وسلّم وعلى آله الأئمّة من ولده الأطهار، الكرام الأبرار، عليهم أفضل السلام «لَنْ يَنَالَ اللهَ لُحُومُهَا وَلا دِمَاؤُها، وَلَكِنْ يَنَالُهُ التَقْوَى مِنْكُم» [٢٢: ٣٧].

تقبّلَ اللهُ منّا ومنكم، وكتب لنا ولكم حجَّ بيته الحرام، والوصولَ إلى مشاهده العظام، ومواقفه الكرام، بإعزاز نصرنا وتمام أمرنا وإنجاز متقدِّم وعدهِ لنا، إنّه لا يُخلف الميعاد، ولا يُعجزه ما أراد.

[الخطبة الثانية:]

بسم الله الرحمن الرحيم.

[١] القرآن ٢: ١٢٥

الحمد لله المبدئ المعيد، الكريم المجيد، الفعّال لما يريد[١]، خالق الخلق، وباسِط الرزق، مُنزل القَطر، ومدبّر الأمر، وارث السماوات والأرض وما عليها، وإليه ترجعون.

الله أكبر! الله أكبر! لا إله إلاّ الله.

والله أكبر! الله أكبر! ولله الحمد.

أشهد أنّ لا إله إلاّ الله وحده لا شريك له، وأشهد أنّ محمداً عبده المصطفى، ورسولُه المرتضى، وأمينه على ما أوحى، والمنقذُ من الضلالة والردى، صلى الله عليه وعلى آله الكرام المهديّين، الأئمّة الراشدين الطاهرين: علي أمير المؤمنين وسيّد الوصيّين وخيرة المسلمين، وفاطمةَ الزهراء سيّدةِ نساء العالمين، والحسن والحسين سيّدَي شباب أهل الجنّة، والأئمّةَ من ولد الحسين الطاهرين، بقيّة رسول الله وثِمَاره، ووارثيه وحُجَجِه على العباد، جبال الدين، وسادات المؤمنين، وأولياءَ العالمين، وعلى الإمام المرتضى والوليّ المصطفى، عبد الله أبي محمد الإمام المهدي بالله أمير المؤمنين، وارث فضل الأئمة المهديّين من آبائه الخلفاء الراشدين، وصفْوَة الصفوة من الأوّلين منهم والآخرين، الذي قامت به دولة المؤمنين، وبسيفه ذلّت رقابُ المنافقين، فأعاد الإسلام غضًا ناضرا، والدين مضيئًا باهراً، والحقّ مشرقًا زاهراً، وأحيى به الله من الدين ما اندرس، ومن الحقّ ما التبس، وجمع الله له شرفَ الدنيا وفخرها، وآتاه فضل الآخرة وذُخرها، صلوات الله عليه ورضوانه ورحمته وحنانه.

اللهمّ، صلّ على وليّ عهده، ووارث مجده، وخليفته من بعده، المتقلّد الإمامةَ المتوّج بالكرامة، عبد الله أبي القاسم الإمام القائم بأمر الله أمير المؤمنين، ابن المهدي بالله، أمير المؤمنين، سليلِ خير النبيّين وبقيّة الماضين، ونجيب الأئمّة المهديّين، صلاةً تزيدُه بها كرامة وعَلاءً، وشرفًا

[١] القرآن ٨٥: ١٦

وسناءً، ساميةَ القَدْر، عاليَةَ الفخْر، ناميةَ الذكْر، باقيةً على الدهر.

اللهمّ، وكما قلّدتَني خلافتَك التي كَرّمتَها وشرّفتَها، وحظرتها وحرّمتَها، لعنت من غير أهلها مدّعيها، وأخزيت مناوئِها، وقصّرتَ أيدي المتطاولين إليها، واخترتَ لها الواحد بعد الواحد من آبائي المهديّين، الكرام المصطفين، الخلفاء الراشدين، ثمّ أورثتني مقامهم، وأحييت بي ذكرَهم، وأتممتَ فيّ أمرهم، وقفيت بي على آثارهم، ونصَبتني لما نصبتهم، من الاحتجاج بنا على خلقك، والقيام بأمرك، ونصرة دينك، وإعزاز ملّة رسولك، ونصرتني وأظهرتني وأظفرتني، وأعززت بي الأمّة بعد الذلّة، وكثّرتهم بعد القلّة، وجمعتهم بعد الفرقة، وكشفت عنهم مُدْلَهِمَّ الفتنة، ودياجير الظلمة ودياجِيَ المحنة، بدولتي التي أعززتها ونصرتها، وأيّامي التي آثرتها فاخترتها، وسيوفي التي أمضيتها على الدجّال وحزبه، والنفاق وأهله، فجعلتهم بها حصيداً خامدين، فأصبح الحقّ مشرقًا والباطل زاهقًا[1]، فضلاً منك عليّ ونعمة جدّدتها لديّ، إلى نِعَم قبلها، أسبغتها عليّ وأجزلتها، اللهمّ فألهِمْني شُكْرَ نعْمتك، ووفّقني للعمل بما يُرضيك، ويُزلفني لديك، ويقرّبني إليك، فإنّه لا حول ولا قوّة إلاّ بك، عليك توكّلت، وإليك أنيب،[2] وأمري إليك فوّضتُ، وبك اعتصمت.

«صَلاَتِي وَنُسُكِي، وَمَحْيَايَ وَمَمَاتِي، لله رَبِّ العَالَمِينَ» [٦: ١٦٢].

اللهمّ اغفر لي وللمؤمنين والمؤمنات، والمسلمين والمسلمات، الأحياء منهم والأموات، تقبّلْ أعمالهم وزكّ سعيهم واهدِهم وارأفْ بهم، إنّك أنت الرؤوف الرحيم.

[المصدر: إدريس، عيون الأخبار، ٤٢٨-٤٣١؛ المقريزي، المقفّى، ترجمة المنصور]

---

[1] القرآن ١٧: ٨١

[2] القرآن ٤٢: ١٠ و ١١: ٨٨

٧

خطبة المنصور

بالمهدية في عيد الفطر سنة ٣٣٦

[«وكان يوم الفطر يوم الخميس مستهل شوال من سنة ست وثلاثين. وخرج أمير المؤمنين المنصور بالله صلوات الله عليه لصلاة العيد إلى المصلى الذي ابتناه الإمام المهدي عليه السلام خارج المهدية، وليّ عهده المعز لدين الله أبي تميم خلفه، وسار أعمامه أولاد المهدي بالله وإخوته أولاد القائم بأمر الله، وأولاده، خلف المعز لدين الله. وسار في عساكره بالوقار والاستغفار والتسبيح حتى انتهى إلى المصلى، فقضى صلاة العيد، وارتقى المنبر وخطب، فقال: »[1]]

بسم الله الرحمن الرحيم

الحمد لله شكراً لأنعمه التي لا يُحصى لها عدد وتعريضًا للمزيد من فضله الذي لا يَنفَد. ولا إلاه إلا الله إخلاصًا للتوحيد. والله أكبر إجلالاً لذكر الله العليّ المجيد. سبحان الله المستشهدة آياته على قدرته، المتنعة من الصفات ذاتُه ومن الأبصار رؤيته ومن العقول تحديده ذي الكبرياء والعزة والجلال والقدرة والسناء والعظمة له السماوات العلى والأرضون السفلى وما فوقها وما تحت الثرى[2] كلٌ خاضع لعظمته متذللٌ لعزته متصرفٌ بمشيئته واقعٌ تحت قدرته.

وأشهد أنّ لا إله إلا الله وحده لا شريك له وأشهد أنّ محمداً عبده ورسوله اختاره وارتضاه وانتخبه واصطفاه وكرّمه وأصفاه وبعثه بالهدى

---

[1] إدريس، عيون الأخبار، تحقيق اليعلادي، ض ٤٨٠. قابل بالمقفى للمقريزي، ج ٢، ص ١٦٣: «وركب منها يوم الفطر، والأمير أبي تميم ولي عهده خلف ظهره والأولاد والإخوة والعمومة من ورائهما والأعلام والمطارد بين أيديهما، والطبول تضرب في نواحي العسكر، وهو سائر بوقار حتى وصل إلى المصلى فنزل وصلى بالناس ثم صعد المنبر فقالَ.

[2] القرآن ٢٠: ٦

ودين الحق[1] الذي تعبّد به مَن في السماوات من الملائكة المقربين ومَن في أرضه من الثقلَين فاضطلع عليه السلام بما حُمِّل وبلّغ ما به أرسِل صادعًا بأمر ربه صابراً على البأساء والضراء في جنبه إلى أن أظهر الله دينه على الأديان وأزهق بحقه أباطيل الأوثان. صلى الله عليه وآله وسلّم وشرّف وكرّم.

عباد الله، أوصيكم بتقوى الله وطاعته وخشية الله ومراقبته والتقرب إلى الله بما يُرضيه فإنّه بما في قلوبكم خبير وبأعمالكم بصير لا تخفى عليه خافية[2] ولا يَعزُبُ عنه في السماوات والأرض مثقال ذرة[3] ولا يُنجي من سخطه ولا يوصل إلى رحمته إلا طاعته «وَمَن يُطِعِ اللهَ وَرَسُولَهُ فَقَدْ فَازَ فَوزاً عَظِيمًا» [٣٣: ٧١].

ألا وإنّ الله عز وجل جعل يومكم هذا عيداً مُعظمًا على الأيام ختم به شهراً مفضلاً على الشهور وافتتح به أيام شهور الحج إلى البيت العتيق الذي كرّمه وعظّمه وجعله قبلة الصلوات ومحل البركات ومنزل الرحمات ومثابة للناس وأمنًا[4] ومناراً للدين وعلمًا. فتقرّبوا إلى الله في يومكم هذا بأداء فطرتكم التي هي زكاة صومكم وسنة نبيكم سيد الأنبياء صلى الله عليه وعلى آله وسلم كل امرئ منكم عن نفسه وعن كل واحد من أهله ذكورهم وإناثهم، صغيرهم وكبيرهم، نصف صاع من بُرّ أو صاعًا من شعير أو صاعًا من تمر من طعام أهليكم لا من غيره فليس بمقبول إلا ذاك. وأكثروا من الدعاء واستشعروا الحذر والرجاء. «يَا أَيُّهَا الذِينَ آمَنُوا اتَّقُوا اللهَ وَلْتَنْظُرُ نَفْسٌ مَا قَدَّمَتْ لِغَدٍ» [٥٩: ١٨] فقريب والله كأن قد.

وإنّه عز وجل لم يهملكم إهمال الهمج ولم يجعل عليكم في الدين من

---

[1] القرآن ٩: ٣٣ و ٤٨: ٢٨

[2] القرآن ٦٩: ١٨

[3] القرآن ٣٤: ٣

[4] القرآن ٢: ٥٢١

حرج[١] ولا عذر بعد إيضاح المنهج وتأكيد الحجج برسوله وأئمة الهدى من ذريته عليه وعليهم أفضل سلام الله ورحمته.

وفّقنا الله وإياكم لما يرضيه ويُزلف لديه ويقربنا إليه فإنا له وبه وصلوات الله أولاً وآخراً على محمد خاتم النبيين وسيد المرسلين وعلى آله الطيبين الطاهرين الأئمة المهديين السادة الأكرمين الذين بالحق قضوا ويقضون وبه عدلوا ويعدِلون.

[الخطبة الثاني؛
وجلس جلسة خفيفة ثم قام فقال:]

بسم الله الرحمن الرحيم

الحمد لله رب العالمين والعاقبة للمتقين والصلوات الغاديات الرائحات الناميات الزاكيات الباقيات على محمد وآله الطاهرين الطيبين الأئمة المهديين السادة الأكرمين الطاهرين الأبرين حمداً حمداً! شكراً شكراً! أنجزتَ وعدك ونصرتَ عبدك على كره الكافرين وصغار الماكرين الأخسرين الأفجرين أحزاب الدجّال اللعين المغضوب عليهم الضالين[٢] الأنجاس الأرجاس الأذلين الأتعاس الأشقياء الأخزياء الملعونين في الأرض والسماء.

حمداً حمداً! وشكراً لك شكراً! عوداً وبدءاً لا مكافئًا نعماءك ولا مجازيًا آلاءك معترفًا بالعجز عن الشكر ولو بكل لسان طول الدهر.

سلام الله وصلواته ورحمته وبركاته وتحياته وزكياته عليكما، يا أميرَي المؤمنين، يا خليفتَي رب العالمين، يا ابني الهداة المهديين، يا أبتاه! يا جداهَ! يا ابني محمد رسول الله! سلام مُسلِّم لله فيما قضاه عليّ من

---

[١] القرآن ٢٢: ٧٨
[٢] القرآن ١: ٧

فقدكما صابراً على ما امتحنني به من بعدكما فيا طول الحسرة وفيض العبرة عليك يا أبتاه يا محمداه! يا أبا القاسماه! يا جبلاه! واشَوْقاه! واألَماه!

وخالق الأرض والسماء باعث الموتى ومميت الأحياء ما أنا في ريب من اختيار الله تبارك وتعالى لك ونقله إيّاك إلى دار كرامته ومستقرّ رحمته التي بوّأها محمداً رسوله عليه السلام جدّك وأمير المؤمنين علي بن أبي طالب أباك وفاطمة الزهراء البتول أمك وآباءك الطاهرين المهديين الأبرار. لكن لوعة المحزون باعثة للشجون مبكيةٌ للعيون. فإنّا لله وإنّا إليه راجعون[1] وله مسلّمون وعلي كل حال تصرّف بنا حامدون ولنعمائه شاكرون.

فقد أعظم الله عز وجل النعمة وضاعف المنّة بما ربط على قلبي من الصبر ثم بما أكرمني به من العز والنصر الذي أرسي به قواعد الإسلام ونوّر به قلوب المؤمنين بعد الإظلام وبعد انقطاع الرجاء لتطاول مدّة البلاء بالفتنة العظمى وأهوالها وبلبالها وزلزالها ظلماء بهماء عمياء صمّاء جاهلية جهلاء بدجّال النفاق وأحزابه المرّاق أعداء الدين وأنصار إبليس اللعين أمهلهم الله استدراجًا وأملى لهم فزادوا في الغي لجاجًا «لِيَمْيزَ اللهُ الخَبيثَ مِنَ الطَّيِّبِ» [٨: ٣٧] وليرى أولو الألباب مصداق وعد الله في الكتاب «آلَمَ أَحَسِبَ النَاسُ أنْ يُتْرَكُوا أنْ يَقُولُوا آمَنَّا وَهُم لاَ يُفْتَنُونَ؟ وَلَقَدْ فَتَنَّا الذِينَ من قَبْلِهِم فَلَيَعْلَمَنَّ اللهُ الذينَ صَدَقُوا وَلَيَعْلَمَنَّ الكَاذِبِينَ» [٢٩: ١-٢] وعداً من الله لا يُخلفه وحكمًا لا يبدله في الأولين من عباده والآخرين إلى يوم الدين فكانت بحمد الله ونعمته على أعدائنا فتنةً أصمّتهم وأعمتهم وأضلتهم وأردتهم وأتعستهم وأركستهم وأذلتهم وأخزتهم ولنا ولأوليائنا محنة أكسبتنا أجراً وذخراً وأعقبتنا عزاً وفخراً

---

[1] القرآن ٢: ٦٥١

كان وجهها شتيماً وعقباها كريماً لما أراد الله عز وجل من تجديد دولتنا وإعزازنا وإظهار نعمته علينا وتكفّله بنصرنا وتمحيص أوليائنا وتمحيق أعدائنا حتى إذا انتهت منتهاها وبلغت أقصى مداها ورجع الشيطان خاسراً ونطق هادراً وأذكى ناره وأدام إصراره وآسف الله جبّاره أذن الله بالنقمة فيه بتسليط عبده ووليه عليه فجلّى الله ظلمها ونوّر بُهَمَها وكشف غماءها وصرف لأواءها بي وعلى يدي كرامة من الله خصّني بها وفضيلة حباني بشرفها ونعمة لي ذخرها وعليّ قصرها ووصل بحديثها قديم النعمة على آبائي الطاهرين وسالف مننه على أجدادي الأئمة المهديين.

شهّرت دون ذلك السيوف فكسرها ودلفت إليّ الزحوف فهزمها وتظاهرت عليّ جنودُ الكفرة فخذلها وطمحت العيون نحوي فطمسها ورُفعت الرؤوس فنكسها وشمخت الأنوف فأرغمها وصُعّرت الخدودُ فأضرعها وأبى جل جلاله إلا إتمام أمري وإعزاز نصري وإظهاري وإظفاري وتأييدي وإعلائي إنجازاً لوعده محمداً عليه السلام بإعزاز ملته وإعلاء حجته ونصر أئمة الهدى من ذريته. فأمضى قضاءه قادراً وكبت أعداءه قاهراً «لاَ مُعَقِّبَ لِحُكْمِه» [١٣: ٤١] ولا رادّ لأمره ولا شريك في الحمد له.

يا أهل دعوتنا يا أنصار دولتنا يا كتامة!

احمدوا الله واشكروه على ما خصّكم به من نعمه وجسيم مننه وفضّلكم به على كافّة الخلق في غرب وشرق. بدأكم عز وجل بالنعمة العظمى ثم شفعكم بالمنة الكبرى ووالى بينهما عليكم من سوابغ النعماء بما لا يُحصى: بصّركم والناس عُميان وعلّمكم والخلق جُهّال وهداكم والعباد ضُلال إلى دينه ونصرة حقه وطاعة وليه علَم الهدى وسراج الدجى وقطب الدين وحبله المتين فأرقاكم بالسبق إلى نصرته والسعي في طاعته والتفيّئ بظل دولته والاستنارة بضياء حكمته حتى إذا قضى الله زلزال

البلاد واختبار العباد وجلّل الأرض الظلام وزلزل الأقدام وعظمت الخطوب واشتدّت الكروب ويئست القلوب عصمكم الله وهدى قلوبكم وثبّت أقدامكم إلى أن جلاها الله عنكم خاصة وعن العباد كافة بنا وعلى أيدينا فكانت عليكم نعمة وعلى العباد حجة فانجلت عنكم والله أنتم بيض الوجوه[١] موفون بعهد الله[٢] معتصمون بحبل الله أحياؤكم سعداءُ وأمواتُكم شهداءُ «عِنْدَ رَبِّهِم يُرْزَقُونَ» [٣: ١٦٩] فهنيئًا لكم هنيئًا!

اللهم إني عبدُك اخترتني وارتضيتَني وشرّفتَني بما أورثتني من مقام أصفيائك وخلافة أوليائك وأغنيتني وأفقرتَ الخلق في دينهم ودنياهم إليّ فرأفتَ بي ولم تجعل لأحد عليّ منّةً سواك وأقمتني لإحياء حقك والشهادة على خلقك فإنّي لا أقول إلا حقًا ولا أنطق إلا صدقًا. وقد بلغني عن آبائي عن جدنا محمد رسول الله صلى الله عليه وسلم أنه قال: ما من خطيب يخطب إلا وقفه الله يوم القيامة فسأله عن كل كلمة وما أراد بها.

فوعزّتك وجلالتك وعلوّ مكانك وعظمتك ما هبتُ عدواً ولا فطقتُ فريًا ولا شكرت على النعماء أحداً سواك.

اللهم إني أصبحت راضيًا عن كتامة لاعتصامهم بحبلك وصبرهم على البأساء والضراء في جنبك تعبّداً لنا واعترافًا بفضلنا وأداء لما افترضه الله على العباد لنا وتوسّلاً إليك بطاعتنا.

اللهم فارضَ عنهم وضاعف حسناتهم وامحُ سيئاتهم واحشُرهم في زمرة نبيك الذي دانوا به ووليك الذي والَوْه وأبقِ نعمتك عندهم وأتممها عليهم وأكْمِل حسناتك إليهم وخلّد العزّ في أعقابهم وأجْزِلْ ثوابهم واهدِهم وظهّر قلوبهم إنك سميع الدعاء قريب مجيب!

المصدر: سيرة جوذر، ٥٦؛ عيون الأخبار، ٤٨٠؛ المقريزي، المقفى، ج ٢، ص ١٦٨ (ترجمة المنصور)

---

[١] القرآن ٣: ١٠٧
[٢] القرآن ٢: ١٧٧

٨

خطبة المنصور

في عيد النحر من سنة ٣٣٦، بالمهدية

[«وركب المنصور من قصره بالمهدية لصلاة عيد النحر على الرسم الذي تقدم في يوم الفطر، فصلى بالناس ثم صعد المنبر فقال:»]

بسم الله الرحمن الرحيم.

الله أكبر! الله أكبر! لا إله إلاّ الله.

والله أكبر! الله أكبر! ولله الحمد والملك والخلق.

تبارك الله ربّ العالمين، مدبّر الأمور، وباعثُ من في القبور.

وأشهد أنّ لا إله إلا الله وحده لا شريك له، الذي لبس العزّة، وارتدى العظمة، وانفرد بالجبروت والأزليّة، توحّد بالملكوت والربوبيّة، العزيز الغفّار، المتكبِّر الجبّار، المتعالي عن الصفات، المعروف بالآيات البيّنات، المعبود في الأرضين والسماوات.

وأشهد أنّ محمداً عبده ورسوله، خاتم أنبيائه، وسيّد أصفيائه، وأكرمُ أوليائه، بعثه بالهدى، مُبصِّراً من العَمَى، مُنقذاً من الضلالة والردى، وأكمل به على العباد نعمتَه وإحسانَه، وأبان بهِ سخَطَه ورِضوانه، فبلّغ عليه السلام الرسالة، وصرّح بالبشارة، وأعلن النِذارة، وكشف اللهُ به

الظلماء، وأبطل الجاهليّة الجهلاء، حتى تآلف النافرُ، وآمن الكافِرُ، وعَبَدَ الجاحدُ، وأذعَنَ المُعانِدُ. وأصبح الحقّ واضحًا بعدَ دروسه، مضيئًا بعد طموسه بأصنام معبودة وقلوب كافرة، وأبْدٍ عليه متظافرة، إلى أن أذن الله بإظهار دينه على الدين كله[١].

صلواتُ الله على محمد سيد الأنبياء، المضطلع بالأعباء، الصابر على البأساء والضرّاء، الباذل لله نفسه، أعزّ الأنفس قدراً، وأجلّها عند الله خطراً وأرفعَها في الملاء الأعلى ذكراً، لا يسأل العباد على ذلك أجراً إلا المودّة[٢] في القربى، كما أَمره ربّه ليَكون الودُّ لأئمّة الهدى من ذريّته سببًا لشفاعته والحشر في زمرته.

الله أكبر! الله أكبر! لا إله إلاّ الله.

والله أكبر! والله أكبر! ولله الحمد والعظمة والمجد.

عباد الله! إنّ يومكم هذا يوم عيد أوجب الله تعظيمه وتكريمه، افتتح به الأيّام المعدودات[٣]، وختم به الأيّام المعلومات[٤]، وجعله علمَ الميقات لحجّ بيته الحرام العتيق المكرّم، تفتَح فيه أبواب السماء لقبول الدعاء، فأدعوا الله مخلصين، وابتهلوا إليه راغبين، تقربًا بما أمركم به ووزَعَكم، من بهيمة الأنعام، وأفضلُها إناث الإبل، وإناث البقر، وفحول الضأن، ومن ضحّى بجذَع من المعز لم يُجزِ عنه، وجَذَع الضأن يجزي. وكل ذبيح قبل الصلاة لحمُ محلّل، وبعد الصلاة قُربانٌ مُتَقَبَّل. وتمام الأضاحي سلامة الأعين والآذان. فاجتنبوا مرضاها ومشوّهاتها، بزيادة الأعضاء ونقصانها، وأحدّوا الشفَارَ لها، وارفقوا عند الذبح بها، «فَإذَا وَجَبَتْ جُنُوبُهَا فَكُلُوا مِنهَا وَأطعِمُوا القَانِعَ وَالمُعْتَرَّ» [٢٢: ٣٦. وادّخروا واحمدوا الله. «لَنْ يَنَالَ

---

[١] القرآن ٩: ٣٣ و ٤٨: ٢٨ و ٦١: ٩

[٢] القرآن ٤٢: ٢٣

[٣] القرآن ٢: ٢٠٣

[٤] القرآن ٢٢: ٢٨

اللهَ لُحومُهَا وَلا دمَاؤُهَا، وَلَكِنْ يَنَالُهُ التَقْوَى مِنْكُم» [٢٢: ٣٧] «كَذَلِكَ سَخَّرْنَاهَا لَكُم لَعَلَّكُم تَشْكُرُونَ» [٢٢: ٣٦].

تقبَّل الله منّا ومنكم قربانَنا، وأجاب دُعاءَنا، وزكّى أعمالَنا، إنّه المنّانُ الكريمُ، الجوادُ الرحيم.

[الخطبة الثانية:]

الله أكبر! الله أكبر! لا إله إلا الله.

والله أكبر! الله أكبر! الله أكبر! لله الحمدُ دائمًا، والملك باقيًا، والعزّ قاهراً، والدين واصبًا[1]. فسبحان مَن تفرّد بالبقاء، وتوحّد بالبهاء، وتمجّد بالسخاء، وقهر الخلق بالفناء، ومنّ بالنعم والآلاء، ابتدأ بجوده، وجزى بعدله، شهد الله وشهد من مجّده أنّه لا إله إلا هو، والملائكة المقرّبون، وأولو العلم المؤمنون، قائمًا بالقسط، متفرّداً بالملك، متوحّداً بالربوبية، لا إله إلا هو العزيز الحكيم[2].

وأنّ محمداً عبده ورسوله خاتم النبيّين، وسيّد المرسلين، وأكرم المصطفين، وأفضل المنتخَبين، صلوات الله عليه وعلى مَن تقدمه من الأنبياء والمرسلين، وخَلَفَه من الأئمّة المهديّين، من ذرّيّته الكرام الطاهرين، ألسن الصدق، وأعلام الحقّ، وهُداة الخلق، ودعاة الرشد، وأدلّة القصد.

اللهمّ، صلّ منهم على مَن بدا ضياؤه، ساطعًا سناؤُه، بحرَ علوم زاخرَ الغوارب، وبدرَ سماءٍ، زاهرَ الكواكب، منوِّر الظلم، وكاشف البُهم، مُحيي السنن، ومميت الفتَن: ذلك عَبْدُ الله وخيرتُه وصفيُّه، أبو محمد الإمام المهدي بالله أميرِ المؤمنين، المرتضى للدين، والهادي إلى الحقّ المبين،

[1] القرآن ١٦: ٥٢
[2] القرآن ٣: ١٨

وسيف الله المنتضى على الكافرين. اللهمّ صلّ عليه أتمّ صلواتك، وواصل لديه تحيّاتك، وجدّد له كراماتك، وزده في نعمائك، وفواضل آلائك، وجزيل عطائك.

اللهمّ، وصلّ على وارث مَقامه، وواصل أيّامه، العلَم الأزهر، والسراج الأنور، محمدٍ أبي القاسم القائم بأمر الله أمير المؤمنين، الذي اصطفيتَه وكرّمته، واخترته وارتضيته، وامتحنته وابتليته، فكان لأنعُمكَ شاكراً، وعلى البلاء صابراً، مسلّمًا تسليمَ أنبيائك الأكرمين، وأوليائك المنتخَبين، لرفع شأنهم وكرامتهم، لا لهوانهم.

لقد كان المبتلى بأعظم فتنة، وأشدّ محنة، من أحقّ الأمم بالخزي واللعنة، لاجترائهم عليك، وارتكابهم معاصيك، وجَحدِهم تنزيلَك، وتكذيبهم رسولَك، وتألّبهم على إطفاء نورك[1]، وتظافرهم على هدم دينك، ولم يكن إلى سواك ضارعًا، ولا إلى غيرك خاضعًا، ولا في نصرك شاكًا، فنطق به مفصحًا، وبيّنه مُوضحًا، تثبيتًا للمؤمنين، واحتجاجًا على الكافرين، ثمّ صرمت أيّامَه، وقَضيتَ حمامه، قبل شفاء غيظه، ودرك ثأره، وبلوغ أمله، فخرج من الدنيا راضيًا بك، ضاحكًا مسروراً بلقائك، واثقًا بجزائك. اللهمّ، فصلّ عليه صلاةً لا تبلغها الآمال، ولا تنتهي إليها الأعمال، تَخُصُّه منها بأكرم فضيلة، وأقرب وسيلة، وزده إحسانًا ورضوانًا، ورأفة وحنانًا، من فضلك الذي لا يُنْقِصه الإعطاء وجودك الذي لا منّ فيه ولا أذى. وإنّا لقضائك عليه لمسلّمون، وباختيارك له راضُون، وبثوابك له موقنون، ودعاؤنا له وصلواتُنا عليه فرض منك نؤدّيه، وحقّ أوجبتَه علينا نُقَضّيه.

اللهمّ، لك الحمد من قبلُ ومن بعدُ على نِعمتك عليّ، بإفضائك إليّ إمامةَ الآباء المهديّين، وخلافة الأئمّة الراشدين، ونَصْبِك إيّايَ لإحياء

[1] القرآن ٩: ٣٢ و ٦١: ٨

الدين، بإقامة سنن سيّد المرسلين، وإعزاز المؤمنين، وإذلال الكافرين، أوانَ طُغيان الشيطان، وحين أناخ الباطل على الحقّ بكَلْكل وجرانٍ، وأتممتَ أمري، وأعززتَ نصري، وأسبغتَ نعمتك عليّ، ورادفت منّتك إليّ، ولم تجعل للمخلوقين عليّ فيها يداً، ولا منكداً.

وإليك أرفع رغبتي، وأوجّه طلَبتي، في إيزاع شكر نعمتك، وقضاء حقّك، وأداء فرضك، والتوفيق لما أَرضاك، وأتقرّب[1] إليك، وأزلف لديك.

اللهمّ، إنّي عبدك ووليّك، فضّلتَني ففضُلت، وعزّزتَني فعَزِزت. فأنا العزيز بك، الذليل لك، الكريم بإكرامك، المتواضع لإعظامك، إجلالاً لعزّتك، وخضوعًا لقدرتك، وإشفاقًا من خَشْيتك، لا راغبًا ولا راهبًا إلا إليك ومنك. وأتْمِم عليّ نعمتك بالتوفيق فيما امترى به إحسانك، وأستوجب رحمتك ورضوانك.

اللهمّ، اغفر للمؤمنين والمؤمنات، الأحياء منهم والأموات، الذين أنعمت عليهم بنا فشكروا، وجاهدوا عن دولتنا فصبروا، مستبصرين في دينهم، مُوفين بعهدهم[2]، مسلّمين لوليّ أمرهم[3]، مصدِّقين بالحقّ لمّا جاءهم، مُسَارعين إلى الخيرات[4]، متنافسين في الصالحات. اللهمّ، ضاعفْ أجرهم، وأعْزِز نصرهم، واكبت بهم قلوب أعدائك، وجُحّاد حقّ أوليائك.

وصلّ ، اللهمّ، على محمد نبيك المصطفى و ورسولك المرتضى، وعلى آله الطيّبين، والأئمّة المهديّين. والحمد لله ربّ العالمين، أوّلاً وآخراً وباطنًا وظاهراً.

[المصدر: المقريزي، المقفى، ج ٢، ص ١٦٨-١٧٢ (ترجمة المنصور)]

---

[1] وأتقرّب: وقرّب، الأصل
[2] القرآن ٢: ١٧٧ و ١٣: ٢٠ وغيرها
[3] القرآن ٤: ٥٩
[4] القرآن ٣: ١١٤ و ٢٣: ٦١

٩

خطبة المعز
في عيد النحر سنة ٣٤١

[«وكتم أمير المؤمنين المعز لدين الله صلوات الله عليه وفاة والده أمير المؤمنين من آخر شهر شوال يوم وفاته إلى عاشر ذي الحجة يوم النحر، فخرج لصلاة العيد وعليه شعار السكينة وهيبة الإمامة، فصلّى صلاة العيد ثم ارتقى المنبر وخطب خطبته التي أظهر فيها وفاة أمير المؤمنين المنصور بالله فقال: »[١]]

بسم الله الرحمن الرحيم، وبه نستعين.

الله أكبر، الله أكبر، لا إله إلا الله.

والله أكبر، الأعزّ الأقدر، الخالق المدبّر، ذو الكبرياء والجبروت، والعزّة والملكوت، الأحد الصمد، الفرد المتفرّد، الأعلى القاهر، الباطن الظاهر، الأوّل والآخر[٢]، مبدعِ السموات والأرض بالقدرة، ومالكها بالعزّة ومدبّرها بالحكمة، وخالقها بما فيها من عجائب الفطرة، وبدائع التركيب والصنعة، الذي كل شيء من موات وحيّ ناطقٌ بالدعاء إليه، والدلالة عليه، والشهادة له بالتوحيد والتعظيم والتمجيد، فتكوينُه الأشياء كلها من عدم شاهدٌ بأن لا شيء قبله، وانتهاؤها إلى الغايات دليلٌ على أن لا غاية له، وإحاطتُه بحدودها منبئٌ بأن لا حدّ له، فالضعف والعجز والفقر والنقص

[١] إيريس، عيون الأخبار، تحقيق اليعلاوي، ص ٥٤١.
[٢] القرآن ٥٧: ٣

الذي لم يخل منه مخلوق أفصح ناطق وأصدق شاهد للخالق وحده جل ثناؤه بالإلهية والفردانية، والقدرة والربوبية، والتمام والكمال، والأزل والدوام، تبارك الله رب العالمين، «أَحْسَنَ كُلَّ شَيءٍ خَلَقَهُ» [٣٢: ٧]، وتكفّل لكل حي رزقَه، ثم هدى بالعقل الذي قامت حجتُه ووجبت طاعته، والكتب والرسل الذين تمّت بهم كَلمتُه[١]، فصلى الله عليهم أجمعين، وعلى محمد سيّد المرسلين الذي رفع ذكره، وأعلى قدره، فأكرمه بالوسيلة، واختصّه لكل فضيلة، وابتعثه هاديًا للعباد، ونوراً في البلاد، علّم به من الجهل، وهدى به من الضُلّ، وكثّر به من القُلّ، وأعزّ به من الذلّ، فألّف به بعد الشتات، ونوّر به دياجي الظلمات، صلوات الله عليه وعلى آله المهديين، الأخيار الطيّبين.

أيها الناس، إنّ الله لم يخلقكم عبثًا[٢]، ولم يُهملكم سدى[٣]، ولم يجعل عليكم في الدين حرجًا[٤]، ولم يضرب الذكر صفحًا، بل للعبادة خلقكم، وبطاعته وطاعة رسوله أمركم، وجعل للطاعة أعلامًا منصوبة وفروضًا مكتوبة، ومن أفضل أعلامها وأكرم أيامها يومُ الحج الأكبر إلى بيت الله العتيق، مَبْوَإِ إبراهيم خليل الله، وقبلة محمد رسول الله صلى الله عليه وسلم، فتقرّبوا إلى الله بما أمركم به ورزقكم إياه، من بهيمة الأنعام، مقتدين بسُنّة محمد نبي الرحمة والهدى، ومستشعرين لله التقوى، فإن الله عز وجل يقول: «لَنْ يَنَالَ اللهَ لحُومُهَا وَلاَ دِمَاؤُهَا وَلَكِن يَنَالُهُ التَقْوَى مِنْكُم» [٢٢: ٣٧] فبالتقوى تُقبل الأعمال وتُدرك الآمال، وكَبّروا الله على ما هداكم[٥]، واشكروه على ما أولاكم.

ألا وإنّ خير الهَدْي الإبل، وخير الإبل إناثُها، وكذلك من البقر، ثم

---

[١] القرآن ٦: ١١٥
[٢] القرآن ٢٣: ١١٥
[٣] القرآن ٧٥: ٣٦
[٤] القرآن ٢٢: ٧٨
[٥] القرآن ٢٢: ٣٧

الفحول من الضأن. وسلامة الضحايا سلامة الأعين والآذان، وأن تكون من حلال الأموال.

نسأل الله لنا ولكم قبول العمل بامتنانه وبلوغ الأمل من رضوانه، ورحمته وإحسانه.

الخطبة الثانية

الله أكبر، الله أكبر، لا إله إلا الله.

والله أكبر، الله أكبر شأنًا وأعظمُ سلطانًا، وأوضحُ آياتٍ وبرهانًا عن أن تُنكر العقولُ توحيدَه، أو ترومَ تحديدَه، خالق السموات والأرض، ومالكهما ومدبّرهما الفرد الصمد، الواحد الأحد، الذي لا شريك له ولا ندّ، الخالق القدير، الرحمن الغفور، النافذ قضاؤه، الكائن ما يشاؤه، المتقن كل شيء صُنعًا، الموسع كلّ شيء رزقًا، والمحيط بكلّ شيء علِمًا[1]، أحمدَهُ وأستعينه وأستهديه، وأفوّضُ إليه وأتوكّلُ في كل الأمور عليه.

أشهد أنّ لا إله إلا الله وحده لا شريك له، وأشهد أنّ محمداً خيرته من عباده، ونجيبه من بريّته، وصفوته من المتطهّرين، ورسوله إلى كافّة العالَمين، وبعيثُه بالإمامة إلى الثقلين، ليبلّغ حجّةَ الرب، ويوضّح محجة الحق، فأدى رسالة الله ورحم ورأف بعباد الله، وصبَرَ على الكبّار، من مكر الكفّار، إلى أن أدال الله للحق على الباطل، والهدى على الأضالل وألهب به المجاهل، بمحمد عليه أفضل الصلاة وأزكاها وأكملُها وأنماها، وأخلدها وأبقاها، وعلى الأئمة المهديّين من عترته الكرام الأبرين الذين اختارهم للخلافة، وارتضاهم للإمامة، وأكّد بوصيّة الرسول حجّتهم وأوجب في التنزيل طاعتهم، بعد تفضيله إياهم على العالمين بأبوّة محمد سيد

[1] القرآن ٦٥: ١٢

المرسلين، وعليّ أفضل الوصيين، مَن أمُّهم سيدة النساء، خامسة أصحاب الكساء، صلوات الله عليهم أجمعين، وعلى أميرَي المؤمنين المهدي بالله والقائم بأمر الله، سيّدَي الورى وإمامَي الهدى اللذين أعلى الله بهما دعوة الحق، وأنطق بهما الإيمان والمؤمنين، وأقام بهما دعائم الدين، وأزهق بحقهما باطل المدّعين[1] وأكاذيب المتخرّصين، وقطع بسيوفهما دابر الظالمين[2].

اللهم اخصص الإمام الفاضل، والوصي العادل، والبر الكامل، والغيث الوابل، ذا الآيات الباهرات، والمعجزات النافذات، الباذل نفسه الكريمة في حين الأزل والكُرُبات، الصابر في البأساء والضرّاء حتى طهّر الأرض من جبابرة الأعداء، عبدك ووليك ونجيبك وصفيّك أبا الطاهر إلمنصور بك، والمتوكل عليك والمفوِّض إليك، العامل بما يُرضيك ويقرّب إليك ويُزلف لديك، الذي فجعْتَنا بفقده، وأوحَدْتَنا من بعده، وأفردْتَنا منه وأوحشتنا، فقبلت دعاءه، وأجبت نداءه، وجمعتَ بينه وبين أحبّته في مستقر جنتك وسعة رحمتك.

وإن القلق، وشدة الحرق، عليك يا أبتاه، يا سيّداه، يا إسماعيلاه، يا أبا الطاهراه، يا بحر علوم الأئمة الطاهرين، الهداة المهديين، يا بقية أبناء الرسول، وأبناء الوصيّ والطاهرة البتول، يا إمام الأمة ومفتاح باب الرحمة، يا سراج الهدى وشمس الورى، ومجلي الطخياء، يا مخصوصاً من الله بتعجيل الكرامة، عظُم والله علينا المصابُ بك، وجل البلاء، وعدِم العزاء لفقدك، وقصرت الألسن عن إحصاء فضائلك، وتعداد مناقبك. فوالذي اختصّك بكرامته، وحباك بجزيل عطائه، وشرّفك بأبُوّة رسوله، لولا ما أوعزتَ إليّ به، وأكّدته عليّ، من القيام بحق الله والذبّ عن أمة جدك رسول الله، واستنقاذهم من غمرة الجهالة، وبحار الضلالة،

[1] القرآن ١٧ : ٨١
[2] القرآن ٦: ٤٥

ومهاوي الفتن، ومعاطب المحن، وما تقرر عندي، ورسخ في صدري، من الجزاء بمقدار الوفاء لله ولرسوله، ولأئمة الهدى، لضربتُ على وجهي سائحًا في البلاد، قاليًا للمهاد، راضيًا ببُلغة مِن الزاد، إلى أن يُلحِقَني الموت سريعًا بك، فأفوز بقربك، ورحمة ربك.

لكنّي فكّرتُ ونظرت وتدبّرت، فلم أر لي وجهًا أستوجبُ به درجتَك واللحاقَ بشرفك سوى الصبر والاحتساب، فتجلّدت، وصبّرني ربّي فصبرتُ، وغلب عليّ اليقين فأمسكت، فأقول: إنّا لله وإنّا إليه راجعون[١]، ولا حول ولا قوة إلا بالله العليّ العظيم، والرحمن الرحيم، له الحمد على ما أبلى، والشكرُ على ما أولى.

معاشر أوليائنا، والقائلين بطاعتنا، والمتمسّكين بولايتها، هذه والله المحنُ الشدّاد، المُنضجة للأكباد، هذه الزلازل العظام التي لا تثبت لها الأَقدامُ، هذه المشاهد التي لم تألُكم أئمتُكم لها تبيينًا ولم تزل راغبة إلى الله في تثبيت أقدامكم وعصمة قلوبكم عند حلولها بكم، ووقوع المحنة فيها عليكم. فتثبتوا تسلَموا، ولا تضِلوا فتندَموا، فلن يُخليَ الله أرضَه وعصره في كل زمان من قائم لله بالحق، شاهد على الخلق، يُقِرُّ به المؤمنون، ويجحَدُ به الكافرون الضالون الأخسرون.

إنّ الله بحمده خلق الخلقَ من غير حاجة كانت منه إليهم، لكن لعبادته وإظهار فضله وجوده عليهم، وجعلَ الحياة فيهم قوةً عاملة، والموتَ كأسًا دائرة، وما بعد الموت جزاءً للعمل، وبيّن لكم بين هذين نهجَ السبل، برسُله المنتجبين، وبأئمة الهدى المختارين، وجعل ثوابهم وحظّهم على مقدار بلاغهم وقيامهم، واضطلاعهم بأمره، وإرشاد خلقه، وجعل بينهم درجات في الفضل فقال جلّ ثناؤه: «ثُمَّ أَوْرَثْنَا الكِتَابَ الذينَ اصْطَفَيْنَا من عِبَادِنَا، فَمِنْهُم ظَالِمٌ لِنَفْسِهِ وَمِنْهُم مُقْتَصِدٌ، وَمِنْهُم سَابِقٌ بِالخَيرَاتِ بِإِذْنِ

[١] القرآن ٢: ١٥٦

الله، ذَلِكَ هُو الفَضْلُ الكَبِيرُ» [٣٥: ٣٢]. تبارك الله ربّ العالمين، الذي لم يرضَ بالدنيا ثوابًا للمؤمنين، ولا عقابًا للكافرين.

أيها الناس، ما من حيّ إلا وهو رهين بالموت، ولا موتَ إلاّ وبعده نُشور، ولا نشورَ إلاّ بحساب، فثواب أو عقاب. فطوبى لمن لقي الله متمسّكًا بحُجْزة أوليائه، معتصمًا بعصمتهم، قائمًا بلوازم الطاعة المفروضة عليهم بحججه وأصفيائه، متفيّئًا بظلال ألوية عترة سيّدنا محمد رسول الله سيّد المرسلين، يومَ لا ينفع إلاّ الدين، ولا يُنجي إلاّ صحة اليقين، «يَوْمَ تَجِدُ كُلُّ نَفْسٍ مَا عَمِلَتْ مِنْ خَيْرٍ مُحْضَراً، وَمَا عَمِلَتْ مِنْ سُوءٍ تَوَدُّ لَوْ أَنَّ بَيْنَهَا وَبَيْنَهُ أَمَداً بَعِيداً وَيُحَذِّرُكُم اللهُ نَفْسَهُ وَاللهُ رَؤُوفُ بِالعِبَادِ» [٣: ٣٠].

أيها الناس، إنّما الأعمالُ بخواتمها، والجزاء من الله بحسب الوفاء لله ولرسوله، ولأئمة الهدى من ولد الرسول، وقد شاهدتُم سيّد الأئمة، وراعيَ الأمة، وسراجَ الدجنة، في مواطن ومشاهد قضى فيها فرض ربّه عليه، وأدّى وديعة جدّه محمد لديه، وبيّن لكم من سننه ما إن اقتدَيْتُم به لن تضلّوا ولن تَنْبَتَّ أيديكم من رحمة الله، ولن تعشُوَ أبصارُكم عن قصد السبيل الأقوم، والتمسّك بالدليل الأعظم، وما من وليّ سالف، إلا وبعده وصيٌّ خالفٌ، قائم لله بحقه مُستنجزٌ ثوابه، عاملٌ بما يرضيه حسب طاقته، ومنتهى استطاعته، «لاَ يُكَلِّفُ اللهُ نَفْسًا إلاّ وَسْعَها» [٢: ٢٨٦]، ولا يرتضي للقيام بدينه، وهداية خلقه، ورعاية أمة نبيّه إلاّ الأفاضلَ الأمجاد، الآحادَ الأفراد، ذوي الهمم العالية، والأخلاق الرضيّة، والنفوس الأبيّة، من خالص الذرية. وقد جرت سنّة الله في خلقه، ونفذ في حكمه ما لا يُستطاع له جَحد، ولا للقول به ردّ، من مواصلة الرسل لتبيين السبيل في الزمان بعد الزمان، لإعلان دينه حسب الإمكان، فأوجب للعباد الثوابَ بطاعتهم وإجابة دعوتهم وقبول هدايتهم، والعقابَ بإسخاطهم وجحدهم

وإنكارهم، وليس للمؤمن بأوّلهم جَحْدُ آخرهم، ولا ينفع جاحدَ أوّلهم تصديقُ آخرهم، للثواب والرحمة من العذاب الأليم، والخزي المقيم. وقد قرن الله طاعة أئمة الهدى بطاعة الرسل، وطاعة الرسل بطاعته، فقال: «أطِيعُوا اللهَ وَأطِيعُوا الرَسُول وَأولي الأمْرِ منْكُم» [٤: ٥٩]. بذلك جرت عادته في الأنبياء والمرسلين «فَلَنْ تَجدَ لسُنَّة الله تَبْديلاً، ولَنْ تَجدَ لسُنَّة الله تَحْويلاً» [٣٥: ٤٣]. وهل لُمقرّ نبوّةَ موسى ورسالة عيسى عليهما السَلام حاجةٌ بتفضيل سيّدنا محمد خاتم النبيّين وسيّد المرسلين إذا أنكر نبوّته، وهل له انتفاع بأعماله أو ثوابٌ لعبادته؟

النور، أيها الناس، فينا مَصون، وعطاء ربّك لنا غيرُ ممنون، فأين تذهبون، وفي أيّ أرض تتيهون، «هَيْهَاتَ هَيْهَاتَ لِمَا تُوعَدُونَ» [٢٣: ٣٦]. فأطيعونا تهتدوا، وتمسّكوا بحبلنا ترشَدوا، واعملوا بما تفوزون به في أخراكم تسعدوا، ولا تجعلوا أكبر هَمِّكم دنياكم، فإنّ أمير المؤمنين عليّ بن أبي طالب أبا الأئمة المهديّين صلوات الله عليه وعليهم أجمعين، قال: «إنّ الله أحلّ حلالاً وأعان عليه، وحرّم حرامًا وأغْنَى عنه»، فدعُوا ما قلَّ لما كثُر، وما ضاق لما اتّسع، فقد أمركم بالعمل، وتكفّل لهكم بالرزق، فلا يكون طلبُ المضمون لكم أولى بكم من طلب المفروض عليكم.

اللهمّ، أوزعني شكرَ نعمتك ووفّقني لما يُرضيك ويقرّب إليك، ويوجب المزيدَ من فضلك، والذخر عندك بإتمام نعمتك عليّ في الدنيا والآخرة، إله الخلق ربّ العالمين.

اللهمّ أيّدْني بنصرك، وافتح لي على أعدائك فتحًا تُحيي به الدين، وتُعزّ به ملّة محمد سيّد المرسلين، وارزُقنا زيارة قبره والارتقاءَ على منبره، وحلولَ داره، وقضاءَ الحجّ إلى بيتك الحرام والوقوفَ بتلك المشاهد العظام، براياتنا، وقد جدّدْتَ لنا العزّ ولأوليائنا، وقد أيّدتنا وإيّاهم بالنصر، وأكْرمتَنا بالظفر، وأظهرتنا على القوم الظالمين، وأخضعتَ لنا رقاب

المعاندين العاصين. وقد تقدّم منك الميعادُ، للآباء والأجداد، ولا خُلفَ لوعدك، ولا رادّ لأمرك، والرضا والتسليم بما قضيْتَ، عجّلتَ أو أجّلت.

اللهمّ، واجعل ما مننت به من إحسانك، وما تُجدِّدُ لي من فضلك ونعمتك عليَّ وعلى العباد، رُحْمةَ منك.

اللهمّ، واقرن بكل عزّ تجدّده لي ذُلاً تُسكنُه قلبي لعظمتك وجلالك وهيبتك، فلا عزّ إلاّ في الخضوع والعبودية لك، ولا غنىَ إلاّ في الفقر إليك، ولا أمنَ إلاّ في خوفك، ولا سعادة في الدنيا والآخرة إلاّ برضاك، يا ربّ العالمين.

اللهمّ، اغفر للمؤمنين والمؤمنات، والمسلمين والمسلمات، الأحياء منهم والأموات، واخصص أولياءَ دولتنا وأنصارَ دعوتنا المُجاهدين الصابرين الشاكرين، من رحمتك، بما استوجبوه بطاعتك، وقضاء فروضك، وموالاة أوليائك، ومعاداة أعدائك.

وصلّى الله على محمد سيّد المرسلين في الأوّلين والآخرين، اذكروا الله العظيم يذكُركم[1]. وأستغفرُ الله لي ولكم، والحمد لله وصلواته وسلامه على سيّدنا محمد وآله أجمعين.

[المصدر: سيرة جوذر، ٧٦-٨٤؛ إدريس، عيون الأخبار، تحقيق اليعلاوي، ٥٤١-٥٤٨.]

[1] القرآن ٢: ١٥٢

١٠

خطبة المعز

[«ونحن نذكر طرفًا مما جاء عن أئمة الحق عليهم السلام نوضح به عالي منازلهم، وسامي مراتبهم، وما يجب لهم، وأن يعتقد فيهم من ذلك ما قال مولانا المعز لدين الله صلوات الله عليه في خطبة له، وهو:»[1]]

الحمد لله موحّد الآحاد أدلة على وحدانيته، وممجّد الأمجاد بمجد ربوبيته، مؤزّل الأزل بأزل لاهوتيته، قارن الدهر بالزمان بإبداع ربوبيته، علّل المعلول لعلته، وعلى المتحرّك ومحرّكه بحركته، وارتفع عن كليهما بعز سلطان قدرته، كان قبل الحركة والسكون، والظهور والكمون، مكوّر الأكوار، ومدوّر الأدوار، ومقدّر الليل والنهار، الباطن بإبداع العقل والحواّس، الظاهر بتصوير الصُوَر والأشخاص. أحمده على ما به أفردنا وخصّنا وانتجبنا بحَرْف اللام في الظلال، وأبرزنا في أشخاص بلا أمثال، وجعلنا سببًا لعز سلطانه الكبير المتعال فنحن أبوابه وخُزّانه، ووجهه وجنبه ويداه المبسوطتان[2] في عباده، نحن باب حِطّته الذي من دخله غفرت ذنوبُه، وكُشِفت كروبُه، نحن باب إلى بيته المعمور وسَقْفه المرفوع[3]،

[1] حاتم بن إبراهيم الحامدي، تحفة القلوب، فصل ١٥.
[2] القرآن ٥: ٦٤.
[3] القرآن ٥٢: ٤ و ٥

والصراط المستقيم[١]، والنبأ العظيم[٢].

أيها الناس! قد بيّنّا لكم ذكراً، فاذكروا إتمام النعمة عليكم بنا، وكمال الدين الذي رضى الله لكم دينًا دين الإسلام[٣] الذي لا يُبتغى غيره ولا يُقبل سواه، «وَمَن يَبْتَغِ غَيْرَ الإِسْلاَمِ دِيْنًا فَلَنْ يُقْبَلَ مِنهُ وَهُوَ فِي الآخِرَةِ مِنَ الخَاسِرِينَ» [٣: ٨٥]، وإبراهيم أولاه، ومحمد أخراه، ونحن كماله وتمامه ومنتهاه «إِنَّ الشَيْطَانَ لَكُم عَدُوٌ فَاتَّخِذُوهُ عَدُواً إِنَّمَا يَدْعُو حِزْبَهُ لِيَكُونُوا مِن أَصْحَابِ السَعِيرِ» [٣٥: ٦]، ولم يزل يُظهر الله بظهورنا في كل وقت وأوان شيطانًا، ليُظهر بنقصه فضلنا، وبفساده صلاحنا. قال النبي صلى الله عليه وعلى آله: «قرن بكل نبى شيطان، وقُرن بي شيطانان»، فلا تشتروا الضلالة بالهدى[٤]، بطاعة مَن عتا وطغى وكذّب وتولّى، وسفك هو ومن مضى من سلفه الدماء في الشهر الحرام، والناس حُرُم، كُفراً بالله وتكذيبًا بما وعد الله من الأمن لأولياء الله، أولئك الذين «لَعَنَهُم اللهُ بِكُفْرِهِم» [٢: ٨٨[٥]]، وجعل قلوبهم قاسية بظلمهم[٦]، «ألاَ لَعْنَةُ اللهِ عَلَى الظَالمِينَ» [١١: ١٨].

اللهم اغفر لي وللمؤمنين والمؤمنات، «ولاَ تَزِد الظَالمِينَ إلاَ تَبَاراً» [٧١: ٢٨[٧]]. «وَالسَلاَمُ عَلَيَّ يَومَ وُلِدْتُ، وَيَومَ أَمُوتُ، وَيَومَ أُبْعَثُ حَيًّا» [١٩: ٣٣]، في الكون بشراً شريفًا، وفي المعاد نوراً إلهيًا لطيفًا، منه بدأ وإليه يعود.

[المصدر: تحفة القلوب، تحقيق عباس همداني، فصل ١٥]

---

[١] القرآن ١: ٦ و غيرها

[٢] القرآن ٣٨: ٦٧ و ٧٨: ٢

[٣] القرآن ٥: ٣

[٤] القرآن ٢: ١٦ و ٢: ١٧٥

[٥] أيضا آية ٤: ٤٦

[٦] اقتباس من القرآن ٢٢: ٥٣ و ٣٩: ٢٢ و ٥: ١٣

[٧] «ربِّ اغفر لي ولوالدَي ولمن دخل بيتي مؤمنًا وللمؤمنين وللمؤمنات ولا تزد الظالمين إلاّ تباراً»

١١

خطبة قرواش بن المقلد للحاكم، سنة ٤٠١

[«فمن الحوادث فيها أنه ورد الخبر بأن أبا المنيع قرواش بن المقلد جمع أهل الموصل وأظهر عندهم طاعة الحاكم صاحب مصر وعرفهم ما عزم عليه من إقامة الدعوة له ودعاهم إلى قبول ذلك فأجابوه جواب الرعية المملوكة وأسروا الأباء والكراهية وأحضر الخاطب في يوم الجمعة الرابع من المحرم فخلع عليه وأعطاه النسخة ما يخطب به فكانت: »[١]]

الله أكبر الله أكبر لا إله إلا الله، والله أكبر لله الحمد، الحمد لله الذي[٢] انجلّت بنوره غمرات الغضب وانهدّت[٣] بقدرته أركان النُصُب وأطلع بقدره[٤] شمس الحق من الغرب، الذي محا بعدله جور الظلمة وقصم بقوته ظهر الغشمة، فعاد الأمر إلى نصابه والحق إلى أربابه، البائن بذاته، المتفرد بصفاته، الظاهر بآياته، المتوحد بدلالاته، لم تفته[٥] الأوقات فتسبقه الأزمنة، ولم تُشبِه الصور فتحويه الأمكنة، ولم تره العيون فتصفه الألسنة، سبق كل موجود وجودُه وفات كل جود جوده؛ واستقر في كل

[١] ابن الجوزي، المنتظم، ج ٧، ص ٢٤٨-٢٤٩.

[٢] والله أكبر ولله الحمد، الحمد لله الذي: وله الحمد الذي، ابن الجوزي

[٣] وانهدت: وانقدت، ابن الجوزي

[٤] بقدره: بنوره، ابن الجوزي

[٥] تفته: تفنه، ابن تغري بردي

عقل توحيده وقام في كل مرأي شهيده. أحمده بما[١] يجب على أوليائه الشاكرين تحميده وأستعينه على القيام بما يشاء ويريده، وأشهد له بما شهد أصفياؤه وشهوده وأشهد أنّ لا إله إلا الله وحده لا شريك له، شهادة لا يشوبها دنس الشرك ولا يعتريها وهم الشك، خالصة من الإدهان، قائمة بالطاعة والإذعان.

وأشهد أنّ محمداً عبده ورسوله صلى الله عليه اصطفاه واختاره لهداية الخلق وإقامة الحق، فبلّغ الرسالة وهدى من الضلالة والناس حينئذ عن الهدى[٢] غافلون وعن سبيل الحق ضالون، فأنقذهم من عبادة الأوثان، وأمرهم بطاعة الرحمن حتى قامت حجج الله وآياته وتمت بالتبليغ كلماته[٣]، صلى الله عليه، وعلى أول مستجيب له علي أمير المؤمنين وسيد الوصيين، أساس الفضل والرحمة وعماد العلم والحكمة، وأصل الشجرة الكرام البررة النابتة في الأرومة المقدسة المطهرة، وعلى خلفائه الأغصان البواسق من تلك الشجرة وعلى ما خلص منها وزكا من الثمرة.

أيها الناس، «اتَّقُو اللهَ حَقَّ تُقَاته» [٣: ١٠٢] وارغبوا في ثوابه واحذروا من عقابه، فقد تسمعون[٤] ما يَتلى عليكم في كتابه، قال الله تعالى: «يَومَ نَدْعُو كُلَ أنَاس بِإمَامهم» [١٧:٧١] وقال: «يَا أيَّهَا الذينَ آمَنُوا أطِيعُوا اللهَ وَأطيعُوا الرَسُولَ وَأولِي الأمْرِ منكُم»[٥] [٤: ٥٩]، فالحذر ثم[٦] الحذر أيها الناس[٧]، فكأن قد[٨] أفضت بكم الدنيا إلى الآخرة وقد بان أشراطها ولاح سراطها، ومناقشة حسابها والعرض على كتابها: «فَمَن

[١] بما: كما، ابن تغري بردي
[٢] عن الهدى: من الهوى، ابن الجوزي
[٣] القرآن ٦: ١١٥
[٤] تسمعون: ترون، ابن الجوزي
[٥] يا أيها الذين...الأمر منكم: -، ابن تغري بردي
[٦] ثم: -، ابن الجوزي
[٧] أيها الناس: -، ابن تغري بردي
[٨] فكأن قد: فكأني، وقد، ابن تغري بردي

يَعْمَلْ مِثْقَالَ ذَرَّةٍ خَيراً يَرَهُ وَمَن يضعْمَلُ مِثْقَالَ ذَرَّةٍ شَراً يَرَهُ» [٩٩:٧ و ٨]. اركبوا سفينة نجاتكم قبل أن تغرقوا «وَاعْتَصِمُوا بِحَبْلِ الله جَمِيعًا وَلاَ تَفَرَّقُوا» [٣:١٠٣]، واعلموا أنّه «يَعْلَمُ مَا فِي أَنْفُسِكُمْ فَاحْذَرُوهُ» [٢: ٢٣٥] [1] وأنيبوا إلى الله خير الإنابة وأجيبوا داعي[2] باب الإجابة، قبل «أَنْ تَقُولَ نَفْسٌ يَا حَسْرَتَا عَلَى مَا فَرَّطْتُ فِي جَنْبِ الله وَإِنْ كُنْتُ لَمِنَ السَاخِرِينَ، أَوْ تَقُولَ لَو أَنَّ اللهَ هَدَانِي لَكُنْتُ مِنَ الْمُتَّقِينَ، أو تَقُولَ حِينَ تَرَى العَذَابَ لَو أَنَّ لِي كَرَّةً فَأَكُونَ مِنَ الْمُحْسِنِينَ» [٣٩:٥٦-٥٨]. تيقظوا من الغفلة والفترة قبل الندامة والحسرة، وتمنى الكرة[3] والتماس الخلاص «وَلاَتَ حِينَ مَنَاصٍ» [٣٨: ٣]؛ وأطيعوا إمامكم ترشدوا وتمسكوا بولاة العهد تهتدوا، فقد نصب لكم علمًا لتهتدوا به وسبيلاً لتقتدوا به؛ جعلنا الله وإياكم ممن تبع مراده وجعل الإيمان زاده، وألهمه[4] تقواه ورشاده، واستغفر الله العظيم لي ولكم ولجميع المسلمين

ثم جلس وقام فقال:

الحمد لله ذي الجلال وخالق الأنام ومقدر الأقسام، المتفرد[5] بالبقاء والدوام فالق الأصباح وخالق الأشباح وفاطر الأرواح؛ أحمده أولاً وآخراً وأشكره[6] باطنًا وظاهراً، وأستعين به إلهًا قادراً وأستنصره وليًا ناصراً. وأشهد أنّ لا إله إلا الله وحده لا شريك له، وأنّ محمداً عبده ورسوله،

[1] واعلموا ... فاحذروه: -، ابن تغري بردي
[2] القرآن ٤٦: ٣١
[3] الكرة: الكر، ابن تغري بردي
[4] وألهمه: والهمة، ابن تغري بردي
[5] المتفرد بالبقاء: المتفرد بحقيقة البقاء، ابن تغري بردي
[6] وأشكره: أستشهده: ابن الجوزي

شهادة من أقرّ بوحدانيته إيمانًا، واعترف بربوبيته إيقانًا[١]، وعلم برهان ما يدعو إليه وعرف حقيقة الدلالة عليه. اللهم صل على وليك الأزهر وصديقك الأكبر علي بن أبي طالب أبي الأئمة الراشدين المهديين[٢]،؛ اللهم صل على السبطَين الطاهرَين الحسن والحسين، وعلى الأئمة الأبرار، الصفوة الأخيار، من أقام منهم وظهر، ومن خاف منهم واستتر[٣]؛ اللهم صل على الإمام المهدي بك والذي بلغ بأمرك وأظهر حجتك ونهض بالعدل في بلادك هاديًا لعبادك؛ اللهم صل على القائم بأمرك وعلى المنصور بنصرك اللذَين بذلا نفوسهما في رضاك وجاهدا أعداءك؛ اللهم صل على المعز لدينك المجاهد في سبيلك، المظهر لآياتك الحقية والحجة العلية؛ اللهم صل على العزيز بك الذي مهدت به البلاد وهديت به العباد؛ اللهم اجعل توافي صلواتك وزواكي بركاتك، على سيدنا ومولانا إمام الزمان وحصن الإيمان وصاحب الدعوة العلوية والملة النبوية، عبدك ووليك المنصور أبي علي الحاكم بأمر الله أمير المؤمنين، كما صليت على آبائه الراشدين وأكرمت أجداده المهديين[٤]. اللهم وفّقنا لطاعته واجمعنا على كلمته ودعوته واحشرنا في حزبه وزمرته[٥]؛ اللهم اعنه على ما وليته واحفظه فيما استرعيته وبارك له فيما أتيته وانصر جيوشه وأعل أعلامه في مشارق الأرض ومغاربها، إنّك على كل شيء قدير.

[المصدر: ابن الجوزي، المنتظم، ٧: ٢٤٨-٢٥١: ابن تغري بردي، النجوم، ٤: ٢٢٤-٢٢٧]

---

[١] إيقانا: إتيانا، ابن الجوزي

[٢] المهديين: المهتدين، ابن الجوزي

[٣] واستتر: فاستتر، ابن تغري بردي

[٤] أجداده المهديين: أولياءك المهتدين، ابن تغري بردي

[٥] اللهم وفقنا لطاعته ... حزبه وزمرته: -، ابن الجوزي

١٢

خطبة الآمر

[«ونقلتُ من خطبه عليه السلام ما وجدته في حريرة مُنتسخًا للحرة السيدة الملكة الصليحية، وقد أطلق عليها العلامة الشريفة لأمير المؤمنين، وهي هذه بفصّها ونصّها:»[1]]

بسم الله الرحمن الرحيم.

الحمد لله الذي قصُرت الفِطَنُ عن معرفة حقيقة ذاته، وعجزت الألسن عن تعديد صفاته، وخضع لِعزّه مَنْ في أرضه وسماواته، ودلّ على وحدانية[2] عظيم ملكه باهر آياته، لا رادّ لأقضيته، و«لاَ مُبَدِّلَ لِكَلِمَاتِهِ» [٦: ١١٥[3]]، نحمده على نعمه التي ما زال يُجرينا فيها على جميل عاداته، ونشهد أنّ لا إله إلاّ الله وحده لا شريك له شهادةً تمحو عن قائلهم عظيم سيئاته، وتقضي بمُضاعف حسناته، ونشهد أنّ جدّنا محمداً عبده ورسوله أرسله ومكارم الأخلاق من آياته، وصلّى الله عليه وعلى أبينا أمير المؤمنين علي بن أبي طالب المتصدق بخاتمه في صلاته، وعلى الأئمة الطاهرين من ذريتهما براهين الهدى وعلاماته، سلّم تسليماً.

أيّها الناس، حتّام أنتم «فِي غَمْرَةٍ سَاهُونَ» [٥١: ١١]، وعن ما أمامكم

---

[1] إدريس، عيون الأخبار، ج ٧، ص ٣٢٢.

[2] وحدانية: وحدانيته، أ

[3] أيبضا آية ١٨: ٢٧

من هول المطلع لاهون، وللبصائر لا تستعملون، وبما يدعون إليه[1] لا تعملون، «كَلاَّ سَوْفَ تَعْلَمُونَ، ثُمَّ كَلاَّ سَوْفَ تَعْلَمُونَ» [١٠٢: ٣-٤]؛ فرحم الله امرءً نظر إلي أمامه، واهتدى بمراشد إمامه، وأرضى خالقَه في نقضه وإبرامه، وهجر الهُجْرَ في منطِقه وكلامه.

عباد الله، وهذا شهر رمضان المبارك قد نَزَل بكم نزول الضيف فبالغوا في إكرامه، وتوفّروا في صلاته[2] وصيامه، واجتهدوا أن تقطعوا أيّامه نُسُكًا ووَرَعًا، ولياليه سُجَّداً ورُكَّعًا، وأن تصوموا فيه عن الخطايا والمآثم، صيامَكم عن المشارب والمطاعم.

إنّ أحسم ما تُلِيَ على صَهَوات المنابر، ورَعَتْه أسماع البوادي والحواضر، كلامُ عَلام الغيوب والمُطّلِع على السرائر؛ قال الله تعالى في كتابه المكنون: «وَإِذَا قُرِئَ القُرْآنُ فَاسْتَمِعُوا لَهُ وَاَنْصِتُوا لَعَلَّكُم تَرْحَمُونَ» [٧: ٢٠٤]. أعوذ بالله وقدرته من الشيطان ونزغته، بسم الله الرحمن الرحيم: «شَهْرُ رَمَضَانَ الذي أُنْزِلَ فيه القُرْآنُ، هُدًى للنَاسِ وَبَيِّنَاتٍ مِنَ الهُدَى وَالفُرْقَانِ، فَمَنْ شَهِدَ مِنْكُم الشَهْرَ فَلْيَصُمْهُ وَمَنْ كَانَ مَرِيضًا أَوْ عَلَى سَفَرٍ فَعِدَّةٌ مِنْ أَيَّامٍ أُخَرَ» [٢: ١٨٥].

بارك الله لنا ولكم في القرآن العظيم، ونَفَعنا وإيّاكم بالآيات والذكر الحكيم، ونستغفر الله لنا ولمن سَلّم لنا من المؤمنين حقّ التسليم.

[الخطبة الثانية:]

بسم الله الرحمن الرحيم.

الحمد لله باري البريّة، وعالم الخفية، والمنزّه عن الصحابة[3] والذرية،

---

[1] إليه: + الرشاد، أ

[2] صلاته: صلواته، ف

[3] الصاحبة: الصاحب، ف

وصلى الله على جدّنا محمد الهادي إلى المحجة المضيئة، وعلى أبينا أمير المؤمنين علي بن أبي طالب أخيه وابن عمه الذي ارتضاه للوصيّة، وعلى الأئمة الطاهرين من ذريتهما حُجَج الله على خلقه الواضحة الجليّة[١]، وسلّم تسليمًا.

أيّها الناس، إنّ الله تعالى رَفَعَ جدّنا محمداً إلى الدرجة العليّة، وأناله من الشرف ما لم يصل إليه منتهى أمل[٢] ولا أمنية، وأمر سبحانه بأمر بدأ فيه بنفسه وثنّى بملائكته قدسه تشييداً لفخره وتعظيمًا، فقال جلّ من قائل: «إِنَّ اللهَ وَمَلائِكَتَهُ يُصَلّونَ عَلَى النَّبِيِّ يَا أَيُّهَا الذِينَ آمَنُوا صَلّوا عَلَيهِ وَسَلِّمُوا تَسْلِيماً» [٣٣: ٥٦]. اللهمّ صلّ على جدّنا محمد رسولك الكريم، والهادي إلى صراطك المستقيم، والمنزّل عليه «وَإِنّكَ لَتُلَقَّى القُرْآنَ مِن لَدُن حَكِيمٍ عَلِيمٍ» [٢٧: ٦]، وصلّ يا ربّ على آل محمد.

اللهمّ صلّ على جدّنا محمد الذي أشرق بمبعثه وجه الزمن البهيم، وبشّر بظهوره كل نبي كريم، وأنزلت عليه واصفًا له «وَإِنّكَ لَعَلَى خُلُقٍ عَظِيمٍ» [٦٨: ٤]، وصلّ يا ربّ على آل محمد، وصلّ اللهمّ على أبينا أمير المؤمنين علي بن أبي طالب الذي كان منه بمنزلة هارون من موسى الكليم، وعلى أمّنا فاطمة الزهراء الحورية، وعلى ولدَيها الإمامَين أبي محمد الحسن وأبي عبدالله الحسين أفضل البرية، وعلى علي بن الحسين زين العابدين، ومحمد بن علي باقر[٣] علوم الدين، وجعفر بن محمد الصادق الأمين، وعلى إمام الحقّ إسماعيل، ومحمد نجله، حائزي[٤] شرف الخلافة الأصيل والمحتويين على جُمَل الفضل والتفضيل، وعلى الأئمة المستورين عن عدوهم العادل في أفعاله كلها عن سواء السبيل، وعلى نُجُوم الحق[٥]

---

[١] الجليّة: الجليلة، ف

[٢] أمل: أمر، أ

[٣] باقر: الباقر، ف

[٤] حائزي: حائز، ف

[٥] الحق: الهدى، ف

الثواقب، وشُمُوس الطالعة[1] من المغارب، المهدي بك، والقائم بأمرك، والمنصور بنصرك، والمعز لدينك، والعزيز بك، والحاكم بأمرك، والظاهر بإعزاز دينك، والمستنصر بك، والمستعلي بك، المنقولين إلى جوارك الأمين، والحالّين في أصحاب اليمين[2].

اللهمّ، وأنّا عبدك الآمر بأحكامك، والشاكر لإنعامك، نَظَمْتَ لي بفضلك عقود السعود، وتوّجتَني تيجان العُلى مكلّلة بدُرّ التوفيق المنضود، وأورَثْتَني مقام الخلافة المنتقل إليّ عن الآباء الكرام والجدود، وجعلتَ أيّامي في محاسن الوجود، وأذْلَلْتَ لي أعناق الأسود، وجمعتَ على طاعتي قلب السيّد والمسود.

اللهمّ، فكما خصّصتَني بهذا الفضل المبين، وجعلتني حُجّتك البالغة على العالمين، فصِلْ بي[3] وبعقبي حبل الإمامة كما وَعَدْتَ إلى يوم الدين، واجعل مَنْ اتّبعني من الآمنين الفائزين.

اللهمّ، وارض عن السيّد الأجلّ الأفضل ابن السيّد أمير الجيوش رضاك عمّن أحسن عملاً[4]، واجعل رِفْدَ رحمتك إليهما متّصلاً.

وانصر اللهمّ جيوشي وكتائبي حيث كانوا ويكونون براً وبحراً، واستأصل بسيوفهم شَأفَة أعدائك الذين تمرّدوا طغياناً وكفراً وامنح المسلمين عليهم ظَفَراً ونَصْراً.

واغفر اللهمّ للمسلمين والمسلمات والمؤمنين والمؤمنات، الأحياء منهم والأموات، إنّك وليّ الحسنات، وغافر السيئات.

«إنَّ اللهَ يَأمُرُ بالعَدْلِ وَالإحْسَانِ وَإيْتَاءِ ذي القُرْبَى، وَيَنْهَى عَنِ الفَحْشَاءِ وَالمُنْكَرِ وَالبَغْي، يَعِظُكُم لَعَلّكُم تَذَكَّرُونَ» [١٦: ٩٠] اذكروا الله

---

[1] شموس الطالعة: شموس الهدى الطالعة، أ
[2] القرآن ٥٦: ٢٧
[3] فصِلْ بي: فصِلْ يوم الدين بي، أ
[4] القرآن ١٨: ٣٠

العظيم[١] يذكركم، واشكروا يزدكم.

والحمد لله ربّ العالمين، وصلواته على رسوله سيّدنا محمد وآله الطاهرين.

[المصدر: إدريس، عيون الأخبار، جزء سابع، ص٢٢٣-٢٢٧]

---

[١] العظيم: -، أ

١٣

خطبة الآمر

عيد الفطر

[«ومن خُطَبه أيضًا عليه السلام ما وجدته مكتوبًا في حريرة عليها العلامة الشريفة «الحمد لله ربّ العالمين» وهذا ذكرها:»[١]]

الله أكبر! الله أكبر! ولا إله إلاّ الله، والحمد لله، والله أكبر! الله أكبر! ولله الحمد، الله أكبر على ما هدانا، وله الشكر على ما أولانا.

بسم الله الرحمن الرحيم.

الحمد لله الذي نَصرَ بنا معشر الأئمة من أهل بيت نبيه دين الإسلام الواجب، ورمى عدوّنا المُناصِب بالعذاب الواصب[٢]، ومُتوَقَّد محرقات الشُهُب الثواقب[٣]، وأنفذ في مخالفينا أحكام سيوفنا القواضب، الماضية المضارب، ونَشَرَ بنا أعلامًا للعدل سام[٤] ذكرها في المشارق والمغارب، نحمده على نعمه التي جادتنا أنواؤها بطلّ وابل من الإحسان ساكب، وحقّقت من آمالنا كل دان وعازب، ونشهد أنّ لا إله إلا الله وحده لا شريك له شهادةً أوردها اليقين من نميره أعذب المشارب، وأحلّها من

[١] إيريس، عيون الأخبار، ج ٧، ص ٢٢٧.
[٢] اقتباس من القرآن ٣٧: ٩
[٣] اقتباس من القرآن ٣٧: ١٠
[٤] سام: سنا، ف

توحيد ذي الجلال والإكرام أعلى المراتب، ونشهد أنّ جدّنا محمداً عبده ورسوله هدى به إلى الدين الحنيفي أفضل الشرائع والمذاهب، وأيّده بالقرآن الباهر الآيات والعجائب، وعضّده بأبينا أمير المؤمنين علي بن أبي طالب أخيه ووصيّه وخطيب شرعه وموضح مشكلاته الغرائب، صلى الله عليهما وعلى الأئمة من ذريتهما صلاةً يبلّغهم بها من شرف المعاد أقصى المراتب.

أيّها الناس، الزموا كتاب الله العزيز وسُنّة رسوله، واعملوا بما تضمّناه[1] من أمره وتمثيله، واعتمدوا عليهما في فروع الدين وأصوله، ولا تعدّوا ذلك إلى ما نهى الله عنه من الخوض في كلام الإلحاد وأباطيله، فإن ذلك من مصائد الشيطان وأضاليله، فقد سمعتم قول الله تعالى «وَأَنَّ هَذَا صِرَاطِي مُسْتَقِيمًا فَاتَّبِعُوه وَلا تَتَّبِعُوا السُّبُلَ فَتَفَرَّقَ بِكُمْ عَنْ سَبِيلِه» [٦: ١٥٣]، وأطيعوا[2] لمواعظنا الصادرة عن محض النصيحة والإشفاق، «وَلاَ يَصُدَّنَّكُم الشَيطَانُ» [٤٣: ٦٢] وأعوانه أهل الزيغ والنفاق عن الشرائع وما أوضحته من طرق العبادة، فإنّ الله تعالى أمدّها من كتبه ورسله ومعجزاتهم بأقوى مادّة، وجعل العقول لها خادمة، ولم يجعل العقولَ على الشرائع حاكمة، لأنّ الشرائع صدرت عنه وهو الخالق المنفرد[3] بعلم الغيوب والكمال، والعقول خَلَقَها كسائر صفات المخلوقين في النقص، وتحكيم النقص على الكمال لا يوصف به ذو الجلال؛ فكونوا على ما أمركم الله عاكفين، وعن ما نهاكم عنه صادفين، وسلّموا له تسعدوا وتسلموا، ولا تطلبوا النجاة بالجدال فتضلّوا وتندموا.

عباد الله، ويومكم هذا عيدٌ شرّف الله به دين الإسلام، وختم به شهر الصيام، الذي ميّزه على الشهور وفضّله، وفرض صومه تذكيراً بنعمته

---

[1] تضمّناه: تضمّنا، أ

[2] وأطيعوا: واصتيخوا، ف

[3] المنفرد: المتفرّد، أ

بكتابه الذي فيه أنزله، ووعد كُلاً من المحسنين فيه والمنيبين عن مضاعفة الحسنات ومغفرة السيئات بما يحقّق أمله، واستقبل به أشْهُر حجّ بيته الحرام الذي كفل لكل حُجّاجه ومعتمريه بما يمحو زَلَله، ويوصله إلى نفيس ما قسم له. فانتضوا رحمكم الله من العزمات أمضاها، وامتطئوا من الاجتهادات أوفاها، وأُمّوا بركات تلك المعالم، واستجيروا بحرم الله الشامل المراحم، تَظْفَروا بصَفْحِه عن الجرائم، وتفوزوا بما عنده من النعيم الدائم. وكونوا لحرمة هذا العيد حافظين، وبما يرضي الله فيه عاملين ولافظين. وعودوا على فقرائكم بالمعونة من أموالكم والرأفة، تأمنوا عاجل العدو وآجل المخافة. وفّر الله حظوظَكم من أنوار اليقين، واستعملكم بما ارتضاه لكم من الدين وحماكم من مضالّ الشيطان اللعين.

إن أكملَ الهدايات وأوضحها أدلّةً وسبلاً كلامُ الله وما تضمّنه من قوله «وَتَمَّتْ كَلِمَةُ رَبِّكَ صِدْقًا وَعَدْلاً» [٦: ١١٥]، وهو القائل سبحانه «وَإِذَا قُرِئَ القُرْآنُ فَاسْتَمِعُوا لَهُ وَأَنْصِتُوا لَعَلَّكُم تُرْحَمُونَ» [٧: ٢٠٤]. أعوذ بالله وما مَن به من الإرشاد والنور، من الشيطان وما يدعوا إليه من الإلحاد والغرور؛ بسم الله الرحمن الرحيم «وَمَا أُمِرُوا إلاّ لِيَعْبُدُوا اللهَ مُخْلِصِينَ لَهُ الدِينَ حُنَفَاءَ، وَيُقِيمُوا الصَلاَةَ وَيُؤْتُوا الزكاةَ وَذَلِكَ دِينُ القَيِّمَةِ» [٩٨: ٥]. بارك الله لنا ولكم في القرآن الكريم، ونفعنا وإياكم بالآيات والذكر الحكيم، ونستغفر الله لنا ولمن سلّم لنا من المؤمنين حقّ التسليم.

[الخطبة الثانية:]

بسم الله الرحمن الرحيم

الحمد لله الذي أعزّ بنا معشر الأئمة من أهل بيت نبيه حزبَ الإيمان ونَصرَه وأصلح شأنَه، وصلى الله على جدّنا محمد رسوله الذي أكمل دينه

ومعجزه وبرهانه، وعلى أبينا علي بن أبي طالب أخيه ووصيّه الذي عَضَّدَه به وأيّده وأعانه، وعلى الأئمة من ذريتهما صلاةً يُضاعَفُ لهم في دار كرامته تشريفه وإحسانه.

أيّها الناس، إنّ الله أمركم بالصلاة على نبيه المبعوث إلى البرية جمعًا، وأكرم رسله أصلاً وفرعًا، فقال جل منعمًا كريمًا: «إِنَّ اللهَ وَمَلائِكَتَهُ يُصَلُّونَ عَلَى النَبِيِّ يَا أَيُّهَا الذينَ آمَنُوا صَلُّوا عَلَيْهِ وَسَلِّمُوا تَسْلِيمًا» [٣٣: ٥٦]. اللهمّ صلّ على محمد الذي أمددتَ الخلق من شرعه ببالغ التسديد والتقويم، وهديْتَهم إلى النجاة وصراطها المستقيم، وعلى آل محمد. اللهمّ صلّ على محمد الذي دعوتَ به إلى دار السلام ونعيمها المقيم، ونجّيْت به من الجحيم، وعذابها الأليم، وعلى آل محمد؛ اللهمّ صلّ على أبينا أمير المؤمنين أخيه ووصيّه وشقيق نقعته المساهم، ونصيحه الصادق ووزيره الحازم، وفارج غمّائه في المأزق المتلاحم، وعلى أمّنا فاطمة الزهراء غذية ما خُصّت به النبوة من الوحي وشرف الأخلاق والمكارم، وعلى الحسن والحسين إمامَي الملّة ونيِّرَي فَلَك الدين وجماله في المحافل والمواسم، وعلى الأئمة من ذريّة الحسين الجارين على سُنَن نبيّهم في الآثار والمراسم، والمقيمين لشرعه المعالم، والمفتقر إلى علمهم كل عالم، أئمة الرشاد، وخيرة الله من العباد، الذين جُعِلَ لكل قوم منهم إمامٌ هاد، وهم أفضل العباد والزُهّاد، وأهل الجدّ في إقامة الدين الحنيف والاجتهاد؛ ضلّ قومٌ اتّخذوا من غيرهم وليًا، وجهلوا من فضلهم واضحًا جليًا، ونبذوا الحقّ بنبذهم وراءهم ظهريًا وجاءوا من عنادهم وشقاقهم شيئًا فريًا.

اللهمّ إنّي عبدك، الداعي إلى سبيلك، المكافح لأعداء رسولك، المبيّن لآياتك، الدليل على ما وعدت به أولياءك من جنّاتك، المُوضّح لبراهينك ودلالاتك، المبتغي لعفوك ومرضاتك؛ اللهمّ فانْصُرْني علي الكافرين والجاحدين، وأظْهِر بي العدلَ وأعزِ الدين، وأيّد الغازين والمجاهدين، وارْحَم

حَوْزَة المؤمنين، ودافع عن الإسلام والمسلمين، واهْد إلى واضح سبيل الحقّ المسترشدين، وكُنْ لي خير وليّ ومعين، برحمتك يا أرحم الراحمين. والحمد لله ربّ العالمين، وصلى الله على سيدنا محمد وآله الطاهرين.

[المصدر: إدريس، عيون الأخبار، جزء سابع، ص ٢٢٧-٢٣١]

الفهرس